R. S. Brain

Handbook on Viticulture for Victoria

R. S. Brain

Handbook on Viticulture for Victoria

ISBN/EAN: 9783743324640

Manufactured in Europe, USA, Canada, Australia, Japa

Cover: Foto ©ninafisch / pixelio.de

Manufactured and distributed by brebook publishing software (www.brebook.com)

R. S. Brain

Handbook on Viticulture for Victoria

Royal Commission on Vegetable Products.

HANDBOOK ON VITICULTURE

FOR

VICTORIA.

By Authority:
ROBT. S. BRAIN, GOVERNMENT PRINTER, MELBOURNE

1891.

CONTENTS.

	Page
NINTH PROGRESS REPORT OF THE VEGETABLE PRODUCTS COMMISSION	v
MEMBERS OF THE BOARD OF VITICULTURE	ix

INTRODUCTION.
    Preliminary—Reasons for issuing Handbook—Necessity for co-operation in order to insure greater uniformity in wines of each district—Example of older wine-producing districts of Europe xi

CHAP. I.—*History and Description of the Vine.*
    Root—Stem—Leaf—Flower 1

CHAP. II.—*Physiology.*
    Rise of sap—Transpiration—Assimilation—Respiration—Flowering—Fecundation of the ovule—Setting of the fruit—Ripening of the fruit—Importance of leaves ... ...

CHAP. III.—*Factors influencing the Growth and Products of the Vine.*
    Necessity of serious consideration on account of our past experience being very limited—Influence of climate—Irrigation of vineyards—Influence of aspect—Division of the colony into three climatic regions—Influence of soil—Influence of variety 15

CHAP. IV.—*Ampelography.*
    European vines—American vines—Indigenous Australian vines ... 29

CHAP. V.—*Selection of Site, and Choice of Suitable Varieties.*
    Importance of considering the character of wine which it is desired to make before selecting site—General requirements which should be fulfilled by a site—Advantages or otherwise of each climatic region ... 66

CHAP. VI.—*Preparation of Soil.*
    Necessity of deep preliminary cultivation—Methods of preparing the soil; subsoiling or trenching—Drainage 74

CHAP. VII.—*Laying-out of Vineyard.*
    Distance apart of vines—Arrangement of vines—Marking out the vineyard—Extent and disposition of blocks 80

CHAP. VIII.—*Propagation of the Vine.*
    Propagation by seed—Propagation by cuttings—Selection of cuttings—Different sorts of cuttings—Length of cuttings—Preservation of cuttings—Stratification—Propagation by layers—Ordinary layering—Complete burying of the vine—Reversed layering—Multiple layering 88

                                                                                    Page
CHAP. IX.—*Planting.*

Are cuttings or rooted vines to be preferred?—Planting of cuttings in the vineyard—Depth for planting—Proper time for planting—Inclination of cuttings—Method of planting—Plantation of cuttings in a nursery—Plantation of rooted vines in the vineyard 98

CHAP. X.—*Forming the Young Vine.*

Proper height of vines—Forming the stem in the first region—Forming the stem in the second and third regions 105

CHAP. XI.—*Pruning.*

Position of fruit-bearing wood on the vine—Long or short pruning—Laws which govern the operation of pruning—Short spur pruning—Rod pruning—Necessity of providing for wood as well as fruit—Mixed system of pruning—System giving great extension—Other systems of pruning—Time for pruning—Pruning instruments 110

CHAP. XII.—*Summer Pruning.*

Disbudding—Topping—Gooseberry style—Tying up—Nipping off the terminal bud of a shoot—Annular incision—Stripping the leaves off ... 122

CHAP. XIII.—*Cultivation.*

Necessity of keeping soil in a loose state—Winter cultivation—Summer cultivation 130

CHAP. XIV.—*Grafting.*

easons for grafting—Ordinary cleft graft—English cleft graft—Time for grafting—Value of different stocks 134

APPENDICES.

A. Abstract of Evidence taken by the Royal Commission on Vegetable Products 140
B. List of Members of Central Vine-growers' Association 145
C. List of the Vine-growers of Victoria 149
D. List of Applications from Vine-growers under the Bonus Regulations ... 170
E. List of Vine-growers' Associations and Office-bearers 179

INDEX 180

NINTH PROGRESS REPORT OF THE ROYAL COMMISSION ON VEGETABLE PRODUCTS.

To His Excellency the Right Honorable JOHN ADRIAN LOUIS, *Earl of Hopetoun, Viscount Aithrie, and Baron Hope, in the Peerage of Scotland; Baron Hopetoun of Hopetoun, and Baron Niddry of Niddry Castle, in the Peerage of the United Kingdom; Knight Grand Cross of the Most Distinguished Order of Saint Michael and Saint George; Governor and Commander-in-Chief in and over the Colony of Victoria and its Dependencies, &c., &c., &c.*

MAY IT PLEASE YOUR EXCELLENCY:

We have the honour to acquaint Your Excellency that, since the date of our last Report, we have confined our inquiries to the collection of practical evidence regarding the cultivation of Perfume Plants and Essential Oils, the cultivation of the Sugar Beet and the manufacture of Sugar therefrom, and the various branches of Agricultural Education as taught in Great Britain and

Europe, with a view to the development of Agricultural Education in this colony. The Minutes of Evidence on these several subjects ar submitted herewith.

In our last Report to Your Excellency we stated that we were fully convinced of the value attached by the public to the Handbooks we have already issued, founded on the evidence given before us, on the subjects of Silos and Ensilage (No. 1), and (No. 2) on the cultivation of Perfume Plants and the production of Essential Oils and Medicinal Drugs. The published returns of the Government Statist show that in the first instance very great advantage to agriculture in Victoria has resulted from the dissemination of the information regarding Ensilage, and in the latter a flourishing Government Perfume Farm is now existing at Dunolly, where eight months ago there was nothing to be seen but the primitive bush. This official example is, to our knowledge, already bearing fruit, and we have every reason to believe that a new industry has been added to the colony.

Accompanying the present Report, we beg to hand to Your Excellency a third Handbook, which is entirely devoted to the important industry of Vine-growing.

This work has been prepared by Mr. François de Castella, one of the experts attached by the Government to the Board of Viticulture, who from training and education is specially qualified to compile from the evidence given by the witnesses, and from his own experience in this colony, a Manual which shall be of practical service to the vine-growers of Victoria.

This Handbook will be followed by a second, dealing with Cellar work and the making of Wine, and subsequently other publications on the cultivation of the Fig, the Olive, &c., will be issued by the Commission.

We have the honour to be,
    Your Excellency's most obedient servants,

    WALTER MADDEN, Vice-President. (L.S.)
    FREDK. T. DERHAM, Member. (L.S.)
    JOHN L. DOW, ,, (L.S.)
    JAMES BUCHANAN, ,, (L.S.)
    CHARLES YEO, ,, (L.S.)
    JAMES McINTOSH, ,, (L.S.)
    JOSEPH KNIGHT, ,, (L.S.)
    ANDREW PLUMMER, M.D., ,, (L.S.)
    T. K. DOW, ,, (L.S.)
    JOHN WEST, ,, (L.S.)
    D. MARTIN, ,, (L.S.)

JOHN J. SHILLINGLAW,
              Secretary.

Public Offices, Melbourne,
    5th May, 1891.

NOTE.—The Honorable J. F. Levien, President of the Commission, absent in Europe. The Honorable George Graham, Minister of Agriculture, has not signed this report, owing to the fact that he is a member of the present Ministry, and as such among His Excellency's Advisers.

MEMBERS OF THE BOARD OF VITICULTURE.

THE HONORABLE GEO. GRAHAM, MINISTER OF AGRICULTURE, *President.*

JOHN M. HIGHETT, ESQ., M.P., *Chairman.*

EMILE BLAMPIED, ESQ., *Great Western.*
THOS. BLAYNEY, ESQ., *Nagambie.*
FREDK. BÜSSE, ESQ., *Barnawartha.*
PAUL DE CASTELLA, *Yering.*
ALEXANDER CAUGHEY, ESQ., *Gooramadda.*
CHARLES CRAIKE, ESQ., *Geelong.*
JOHN JOHNS, ESQ., *Katandra.*
MICHAEL KAVANAGH, ESQ., *Mooroopna.*
FRANCIS MELLON, ESQ., *Dunolly.*
JOHN C. VAN STAVEREN, ESQ., *Nathalia.*
JAMES WILLIAMS, ESQ., *Numurkah.*

SIR ARCHIBALD MICHIE, K.C.M.G., Q.C., *Treasurer.*

ROMEO BRAGATO, ESQ., and FRANÇOIS DE CASTELLA, ESQ., *Experts.*

JOHN J. SHILLINGLAW, ESQ., *Secretary, Public Offices, Melbourne.*

INTRODUCTION.

Although the vine has been successfully cultivated in Victoria for many years, a fresh impetus seems to have been given to the wine-growing industry during the last few years, which fact is undoubtedly due to the inquiries of the Royal Commission on Vegetable Products and to the work of the Board of Viticulture.

A considerable number of persons, more especially young men with small capital, are leaving the cities and turning their attention to the country districts; many of our farmers, finding that the cultivation of cereals scarcely pays, are looking out for some product which will enable them to make more money out of their holdings. Amongst other cultures, that of the vine presents itself as being one of the most remunerative.

Many excellent works have been written on Viticulture, but they are mostly in French or some other foreign tongue, the few English ones which exist being either out of print or only treating of the culture of vines under glass, as practised in England.

The constant demand for some elementary work, in which beginners may learn something of practical Viticulture, has led to the elaboration of this little handbook, which it is hoped may be of service to those requiring information on the subject.

The compilation of such a work is not so easy a task as might at first sight be supposed. The colony of Victoria embraces every description of climate, from Alpine to semi-tropical, or, in other words, every climate in which the vine can be profitably cultivated. To write a book which it is intended should teach people in different circumstances—and who must therefore necessarily adopt different cultural methods—is on this account, in order to avoid confusion, a task requiring great care. In the following pages every endeavour has been made to point out what influence the surrounding circumstances have on the vine, and in what way the different vineyard operations should be altered in consequence. This is the reason why the three first chapters constitute a sort of introduction, a thorough comprehension of which will render the remainder of the work far more intelligible. These first chapters consist chiefly of theoretical considerations, which may be but of small interest to many practical farmers. As such, they have been made as independent as possible of the rest of the work, in order that practical men may, if they so choose, pass them over and proceed at once to the practical part, in which scientific terms and formulæ have been avoided as much as possible, in order to render it readily intelligible to all.

It is unnecessary to enlarge upon the advantages to be derived from the cultivation of the vine. They are evident to any one who considers the subject, and this work is intended rather to give information to those who have already decided to plant than to persuade those who have not.

The cultivation of the vine differs essentially from that of most other plants. Wine does not, like many agricultural products, command a more or less fixed price, varying only with the condition of the market. It varies enormously in value. Without taking into consideration badly-made wine, which may be considered as worthless, we shall often find sound wines of the same age one of which will be worth four times as much as another. This difference in price depends chiefly upon the quality of the wine, and often on the relative rather than on the absolute quality—or, in other words, its suitability for the market which it is intended to command.

At the present moment the market for Victorian—and we may say for Australian—wine is very indefinite. Every one admits that the London market is the one upon which we chiefly rely, and which we must use our best endeavours to satisfy. The production of wine in Victoria is so insignificant that up to this time we have not been looked upon as a wine source by the large London merchants. This, however, is correcting itself. The amount of wine which we shall in a few years produce will be very considerable, and it is absurd to suppose that every grower will then be his own wine merchant, maturing and retailing his wine, as he often has to do at present. Instead of this unsatisfactory state of things, there will be purchasers as soon as the fermentation is properly terminated and the wine is in a fit state to travel. Competition will bring about differences in price in favour of the most suitable wines, and the grower will naturally find that these are the most advantageous for his business. At present any well-made wine of moderate alcoholic strength is of pretty much the same value, but it is scarcely reasonable to suppose that this state of things will continue.

In each district there will be one class of wine which will surpass all others in point of excellence, and it is this type which the grower should endeavour to produce. Different districts will doubtless produce different wines, but all the vine-growers of one district should endeavour to make their wines of that type. Instead of interfering with each other by doing so, they will materially assist one another, as they will render it possible for merchants to obtain a sufficient quantity of the same wine to supply their customers with an article of unvarying character.

This is not possible at present, on account of the great number of different wines made by each vineyard, and the hopeless confusion of names.

Instead of having in each district a host of different names, such as Hermitage, Shiraz, Carbinet, Burgundy, Chasselas, Riesling, Tokay, &c., let each district produce a definite type of wine. Names derived from the sort of grape really mean nothing. Two Rieslings—for instance, one grown on the Yarra and the other on the Murray—differ as much as Hock and Sherry.

Each district now has its Vine-growers' Association. Let all the vine-growers join it, and agree amongst themselves to produce one class of wine, or two at most—say one white and one red—and instead of the host of names mentioned above, the wine will then come to be known by the name of the district in which it is produced. We should have, for example, Rutherglen, Great Western, Bendigo, Mooroopna, and so forth.

Such a change will inevitably come, and the sooner it comes the better for the wine industry. A man will then have some idea of the contents of a bottle from the label.

In all old wine-growing countries this is the course which has been adopted. Fortunately for them, difficulty of communication and the experience of centuries, which showed them what sort of wine could be best produced in the district, brought this about. It is thus that such districts as Bordeaux, Burgundy, Chablis, Sauternes, Champagne, all produce distinct types of wine, and the names of these districts have become famous throughout the civilized world. At the Cape the depreciation of wine was so great that they had to adopt this system, which has so far been attended with most beneficial results.

Very often the growers do not know what sort of wine it is best for their own interests to produce; a few of them do not even know bad wine from good. By belonging to a Vinegrowers' Association, and meeting occasionally to discuss affairs in a friendly spirit, comparing their wines without jealousy, and obtaining the opinion of qualified judges upon the suitability or otherwise of such-and-such a description of wine, they will do more good to themselves, their neighbours, and the viticultural industry in general, than can be easily estimated.

The above remarks apply to the local as well as to the home market. It is very satisfactory to note that year by year the local consumption of our wine is increasing, and although at present far from being as considerable as one might wish, the prejudice of our population in favour of beer and spirit, to which they and their ancestors before them have been accustomed, must be taken into consideration.

It is very gratifying to observe the way in which wine is gradually beginning to supersede other drinks with a great many Victorians. It is needless to remark that the effects of this change of opinion are as beneficial to the consumers as to the producers of the wine, for nobody now attempts to deny that sound natural wine is more wholesome than any other beverage man is in the habit of consuming.

We are entitled to hope that from the amelioration in quality, and greater uniformity in character to which we are looking forward, the result will be a largely increased local consumption.

In conclusion, my thanks are due to those authors whose works have furnished much of the matter contained in this Handbook. Although I have availed myself largely of the reports of the Vegetable Products Commission, there are several other works which I have extensively consulted whilst writing the following pages, and to their authors I now tender my grateful thanks.

Among these I would specially mention Baron Sir F. von Mueller, *Select Extra Tropical Plants;* G. Foex (Director of the Agricultural College of Montpellier), *Cours Complet de Viticulture;* L. Portes and

F. Ruyssen, *Traité de la Vigne et de ses Produits*; Dr. Jules Guyot, *Culture de la Vigne et Vinification*; *Etude des Vignobles de France*; George Husmann, *Culture of the Vine in California*; Francisque Chaverondier, *La Vigne et le Vin*; and the works of Dr. A. C. Kelly upon Vine Culture in South Australia.

Board of Viticulture,
Melbourne, 12th May, 1891.

CHAPTER I.

HISTORY AND DESCRIPTION OF THE VINE.

THE culture of the vine has always accompanied the progress of civilization from the earliest ages up to the present time. Although generally said to have been introduced into Europe from Asia Minor modern research tends to prove that it was indigenous throughout Southern Europe. Of late years many fossil vines have been discovered, some of which so closely resemble the varieties of the present day that it is most probable that the vine has existed in Europe since the geological ages.

Wine was made and drunk by the Hebrews, Egyptians, Greeks, and Romans in the very earliest times. The first mention of it in the Bible is in Genesis ix., 20, 21, 24, where we are told how Noah made wine, and drinking some of it, without knowing its strength, was overpowered by it. Even before this, however, it appears that wine was made in Egypt. At the tomb of Apophis a bas-relief was found representing a wine-press which dates from B.C. 3852, or 1,500 years before Noah.

The antiquity of viticulture, although interesting, is of no practical importance to us, and it will suffice to say that as times became more peaceable, the growth of the vine spread over the greater part of the continent of Europe, even penetrating into the south of England, where, however, it is no longer cultivated for wine-making purposes, and at the present day this precious plant is cultivated in every civilized country where climatic conditions render it possible to do so with profit.

The vine belongs to the family of the Ampelideæ, genus Vitis. All the vines of European origin belong to one species, *i.e.*, Vinifera;

they, therefore, all come under the botanical name of Vitis Vinifera, of which the different sorts, or "*cepages*" as they are called in French, are only varieties. In a future chapter it is intended to describe a few species of Vitis other than the Vinifera, amongst which will be the various American vines, as they differ only in some minor respects from the Vitis Vinifera, which is by far the most important. In this chapter we shall confine ourselves to it as the type to which all vines may be compared.

There is a considerable difference between the wild and the cultivated state of the vine—in the former it is one of the most vigorous, fastest growing, and longest-lived of plants, capable of covering hundreds of square yards or climbing to the tops of the highest trees, but bearing little fruit. In the latter, on the other hand, instead of being a creeper as it is intended to be by nature, it is turned into a more or less stunted shrub, its vitality is much diminished, and its life is shortened to a great extent; these apparent drawbacks being amply compensated by the great increase in the yield which is thus brought about:

With the vine as with many other plants a diminution in the vigour of the plant is marked by an increase in the production of fruit. This is one of the wise provisions of nature for the perpetuation of the species. As long as the plant is in full vigour, it centres all its activity on itself, growing in a remarkable manner, but bearing little or no fruit. When, however, it begins to get weakened by any cause, natural or artificial, it seems to feel that its end is approaching, and turns all its activity to reproduction or the production of fruit.

Many vignerons, knowing this, carry things to extremes and weaken the vine, through excessive pruning, to such an extent that its very existence is made difficult to it. Thus, by overdoing things, do they obtain wretched results, for which they blame the soil, the season, or any cause but the right one. The vine resents such barbarous treatment. Growers must adopt a more rational course, and not kill the goose which lays the golden eggs. This is contrary to the opinion held by many vignerons, but is nevertheless true. It is what *Dr. Guyot*, the eminent French authority on viticulture, tried to impress on the vine-growers of France during his whole life. We shall see more of this when we come to pruning.

The vine is a deciduous flowering creeper or shrub with long slender sarmentaceous shoots. The different parts may be described as follows:—

ROOTS.

The roots of the vine are of two sorts, tap-roots and laterals, which between them make up the complete root system of the plant, each having its special functions to perform. These two sorts of roots are very similar in structure, they are both long, slender, and branching, moderately succulent and similar to those of most fruit trees, and differ principally in their direction. The tap-roots of the vine are ramified, and not so distinct as in most other plants; they are more marked in seedlings than in vines grown from cuttings.

When a young vine is grown from seed the root grows much faster than the stem—it is at first entirely cellular, but it soon becomes covered with a thin epidermis (outer skin), which gets thinner towards the extremities; it is only the parts which are covered with this epidermis which are capable of absorbing food from the soil; on them are found the minute absorbent hairs covered with a very thin membrane, through which the nourishing elements of the soil enter the vine in a state of solution. Later on, this thin skin gives place to a regular bark; woody fibres appear in the centre, and the root reaches its adult stage in which it can no longer absorb liquids directly, but serves to transmit those absorbed near the extremities to the other parts of the plant.

The adult root is composed of a pithy centre, surrounded by bundles of fibres (fibro-vascular bundles), separated by medullary rays. Outside is the bark, formed of vascular bundles, surrounded on the exterior by a layer of cork, which serves to protect the root from injuries. This cork layer varies in thickness, it predominates in the roots of some of the American species, rendering them able to resist the attacks of the phylloxera, to which the European varieties succumb. The roots of the American varieties are also tougher and more woody. Between the bark and the interior of the root is to be found the cambium layer, which generates the different tissues.

STEM.

The stem of the vine in its wild state is not divided as it is when cultivated into trunk, crown, and shoots, but is long, slender and ramified, like the stems of most creepers, and is of pretty much the same diameter at different parts of the vine. This is due to the fact that the more rapid the development of the upper part of the vine the more slender will the stem be. This is often noticeable in trellises, and even vines in a vineyard where the main trunk has been formed too quickly. It is better to form it gradually, as a much stronger and better trunk, requiring less support than that of a too-rapidly formed vine, will be obtained.

The shoots of the year are long and more or less slender. They are knotted at regular intervals. At each knot a leaf is to be found, the leaves growing alternately on either side of the shoot. Tendrils grow opposite to the leaves, which help the plant to fix itself to adjacent objects. In most vines every third leaf will be without a tendril opposite to it, the other two having one. The tendrils are then discontinuous, one species of vine (Vitis Labrusca) has continuous tendrils, a tendril (or bunch) being opposite to every leaf. At each knot there is a woody partition right through the shoot separating the pith above and below it, thus making a vine shoot in this respect comparable to that of a bamboo.

At the base of each leaf there are several buds. The main one will only develop itself in the ensuing year; but, in addition to this, there is one which may give rise to a lateral shoot during the current year, *i.e.*, may grow during the same year as the main shoot, and there are two or more secondary buds which, like the principal one, are reserved for the ensuing year, but only develop themselves in case of injury to the main one.

The laterals grow principally if the extremity of the main shoot be broken off, as we shall see when we come to the chapter on summer pruning.

It is on the lateral shoots of the year that the second crop of grapes appears. It has been recommended to break off the extremities of the young shoot when they are about 4 inches long, it being said that the lateral shoots thus brought into existence will between them bear more fruit than the original shoot off which they grow. This has not been proved as yet, but still deserves mention, as it presents an opportunity for some interesting experiments.

Unless the vine be short pruned a great many of the buds will not develop themselves, the ones at the greatest distance from the old wood, or situated near the end of the previous year's shoots, alone developing themselves; this tendency of the vine to continually elongate itself must be carefully considered when vines are pruned long.

The structure of the stem is very similar to that of the root. It also commences, like the root, by being purely cellular, but soon differentiates itself, becoming gradually more and more complicated. In the centre we have a cylinder of pith, very considerable in the young shoots, but which gradually diminishes as the shoot gets older. Outside this several concentric layers of fibro-vascular bundles are situated, the number varying with the age of the vine; they constitute the wood, which is extremely hard and dense in old vines, although soft when the shoots are young. Then comes the cambium, or generating layer, which forms the rings of new wood every year. The cambium layer is composed of mucilaginous cells, and is situated immediately between the young wood and the bark, which is itself composed of several layers, which it is unnecessary to enumerate here. The bark is thin and adherent; it is drier and tougher than that of most other plants, and for this reason the vine is very hardy, and capable of resisting intense cold; it will survive a winter during which the fig, for example, would perish. The outer layer of bark is gradually pushed off and replaced by new layers underneath it. The old ones do not fall off entirely, but remain more or less attached to the under parts, thus giving the old wood of the vine a characteristic but untidy appearance. This peculiar bark is a certain protection to the plant, but is at the same time a great drawback, as it forms a harbour for insects, spores of parasitic fungi, &c., &c.

LEAVES.

The leaves of the vine are large, and more or less deeply indented, being usually divided into five lobes, by as many *sinus*, as the indentations are called. The margin is serrated or divided into teeth, which vary greatly in size and character; they are large or small, blunt or sharp, regular or irregular; sometimes there are two distinct series of them.

The leaf is supported by a rather long stalk or *petiole*, which in structure resembles the young stem of the vine. There are five fibro-vascular bundles in it, each of which separates at the junction with the broad part of the leaf or limb to form one of the main veins, and occupy one of the lobes, the centre one, or mid-rib, being the largest. Each of these primary veins again gives rise to numerous secondary and tertiary veins distributed in such a way as to form a perfect network of fibre. The veins are raised on the under-surface of the leaf, but rather sunk-in if observed on the upper side.

The two surfaces vary also in many other respects. The under-surface is usually downy, whilst the upper is seldom so. The under side is always of a paler colour than the upper.

In structure the leaves of the vine consist of an epidermis or outer skin, which covers both sides of the leaf, and encloses the parenchyma or cellular tissue, the cells of which contain the chlorophyl or green colouring matter.

On the under side of the leaf are to be found the stomata or breathing pores, to the number of 13,600 per square inch. These may be termed the lungs of the plant, as it is through them that the air is brought in contact with the inner tissues, which are thus enabled to absorb necessary gases from the air, and to get rid of those eliminated during the process of nutrition, as well as a large amount of water. On the upper surface there are no stomata.

On the epidermis are hairs, which are either stiff or long and silky, the former on the under side of most vine leaves, especially on the veins, whilst the latter constitute the cottony down occasionally present on the under or on both sides of the leaf.

Flower.

The flowers of the vine are grouped in bunches, which are too familiar to require description. The bunch is botanically termed a raceme, and is an example of indefinite inflorescence. The flower itself is small and insignificant looking, and of a pale green colour. It may be described as follows :—

Calyx small, almost entire, formed of five sepals united at their base. Corolla, usually composed of five petals, alternate with the sepals and cohering above; when the bud opens they are set free at the base, but remain united at the summit, so that the whole corolla falls off in a single piece. Stamens, usually five in number, opposite to the petals, the anthers being ovate and versatile. Alternate with the stamens are five nectariferous glands, which give rise to the fragrant perfume of the flower. Pistil—style short. It is divided into two cells, each with two ovules. This is the complete or hermaphrodite flower of the vine (Figs. 1 and 2) containing both stamens and pistil. In the wild state all the flowers are not complete,

FIG. 1.   FIG. 2.

some plants bear complete flowers, whilst others bear flowers which are only male, the pistil not being formed (Fig. 3). Other plants

FIG. 3.

again bear both male and complete flowers. Amongst cultivated vines only the plants with hermaphrodite flowers are to be found; the others, which are always sterile, not having been reproduced by cuttings. Among seedling vines, however, they are of frequent occurrence, and if found in a vineyard, the vines bearing them should be destroyed or grafted with kinds bearing only complete or hermaphrodite flowers.

In addition to these, some badly-formed flowers may be found either with the petals opening at the top and remaining attached to the flower

FIG. 4.

in the shape of a star, instead of detaching at their base and falling off in a single cap as they ought to do (Fig. 4). Some again may have the stamens and pistils turned into leaves, either partially (Fig. 5) or totally, as in the flower of a double geranium. The first

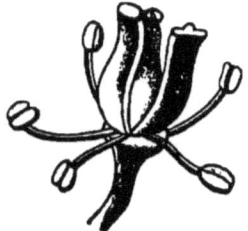

Fig. 5.

are capable of being fecundated by pollen from another flower and giving fruit; they are unable to give rise to fruit otherwise, as the stamens are short and weak, and the pollen often sterile. The second are and must always be sterile.

Tendrils may be looked upon as bunches which have aborted or which bear no fruit. They occur in the same position as the bunches, *i.e.*, opposite to the leaves, the complete bunches being opposed to lower leaves, whilst the tendrils are situated more towards the extremities of the shoots—they serve to attach the vine to the different objects upon which it climbs. The fruit resulting from the fecundation of the above-described flower is a round or slightly oblong succulent berry, which, when ripe, consists of a rather thin skin enclosing a very fluid pulp containing various substances, the most important being glucose or grape sugar and some vegetable acids. In the centre are situated the seeds, varying in number from one to four; in some varieties they are totally absent. The tannin and colouring matter are contained in the skin. The percentage of glucose in the juice, and consequently the strength of the wine, depends upon the amount of fruit on the vine. Vines bearing a light crop will give a stronger wine than those heavily laden with fruit; by regulating the number of bunches on the vines, it is possible to increase or diminish the strength of the wine.

CHAPTER II.

PHYSIOLOGY.

Having described the different parts of the vine, let us see in what manner and to what extent each of them contributes to the development of the plant and production of fruit.

The vine being a deciduous plant, the cycle of its yearly development only extends from the time when the buds burst in the spring till the leaves fall off in the autumn, which, in a temperate climate, embraces a period of something under six months; the other six months of the year are passed in a dormant state.

In this annual cycle of activity it seems to have for primary object the production and proper maturation of its fruit; all the functions of the different organs tending towards this end, as if they had been brought into existence solely for this purpose.

The activity culminates in the ripening of the fruit; after this has taken place, the leaves turn red or yellow, fall off, and the plant hastens to assume its wintry appearance. Not only is this the case in the cultivated vine, where it might be expected since every device of art and an artificial selection during many centuries have been at work striving to increase the yield, but even in the wild state is this so, although to a lesser degree.

In the spring the activity of the vine begins to manifest itself by a rise in the sap; this is followed by the emission of shoots bearing leaves and flower buds, which grow with great rapidity for the first few months.

The rise of the sap is due to the increase in the surrounding temperature; this acts by dilating the bubbles of air which exist in the liquid column contained in the vessels of the stem; by stimulating the leaf buds it causes the emission of organs which provide for a continuation of the rise. The vessels of the vine are large, and the sap flows very freely through them. When a shoot is cut in the spring it bleeds copiously. *Hales* measured this ascensional force of the sap, and found that it was equal to a pressure of about 10 lbs. per square inch. When the plant is in full activity, the rise of sap is still greater, as there are more factors to promote it.

The leaves exert a very considerable influence. The leaves of all plants transpire or exhale through their stomata or breathing pores large quantities of water. Those of the vine are no exception to this rule. *Hales* found that a vine with a leaf surface of 1,820 square inches, or 120 medium-sized leaves, exhaled from 5 oz. to 6 oz. of water daily under ordinary circumstances. This amount, however, is not constant—it varies with the amount of light the plant is exposed to and the moisture of the air. Plants do not transpire in the dark nor in a very faint light. This function is more acted upon by light than heat. It makes room for the fresh sap which is being continually sent up by the roots. This sap becomes concentrated by the loss of water, and by osmosis favours the rise of a fresh quantity. Osmosis is the name given to a physical phenomenon which takes place when two liquids of different density are separated by a thin membrane; both liquids traverse the membrane, but the less dense does so to a far greater extent than the denser one. This process of osmosis takes place throughout the whole of the plant through the cell membranes from the root where the liquids enter the absorbent hairs, in the form of a thin watery solution, to the highest parts of the plant. It is the principal cause of the rise of the sap, which is also promoted by capillary attraction in the long vessels of the plant.

It is unnecessary to enlarge upon the cause of this rise of the sap; it is sufficient for us to know that it does rise, and not only does it rise but it circulates.

After entering the roots through the microscopic absorbent hairs in the form of a thin watery solution, it rises through the vessels of the young wood and finally reaches the leaves, to all the tissues of which it is distributed by the veins. In the leaves it is not only concentrated by loss of water, as we have already seen, but it becomes enriched with many new substances derived from its contact with the atmosphere.

Under the influence of the light of day the chlorophyl or green colouring matter is capable of decomposing the carbonic acid of the air and taking the carbon with which it forms immediate products, which will in turn undergo transformations in order to form the different tissues, &c., of the plants, the oxygen being set free. One of the most important of these immediate products is starch, but there are many others such as oils, acids, &c. The leaves therefore, perform the double functions of transpiration and assimilation—in addition to these, a true respiration similar to that of animals takes place in them, the plant absorbing oxygen and exhaling carbonic acid, and effecting transformations in some of the substances assimilated during the day. This respiration is noticeable at night, but is not so considerable as the absorption of carbonic acid during the day.

Having undergone these different processes in the leaf, the sap descends through the vessels of the bark, and is distributed to the different parts of the plant as required, a part of it finding its way to the roots, where it provides for the elongation of these organs; and at the same time a small quantity which escapes, helps to dissolve certain mineral substances of the soil which are not soluble in water, such as carbonate of lime and phosphates, and thus allows them to enter the vine.

It is evident from all this, that carbon, which is the most abundant solid element in all plants, and which remains in the form of charcoal when almost any vegetable substance is strongly heated without a sufficient supply of air to burn it, is derived solely from the atmosphere, and assimilated by the leaves, none of it being absorbed through the roots. The only substances absorbed by the roots are water, ash, and compounds containing nitrogen (ammonia and nitrates). These do not form a large percentage, and if we except water, which is of course necessary to dissolve the other substances, we shall find that not 8 per cent. of the total weight of the plant comes from the soil, the remaining 92 per cent. being absorbed from the air. Strange as this may seem it is not less true, no scientific fact being more clearly proved. The different organs perform their functions in this manner throughout the summer, the roots requiring moisture without the help of which they would be unable to absorb the necessary mineral substances of the soil, or to replace the water lost by the plant through transpiration. The leaves on their side require heat, light, and air. Although it is necessary that moisture should be present in the soil, it must not be so in too great a proportion as the vine requires air at its roots as well. If the soil be swampy or sour, the vigour of the plant will be greatly impaired, and it will fall an easy prey to any disease to which it may be subject.

About the month of November, in Victoria, the all-important function of flowering takes place; the vine has then increased considerably in size both above and below ground. The flower bud gradually swells till the moment of bursting, when the corolla is forced off in a single piece or capsule, and the different parts of the flower are set at liberty. The pollen of the anthers is deposited on the pistil, and finds its way to the ovules, which, being fecundated, will ultimately become the seeds; the ovary in which they are contained swelling up to form the fruit. The exact moment when this fecundation takes place is not clearly known. Some authors consider that it is just before the capsule is thrown off, and while the anthers are in contact with the pistil, whilst the majority admit that it takes place immediately after the fall of the capsule. It is quite possible that under different circumstances both views may be correct.

If the ovules are not fecundated, the flower withers and falls off, giving rise to no fruit, or in plain words the fruit does not set.

The seedless Sultana grape seems at first sight to be an exception to this rule; but the experiment of *Mr. Knight*, of Sandhurst, in his evidence before the Royal Commission on Vegetable Products, proves that this is not so—the ovules are perfectly fecundated, but the seeds are subsequently absorbed into the pulp of the fruit. The non-setting of the grapes, or "*coulure*" as it is termed in French, is due to several causes. The washing off of the pollen by rain at the time when fecundation should take place is one of them, but in far the greater number of cases it is due to a malformation of the flower.

We have already seen several cases in which it is, so to speak, inherited from parent vines, in which case the faulty vines should be destroyed; but it often happens that it is not the fault of the plant but of the season. Under the influence of prolonged wet weather, even a considerable time before the blossoming, there may be an excessive amount of sap in the plant, rendering it weak and flabby, although in appearance perfectly normal. The stamens then become short and watery, and are incapable of fecundating the pistil, which itself may be sterile. This is amply proved to be the case by the fact that anything which tends to diminish the quantity of sap in the vine also diminishes the non-setting of such varieties as may be subject to this defect. The excessive moisture may also promote this by facilitating the growth of fungus parasites on the delicate reproductive organs, with fatal results to the crop of fruit.

In addition to this non-setting or complete abortion in certain years, it may be observed that although at first the fruit appears to have set properly, after a short time differences will be noticeable between different berries of the bunch, all of which do not take an even development, so that at vintage time the bunches are loose and made up of uneven-sized berries, some of which, containing no seeds (which have been re-absorbed), are scarcely larger than shot, and do not ripen properly, while at the same time there are some normal ones (Fig. 6).

In French this is termed "*millerandage.*" It may result from several causes. Sometimes it will be observed on diseased vines, in which case it would appear to be due to faulty nutrition of the plant; but it occurs far more often in Australia, especially when cold wet weather prevails immediately after

FIG. 6.

the setting of the flower, the young fruit receiving a check to their development, from which they are not able to completely recover. According to *M. L. de Malafosse*, these small berries are due to the development of some late flowers present in most bunches, which usually abort, but are enabled to develop on account of the non-setting of some of the principal flowers; they are not, however, capable of giving normal-sized fruit. Whatever be the manner in which this "*millerandage*" be brought about, it may be said to result in the great majority of cases from the prevalence of unfavorable weather immediately after the blossoming. Once fecundated, the fruit develops itself steadily during the whole of the summer, the rest of the plant also increases in size to some extent, although it does not grow rapidly after the blossoming. The leaves increase in size and number, and in them the various substances found in the mature fruit are elaborated. They are thus of the greatest importance; the fruit cannot be formed without them. In the words of Macagno, another eminent French authority, "the leaves are the laboratory of production of glucose, the green branches the conductors of this precious constitutive element of the must."

We, therefore, see that the leaves do not simply act beneficially by sheltering the grapes from the direct rays of the sun, but are indispensable for the elaboration of the necessary constituents of the mature fruit. The unripe berries contain several free acids, amongst the number tartaric, citric, and malic are the most important. By the action of these acids on such substances as starch, gum, dextrine, lignine, cellulose, &c., grape-sugar or glucose is formed. The fruit during this time becomes richer in sugar and poorer in acid; part of the acid is also neutralized by mineral salts absorbed by the roots, and at the same time the juice becomes denser through loss of water by evaporation. The different processes which take place in the plant, of which the ultimate result is the production of glucose, are exceedingly complex and cannot be gone into here; the above outline sketch will suffice to give an idea of the character of the transformations.

A short time before the maturation takes place—the time being marked for red grapes by their commencing to change colour—a characteristic change seems to come over the vine; it looks sick. This is caused by the sap partly leaving the leaves and transporting itself to the berries. During this time the plant looks more unhealthy than at any other period of its yearly development. This is termed in French the "*veraison*," and continues, although in a less marked manner, until the time when the fruit is ready to be picked.

Once the maturity is complete, whether the grapes be picked or not, the duty of the year being accomplished, the vine hastens to assume its winter appearance. The nutritive materials which have not been required for the fruit are concentrated in or about the buds as a store for next year, to enable the plant to start its growth again.

The leaves turn red or yellow and fall off; the ascensional power of the sap becomes less and less and finally ceases, and the vine assumes its winter or dormant state and is to all intents and purposes dead. It continues in this state until the rise of temperature in the spring determines a rise of sap and commencement of vegetation, when the same cycle is gone through once more.

CHAPTER III.

FACTORS INFLUENCING THE GROWTH AND PRODUCTS OF THE VINE.

Any one who studies the numerous works on viticulture, or strives to obtain information on the subject from practical men coming from different parts of Europe, will be struck by the great confusion which exists, and the startling way in which the systems recommended by each differ from one another, even on what would appear to be the fundamental principles, or such operations as planting, pruning, &c.

It may be imagined that this is so, because each district in the old country has its particular method, handed down from generation to generation, and the prejudice common to uneducated country people makes them unwilling to change it; but the application of more scientific methods would change all this, and bring about a reform, having for result the adoption of one standard system. This, however, is not the case. It is not alone by scientific research that our modern knowledge of viticulture has been obtained. Our ancestors were not scientific men, yet no one can deny that they brought it to a high state of perfection. Their guide was practical experience, extending over many centuries; it taught them slowly but surely, with comparatively few exceptions, the best method to adopt; this is amply proved by the fact that since the results of modern research have been applied to practical viticulture, few alterations have been made in the methods used.

We are thus led to admit that nearly every district in the wine-producing countries of Europe has a distinct viticultural method of its own, and at the same time that all these methods are correct, provided they are adopted in the locality where experience has proved their suitability. In Europe things are thus greatly simplified; in nine cases out of ten a man may, with perfect safety, copy the method adopted by the majority of his neighbours. In Australia we are very differently situated; we have no experience of past generations to guide us, but are confronted at the start by a host of conflicting opinions held by vignerons coming from different countries and climates. The simplest and quickest way out of the difficulty is to try to discover, by more scientific means than our ancestors had at their disposal, what are the rules we are to be guided by, and how they may be varied by circumstances. It is impossible to lay down hard-and-fast rules for viticulture—to say, as many people do, that any particular soil, distance apart, kind of vine, &c., is the best for wine making. We shall see that the same method of culture in two different localities will give different results, different modes of culture in the same locality will also give different results, and lastly, that in certain cases different modes of culture in different localities may give the same result.

The surrounding circumstances have more influence on the vine than on most plants usually cultivated. Their effect is plainly visible in the outward appearance of the plant, but manifests itself to a far greater extent in the wine which is, on this account, a most variable product.

These surrounding circumstances are made up of several factors; it is of the greatest importance that the vigneron should know what they are, in what manner they act, and in what way it is possible to modify their effect by adopting a different system of culture, with the object of obtaining a wine well suited to the requirements of commerce, and at the same time of as high a degree of perfection as possible; as between making a pretty good wine and a very good wine lies all the difference between paying working expenses and making handsome profits.

In this chapter we shall examine what these different factors are and in what way they act; in the following ones we shall see in what way it is possible to modify their effect. These factors are climate, soil, and variety.

CLIMATE.

Although the three factors enumerated above are all of great importance, the climate is, without doubt, the most important one. Its influence in rendering a certain mode of culture more suitable than another is very considerable—in fact, it is of such importance as to be capable of rendering the profitable cultivation of the vine impossible. There is, in other words, a climatic zone, outside of which vine-growing will not pay. Fortunately, this zone is very extensive, and we may say that it embraces all climates which are neither tropical nor very cold. Very few parts of this colony of Victoria are unsuitable for the cultivation of the vine as far as this factor is concerned.

The three elements, heat, light, and moisture, in varying proportions, make up the climate. Two vines so situated as to receive more or less of either of them may be said to be in different climates, as would also be the case if they received the maxima or minima of either of them at different times.

Heat and light may be considered together, as they both being derived from a common source—viz., the sun—on a clear day the plant receives more, and on a cloudy day less of each.

The immediate effect of an increase in the amount of heat and light a vine receives, or, in other words, of transporting it from a colder into a warmer climate, is an increase in the vigour of the plant; but its most important effect is to augment the percentage of glucose contained in the must, and, consequently, the strength of the resulting wine.

It is for this reason that the wines of northern France are lighter than those of the south, which are in turn lighter than those of Spain; or, in taking Victoria, that the wines of the northern districts are stronger than those of the southern ones.

That the effect of the climate should be very considerable is evident when we consider that not only does the plant receive more intense heat and light during the same time, but it receives it during a longer time—the yearly cycle of active growth, increasing in length in the warm climate, since the vines begin to bud much sooner in the spring, although the time of complete maturity of the fruit is not sensibly hastened.

We saw in Chapter II. that during the ripening of the fruit the percentage of acid diminishes as that of glucose increases. Part of this acid is employed in the elaboration of the glucose, and part is neutralized by mineral salts derived from the soil just before complete maturity; in a cold climate the acids are not completely neutralized, and the grapes (and wine) often have a sour crude taste.

To sum up the effect of climate in a few words, we may say the colder it is the more acid, the warmer it is the more alcohol the resulting wine will contain.

The cold climate errs by the resulting wine being too rich in acid, and the warm by it being too rich in alcohol. A perfect wine can therefore be more easily produced in a temperate climate.

The influence of moisture is to some extent contrary to what we have just seen, inasmuch as in a moist climate the percentage of acid and glucose in the must are both diminished. In some cases this is an advantage, but in excess is very injurious, the vine being subject to various fungus diseases (especially if the air be damp), and the wine becoming a watery compound without flavour, bouquet, or keeping qualities. Although it is impossible to alter the climate in the matter of light and heat, we can modify it, as far as moisture is concerned, by having recourse to irrigation, which thus becomes of the greatest importance to vine-growers in very dry countries, where the rainfall is so scanty as to render viticulture unprofitable without its aid.

Irrigation, as applied to vineyards, has given rise to much discussion, most persons, especially in this country, holding different opinions as to the results to be expected from it. In the evidence taken by the Royal Commission on Vegetable Products, whilst most witnesses agree that it largely increases the yield, they express very different opinions as to whether its adoption is advisable or not. Some recommend it, others denounce it in emphatic terms, saying that it facilitates the development of fungus diseases of the vine and ruins the character of the wine.* There is much to be said on both sides; moderation must be observed in this as in most other things. The use of too much water is no doubt injurious, especially in land where the drainage is imperfect, as a vine is most unfavorably placed if growing in swampy or very damp soil. In the cooler parts of the colony vineyards should be very sparingly, if ever irrigated; in fact, in most cases, it is better to dispense with it altogether. It will, however, be readily understood by unprejudiced persons that this is not so in the dry northern districts. In the case of a deficient rainfall the application of a few inches of water in an artificial manner can only be attended with beneficial results if the water be applied judiciously and at a proper time. An excessive amount of sap in the plant at flowering time, or a chill immediately after the setting of the fruit, being usually attended with disastrous results (page 12), care should be taken not to apply water until this dangerous period has safely passed and the berries are of the size of small shot.

---

* In the Appendix will be found an abstract of these opinions.

The application of water too late in the season (just before vintage) is also injurious, and, according to some, liable to promote the growth of a second crop of grapes.

On the whole, we may say that irrigation of vineyards is in many cases beneficial, and sometimes even necessary; it enables the cultivation of the vine to be carried out in localities where it would be impossible under the prevailing climatic conditions, it largely increases the yield, and at the same time enables a lighter wine to be produced in the warmer parts of the colony. In the central parts it may often prove beneficial, although by no means necessary, whilst in the cooler southern parts it cannot be recommended except under exceptional circumstances.

The water of rivers contains far more fertilizing matter than rain water, it therefore follows that irrigation acts beneficially in, to some extent, enriching the land, and by thus delaying its ultimate exhaustion, postponing the time when manuring must be resorted to, or at least by compensating for the increase in production it brings about.

The opponents of irrigation urge that it is not used in France. This, however, is not the case. *Foex*, the director of the Agricultural College of Montpellier (France), mentions several parts of the south of France where vineyards have been irrigated for many years, and recommends the extension of this practice, especially for the production of cheaper wines. *Pulliat* also mentions how the vineyards of the Canton du Valais, in Switzerland, are irrigated, the climate, although cold in winter, being dry in summer.

Much harm has been done to the cause of irrigated vineyards by inexperienced persons who have water placed at their disposal. Thinking that its fertilizing powers are unlimited, and that the more the vines get the better will the result be, they over-do it, and swamp them to such an extent as to either prevent the setting of the grapes or promote the growth of fungus diseases, which destroy the crop; they soon find their error, then rush to the other extreme, denounce irrigation, and resolve never to have recourse to it again. Although the water may not have been applied in sufficient quantity to do this, yet it may have done considerable injury by unduly decreasing the percentage of natural acid in the fruit, and thus rendering the wine less liable to keep well as well as making it more dangerous during fermentation. Although too much natural acid (which would be present were unripe grapes employed) is objectionable, too little is almost as bad.

The failure of irrigated vineyards is frequently caused by neglect of cultivation. Irrigation, to be successful, must be supplemented by thorough and frequent cultivation, for which it is by no means a substitute, as many people seem to think.

A vineyard owes its particular climate to several causes, of which the most important are latitude, altitude, and aspect; it is also greatly influenced by the distance from the coast, proximity to mountain ranges, direction of prevailing winds, &c.

It is unnecessary to discuss the influence of altitude and latitude here—every one knows that the further one goes from the equator, or the higher one rises above sea-level, the colder it will be.

The aspect or exposition o a vineyard, however, although of varying and, as a rule, lesser importance, deserves mention, as one continually hears such very different opinions as to its importance. In reality this varies with the coldness of the climate; in a warm one it is not considerable, the amount of light and heat being so great that a little more or less does not make much difference.

On almost level land the influence of aspect is insignificant. On hilly land it may be very considerable, the side of a hill facing the north evidently being far hotter than that facing the south. In some parts of Europe the eastern aspect is considered far superior to any other for the reason we have already given, that light has more influence on many vegetable functions than heat—the eastern side of a hill being exposed to the morning light, always more intense than that of the afternoon.

Is this aspect always an advantage? In a cold climate it is certainly so, but in a warm climate it is often preferable to choose a site with a cooler aspect, S.S.E. or even S.W. One often hears it said that the vine must be grown on hills and not on flat land. In a cold district this is true, because the hillsides with favorable aspect and shelter will be warmer, the drainage better, and the soil also poorer—sometimes an advantage in a cool climate as we shall see later on.

In a temperate climate the aspect is of small importance, and flat land is often as suitable as hilly, whilst in a warm district the best aspect will often be the southern or south-western slope, or the one which would be worst in a cool district.

The distance from the sea renders the climate more extreme, that is, hotter in summer and colder in winter. Localities situated far inland are, as a rule, more liable to suffer from spring frosts, although producing a stronger wine than places near the coast, where the variations in temperature are not so great.

The proximity to high mountain ranges renders the climate cooler and moister than it would otherwise be. The effect of prevailing winds varies according as to whether they have passed over the sea or over a heated continent, or, in other words, whether they are dry or moist.

From all this it will be seen that it is impossible to lay down any simple rules which would enable a man to say, for example, " the climate of my vineyard is identical with that of Bordeaux." Only complete meteorological observations can enable such a thing to be said with any approach to certainty.

For the purposes of this work, it will be very convenient for us to roughly divide the colony into three climatic regions or divisions as far as viticulture is concerned. These regions would be as follows :—

First, or cool region.—This would embrace the greater part of the colony situated on the coast side of the Dividing Range, and would be very similar to the best wine-growing districts of France, such as Bordeaux, Burgundy, Champagne, &c., and from similarity of climate would be solely but eminently suited for the production of light wines of similar character to those made in the above districts.

Second, or intermediate region, comprising the greater part of the central districts of Victoria, the climate of which is similar to that of the south of France or north of Italy. Sandhurst, Great Western, and similar wine-producing districts would come within this region, which would be admirably suited for the production of good commercial wines, and capable of producing either strong or light wines, according to the sorts grown and methods of cultivation.

Third, or warm region; where the climate is similar to that of Spain, Portugal, or Sicily, and therefore best suited for the production of strong wines, although by careful culture and selection of soil and varieties moderately light wines may be produced. Rutherglen, Mildura, and most places situated in the northern and north-western parts of the colony would be comprised in this region which is the one where the best results would be obtained from the employment of irrigation.

Soil.

The nature of the soil has a most important influence on the growth of the vine and on the quality and quantity of wine which it will produce. Two vineyards, differing from each other only in the soil, may give very different results both as regards the crop per acre and the value of the wine.

The vine is one of the hardiest of plants, and will grow in any soil that is not swampy, too highly mineralized, or otherwise unfit for vegetation. There is scarcely any variety of soil fulfilling these requirements in which profitable vineyards have not, at one time or another, been established; but, as might reasonably be expected, certain classes are more or less suitable than others, more especially, as we shall see, in a certain climate or for a certain variety of vine.

The characters of a soil are physical and chemical. The physical characters are looseness or stiffness, depth, and colour.

The looseness or friability of a soil is of great importance. The advantages of a friable soil over a compact one are manifest—the drainage is better, the absorption of water greatly facilitated, and, as it can be cultivated with far greater ease, it enables one to check the evaporation of moisture during the dry season, as nothing favours the retention of moisture so much as keeping the surface in a thoroughly loose state. The difference between a stiff clay soil, which dries up and cracks in summer, and a sandy or otherwise friable soil, which remains loose and is always moist a few inches below the surface, is too well known to need enlarging upon. A loose soil is therefore an advantage in a very wet as well as in a very dry district.

The depth of the soil is of variable importance, and depends chiefly upon the climate. Although a deep soil is usually considered to be the best for vine-growing purposes, if we examine the different districts in the old country we find that this is far more the case in the southern than in the northern parts. In a warm climate the vine, taking a greater development, requires more room for its roots, which, extending vertically as well as laterally, demand a deeper soil. Under such conditions there is also less danger of a scarcity of moisture during the summer. In a cold district the moisture of the soil is always ample, and the vine, growing with less vigour, can satisfy itself with a much shallower soil, in which it is also better able to mature its fruit, an operation which is not always satisfactorily performed in northern France, where it is not uncommon to see vineyards growing where there is only a thin layer of soil covering an impenetrable rocky subsoil. Such vineyards are in many cases celebrated for the excellence of their product (but, again we say it, only in a cold district).

The colour of a soil is of more importance than might be imagined. Every one knows the difference between the temperature of a house, the outside of which is painted black or painted white. With the soil the influence is more marked, as it acts both upon the roots and the part above ground. A dark-coloured soil absorbs heat, and its own temperature rises, but it reflects very little on to the upper part of the vine, whilst a white or light-coloured soil has the reverse effect; it reflects the rays on to the fruit and leaves, whilst its own temperature increases but slightly. It follows that a dark soil is an advantage in a cold climate where the moisture of the soil is excessive, while in a warm climate a light-coloured soil is preferable, as it insures to a greater extent the retention of moisture. The disease known as *Chlorosis*, which is characterized by the leaves of the vine turning yellow and the whole plant losing its vigour, and which often results from too much moisture in the soil, is less prevalent in dark than in light coloured soils, in which many vines, more especially among those of American origin, suffer very considerably from it.

Soils containing pebbles or gravel are always, and in all countries, highly esteemed for viticultural purposes. This is borne out by the fact that almost all the most celebrated vineyards are planted in soils containing a more or less considerable proportion of pebbles of various kinds. In the best Burgundy vineyards they are calcareous, at Bordeaux quartz, on the Rhine granitic, and in Champagne chalky. In some of the most celebrated vineyards the soil is so stony that it would be unfit for any other culture than that of the vine. At Chateau Lafitte the proportion of water-worn quartz pebbles in the soil is 71 per cent.

The chemical properties of the soil are of great importance, and in order that they should be understood, it will be necessary to revert to what we saw with reference to the composition of the vine. The following table gives a fair idea of the importance of the different elements of which the plant is composed, as well as the sources from which they are derived:—

Carbon ... ... ⎫	Amounting to about 90 per cent., and derived by the vine from the air and rain.
Hydrogen ... ... ⎬	
Oxygen ... ... ⎭	
Sodium ... ... ⎫	Amounting to about 4 per cent. These elements are always far more abundantly provided in the soil than is necessary to the plant.
Magnesium ... ... ⎪	
Sulphur ... ... ⎪	
Chlorine ... ... ⎬	
Iron ... ... ⎪	
Silicon ... ... ⎪	
Manganese ... ... ⎭	
Nitrogen ... ... ⎫	Amounting to something over 4 per cent. Derived like the last from the soil in which they are only present to a limited extent.
Phosphorus ... ... ⎬	
Potassium ... ... ⎪	
Calcium (lime) ... ⎭	

Of these fourteen elements, combined together in varying numbers and proportion, the almost infinite number of substances found in the vine and wine are made up. We see from the above table that the last four, viz.:—Potassium, phosphorus, nitrogen, and calcium (or lime) are the only ones we need consider, as all others are either derived from the air and rain or are so abundantly present in all soils as to be practically inexhaustible. The presence of more or less of these four important elements renders a soil valuable or worthless, and the predomination of any one of them will render such a soil especially suitable for one class of plants. A soil rich in nitrogen is most suitable for wheat, colza, tobacco, &c.; one rich in phosphorus is better suited for turnips, maize, sugar cane, &c.; whilst for vines potash is the most important element, at least as far as the production of fruit is concerned—the presence of phosphorus and nitrogen has more influence on the production of wood. Now, although vines are cultivated with the object of obtaining fruit, there must be wood for the fruit to grow upon. We must have sufficient of all the necessary elements, but as potash is the one of which the greatest portion is taken away by the fruit, it is the one which should be present in considerable proportion in all soils intended for vines.

In many cases poor soils give wines of superior quality, especially in a cold climate where a heavy crop would give too weak a wine.

The number of varieties of soil are very great, and it would be out of place to here give complicated analyses, yet it will be of use to those who intend planting, to briefly review what are the chief types of soil, what are the principal constituents of each, and in what way it acts upon the vine.

All soils more or less resemble one of the following types :— Clayey, sandy, calcareous, plutonic, and peaty soils.

Clay soils give excellent wines, as a rule, in temperate climates, especially if they are not too compact, their principal drawback being their liability to crack and dry up. Wines made in clay soils usually possess all the requisite characteristics of a good wine in moderation and are very pleasant. Their chief constituent, pure clay or silicate of alumina, is not necessary to the vine, so its influence must be more mechanical than otherwise.

Schistose soils are usually metamorphic clays, and therefore give similar results. A loose surface resting on a mellow clay subsoil will give excellent results in a cool district. A clayey soil will in most cases greatly benefit by being irrigated.

Sandy soils contain a greater or lesser proportion of pure silica. The wine they produce is generally light and delicate, more so than that produced by any other. In them the vine grows very freely and begins to bear early, probably on account of the facility with which the roots can spread.

Calcareous or limestone soils.—The presence of lime has a marked influence on the strength of the wine—that made on a limestone soil containing as much as 5 or 6 per cent. more alcohol than wine grown on sandy soil. They are therefore more desirable in a cold than in a warm climate. The vine does not grow very vigorously on such soils, although lime is to be found more extensively in the wood than in the fruit.

Plutonic soils.—Under this category may be classed granitic, porphyritic, basaltic, and the so-called volcanic soils ; they are, as a rule, rich in potash, and therefore admirably suited for viticulture. The Hermitage vineyard in France is situated on granitic soil ; the Tokay of Hungary on basalt. The wines made on such soils are therefore excellent, and these soils will grow vines for many years without becoming exhausted.

Peaty soils are those rich in organic matter, and, consequently, in nitrogen. Although very rich and forming good agricultural soils, they must be said to be less suitable than the others for viticulture. The nitrogen stimulates the woody development, but the fruit is watery and the resulting wine—poor in sugar, acids, and tannin—does not keep well.

The presence of iron in a soil has a great effect in increasing the colour of the wine. It is probably for this reason that our Australian wines are, as a rule, so rich in colour. Some soils in France containing magnesia produce white wines of very high quality.

The richest soil does not produce the best wine. In many instances it is rather the reverse. Some of the best wines in the world are grown on soil so poor as to be almost unfit for any other culture but that of the vine. Rich soils more frequently produce common wines, but in great abundance.

Such are, in a general way, the chief kinds of soils and the manner in which they influence the resulting wine. It must be borne in mind that under each head there will be some which will give better results than others, although the differences between them may be so slight as to be only noticeable in the wine itself, and not apparent to an ordinary observer. Chemical analysis enables us to find out all the elements in a soil as well as the proportions in which they exist; by adding certain elements to one soil, however, so as to make it identical with another, we cannot be sure of obtaining the same results from it, even if the other conditions of climate, &c., be identical.

In many European wine-growing districts, it is common to find two vineyards, only separated by a wall, planted with the same varieties and cultivated in the same manner, producing wines of very different commercial values. No addition of substances to the soil will enable the proprietor of the inferior vineyard to produce wine equal to that of his more fortunate neighbour.

There is a subtle something in the soil that gives this superiority, and which it is impossible to impart by artificial means. Most beneficial results may be obtained by the addition of certain substances with a view of increasing the yield, but the quality of the wine cannot be similarly controlled.

These remarks must not prejudice one against the analysis of soils, which is of great help, as we shall see later.

Variety.

It is our intention to devote a special chapter to the description of the different varieties of vine usually cultivated, but we shall here say a few words about the influence of the variety on the character of the wine, and mention some of the points on which varieties differ from one another.

The variety, or "cepage," as it is concisely termed in French, is considered by many to be the most important factor of the wine. We prefer to give it third place, the climate and soil being what may be termed fixed factors, whilst the selection of sorts is entirely at the discretion of the vine-grower.

It is necessary to distinguish between choice and common varieties. The former are those from which high-class wines are made. The latter are devoted to the production of ordinary wines of commerce—they make up for the inferior quality of their product by being much heavier bearers, and hardier than the more delicate choice varieties.

It is to be regretted that many persons, tempted by the prospect of heavy yields, plant common to the exclusion of choice varieties, and thus sacrifice quality to quantity—an injudicious course of action, the evil effects of which will inevitably be felt as soon as competition begins to be active. The higher class wine, commanding a higher price, amply compensates for the lesser yield.

The distinction between choice and common varieties is not absolute, but relative. It depends to some extent upon the condition of soil and climate.

A vine which is a heavy bearer, but which gives too weak a wine in a cold district, may give excellent results in a warmer one; or a sort may be a choice one in one soil and a common one in another. As an example, we may mention the Gamay of Beaujolais and the Pinot of Burgundy. The soil of the Beaujolais district is granitic and schistose, whereas that of Burgundy is calcareous. In the former the Gamay gives a superior wine to the Pinot ; in the Burgundy district, on the other hand, it is the Pinot alone which gives the celebrated wines which make the name of Burgundy a household word throughout the world, whilst the Gamay is looked upon as an inferior sort.

It is thus of the greatest importance that the variety should be suited to the other conditions; we have in the judicious choice of it a means of producing a wine of, to some extent, what character we wish. In a very warm climate we want to make a wine as light as possible, in a cold one it is a strong wine we must try to make. The strength of wines made from different varieties in the same vineyard will greatly differ. For example, one may give a wine containing 14 per cent. of alcohol whilst another would produce one containing over 20 per cent.

It follows that the variety which gives the best results in the first or cool region would be utterly unsuited for the third region, at least for the production of light wine. Although it might yield a strong sweet wine of high quality as such, the demand for this class of wine is only limited.

All varieties are not influenced alike by an increase in the warmth of the climate—its effect in increasing the alcoholic strength of the wine is more considerable on some than on others. For example, a certain sort might give a wine containing 18 per cent. of alcohol if grown at Lillydale, whilst it might contain 26 per cent. if grown at Rutherglen. The relative strength for a second variety might be— Lillydale 20 per cent. and Rutherglen 23 per cent. The increase in strength would be 8 per cent. for the first sort, and only 3 per cent. for the second, which, in other words, gives more constant results under varied climatic conditions than the first sort.

The time of coming into leaf in the spring and of the ripening of the grapes varies greatly. It is very advisable that the vine-grower should keep a permanent record of the date of the first appearance of the leaves and flowers on his vines. Late budding varities are to be recommended in localities subject to spring frosts, whilst early ripening sorts should be cultivated if the weather about vintage time be usually unfavorable. Some varieties have greater or less power of resisting frost, once they are in leaf, whilst others are capable of bearing fruit on the secondary buds if the main ones have been destroyed. The suitability or otherwise of a variety also depends on its capacity for resisting fungus or insect diseases, or being more suited to a special style of pruning. These peculiarities will be given in the next chapter where each vine will be described in detail.

CHAPTER IV.

AMPELOGRAPHY.

The word "Ampelography" denotes the description of different kinds of vines.

The family of the Ampelideæ is divided into several genera; the only one which interests us here is the genus Vitis, which is in turn divided into several species.

The ordinary grape vine, Vitis Vinifera, being the most important, is the species we shall devote most attention to. There are several others which we must also describe, amongst which are the American vines, which have assumed great importance of late years, on account of the remarkable resistance they oppose to the attacks of the phylloxera.

Each species comprises many more or less distinct sorts, or "cepages," as they are termed in French; the term being very convenient, as these different sorts are not all sufficiently distinct to justify their being classed as different varieties from a strictly botanical point of view, although the term may be used in a general way.

As vines are always propagated by cuttings, and any issue derived from seed may vary considerably from the parent plant, it is more correct to look upon all the vines of a "cepage" collectively, as an individual, of which each vine is a part. In other words, the differences between "cepages" are individual differences, the many millions of each which exist together only making up or being, so to speak, part of the original vine from which they were multiplied in the shape of cuttings.

The differences between these sorts are of the first importance as far as the resulting wine is concerned; they, therefore, are of far greater interest to the practical vigneron than to the botanist.

In this chapter the most important "cepages" are described in alphabetical order under the different species to which they belong.

EUROPEAN VINES.

These are very numerous, and embrace over a thousand sorts, all of which belong to the species Vitis Vinifera, many of which, fortunately, need not be mentioned here.

We shall confine ourselves to those which are usually cultivated in Australia, as well as a few which might be adopted with excellent results, according to circumstances, for wine-making purposes, without mentioning the numerous table grapes, as they come more strictly under the domain of horticulture.

The most usual synonyms of each are given, but it must be borne in mind that the classification of the different sorts is by no means easy. Authorities on the subject often hold very different opinions as to the identity or otherwise of sorts called by different or even by the same name in different districts in Europe.

With regard to the time of ripening of the fruit, we have adopted *Pulliat's* system of dividing the time of ripening of all grapes into three periods. The different sorts ripen during one or other of these.

Sorts marked * are those already extensively cultivated in Victoria; those marked † have with certainty been introduced into the colony, but are not extensively cultivated.

† **Aramon.** Synonyms: *Buchardt's Prince, Ugni Noir, Revalaïre, Okors zem Kek*, &c.

Although only a common red variety it was very extensively cultivated in the south of France before the invasion of the phylloxera, on account of its great prolificacy. Foex estimates its average crop at about 1,000 gallons per acre, and states that it has been known to produce 3,500 gallons per acre. It makes up for its great bearing capabilities by only yielding an ordinary wine, especially if the soil be rich and the crop heavy.

In the third or warm region of Victoria it would prove a valuable sort; its wine, being light, would be very suitable for blending with other sorts, with the object of producing a good commercial wine. It comes into leaf early, and is, therefore, liable to suffer from late frosts. It ripens in the third period, and its thin skin makes the berries liable to rot in a moist climate.

It resists the mildew pretty well, but is somewhat sensitive to the attacks of the oidium. As the Aramon is always cultivated for quantity rather than quality it must be planted in a rich soil which is at the same time deep and free.

In the south of France it is always pruned short.

Foex gives the following description of it :—

Stem strong and very vigorous in rich soil; spreading grower; shoots of a fine light-red colour in summer, greyish in winter; knots prominent and close together, with a dirty white, much-developed bud ; leaves large, not deeply indented, upper side glossy, under side covered with loose down, petiolar sinus open ; bunch voluminous, long, almost cylindrical, or slightly shouldered with a tender, herbaceous stalk; berries large, round, very juicy; not very good for table use, though sufficiently sweet ; of a light black (not intense) colour where the ground is moist, and the yield very considerable. It is not as yet cultivated to any extent in Victoria.

† **Aspiran.** Synonyms : *Spiran, Verdal, Epiran, Riveyran, Piran, Verdai.*

A choice red grape, not cultivated in Victoria as yet, although it would prove a valuable sort in the warm region of the colony. The wine made from it is light in colour—light, delicate, and keeps well. It is one of the choice varieties of the south of France. It is a good bearer, and gives from 250 to 400 gallons per acre.

It comes into leaf medium early, but does not suffer from frost.

The grapes ripen early in the third period.

The *Aspiran* suffers but little from most fungus diseases.

The most suitable soil for it is a deep, free soil, preferably gravelly, and of a reddish colour.

It is usually pruned short. Its grapes are excellent for table purposes.

Foex describes it as follows :—" Rather vigorous grower; shoots semi-erect, slender, of light-red colour, with buds a medium distance apart. Leaves of medium size, five-lobed, deeply indented, teeth deep uneven, rather broad, giving the leaf a very elegant appearance, upper surface of a yellowish-green and smooth, under surface with a slight woolly down near the veins; bunch medium size, close, somewhat shouldered ; berries medium size, slightly oval; skin rather thick, of a purplish-black, covered with bloom ; juicy, of a refreshing taste, very agreeable to eat.

*Aucarot.

This seems to be variety of white Pinot, so we shall refer to it later on.

*Baxter's Sherry.

An ordinary white grape, somewhat extensively cultivated in Victoria, which gives a wine of an exaggerated sherry character. It is a heavy bearer, and gives from 600 to 800 gallons per acre. It comes into leaf and ripens in the second period. It may be described as follows:—Vigorous, rather spreading grower, shoots of a reddish yellow colour, long and slender; leaves large of a peculiar tender, rather flabby texture, divided into five lobes, or sometimes seven lobes, the two extra ones being around the first pair of secondary veins on the midrib, petiolar sinus rather open; upper surface bright green and smooth, under surface covered with fine silky down; a few hairs on the veins. Bunch large, rather loose, with oval berries.

*Black Hambro'. Synonyms: *Black Hamburg*, *Frankenthal*, *Schwartz* or *Blauer Trollinger*, &c., &c.

A very fine black table grape, which can also be used for wine-making purposes; in the third region it will give very good results, as the wine made from it is light and delicate, and it is a heavy bearer, ripens during the second period; it is a vigorous grower with thick shoots, leaves large, not deeply indented, teeth rather rounded off, upper surface smooth, under surface very slightly downy. The secondary veins of the mid-rib are almost white and very distinct, giving the whole leaf a characteristic appearance. Bunch large and rather loose. Berries large, almost round, and thick-skinned. The celebrated vine at Hampton Court is a Black Hambro'.

*Black Prince and *Black St. Peter.

Two more table varieties, which give good results for wine-making purposes in the warmer districts of the colony. They are both very vigorous varieties, and may be pruned long.

Bouschet Hybrids.

The *Bouschet Hybrids* are a group of sorts, being the outcome of the experiments of Louis Bouschet in 1828. He endeavoured to produce by hybridization between the Tinto or Teinturier and the ordinary cepages of the South of France a new variety with the red juice of the former and the many advantages of the latter sorts. His experiments were successful, and he and his sons have since given us many varieties, the best known of which are the *Petit Bouschet* (Aramon x Tinto), *Alicante Bouschet* (Grenache x Tinto), *Terret Bouschet,* and *Aspiran Bouschet.* These sorts are of value for the production of intensely deep-coloured wines.

- **Burgundy.** See *Pinots.*
- **Cabernet Sauvignon.** Synonyms : *Petit Cabernet, Vidure, Navarre, Vinidure, Sauvignonne,* and in Australia it is frequently, but erroneously, called *Carbinet.*

This is one of the choicest red varieties of France. It forms the basis of all the best vineyards of Bordeaux, and is largely cultivated in the cool region of Victoria. The wine made from it cannot be surpassed. As wine made from it is a little rough when young, it is better to mix it with some other sorts at vintage time ; the wine is then ready for market sooner than would otherwise be the case.

It is unfortunately a shy bearer, and is very subject to set badly at flowering time. It is also very liable to fungoid diseases, especially oidium and anthracnosis (black spot). Under very favorable conditions it may give as much as 500 gals. per acre, but the average in good soils cannot be said to be more than 200 gals.

It is only in the cool region of Victoria that the cultivation of the *Cabernet* is to be recommended. In the warm parts the advantages gained from it are not sufficient to make up for the small yield.

It comes into leaf late, and escapes late frosts. It ripens at the end of the second period.

The soil which suits it best is a pebbly soil resting on a clay subsoil, also gravelly, so as to insure thorough drainage, the *Cabernet* suffering, perhaps, more than any other sort from an excess of moisture around its roots.

It is at all times, unfortunately, very subject to fungoid diseases, especially oidium and anthracnose, but is exceedingly so if badly drained.

The fruit-bearing buds of the *Cabernet* are situated at some distance from the old wood. It follows that it must be pruned long ; if short-pruned, it will often prove perfectly sterile.

In addition to its many other advantages, it gives excellent results when grafted on other varieties.

The following are the characteristics by which it may be recognised:—Vigorous, somewhat spreading grower; wood of a reddish rather dark-fawn colour, of medium thickness, with buds of a medium size; the leaves are very characteristic (five-lobed), the indentations or sinus being deep and the lobes overlapping each other towards the outside in such a way as to make it appear that the leaves were pierced with five holes; upper-surface of a fine dark-green colour, free from down and glossy, but uneven; under-surface covered with close short down; teeth large and very uneven. The leaf has a peculiar crisp appearance. Bunch of medium size, conical, slightly shouldered and rather loose. Berries small, round, thick dark skin, covered with a beautiful bluish-grey bloom; they are rather apt to fall off when very ripe.

* **Carmenet.** Synonyms: *Gros Cabernet, Cabernet Franc, Grosse Vindure, Petit fer, Breton, Veronais, Arrouya.*

This variety differs but slightly from the preceding one, the wine made from it being almost identical, although perhaps less perfumed. It is not superior to the *Cabernet* in any respect, and will not do in a limestone soil.

It differs from the *Cabernet* in the following points:—Wood of a paler colour; leaves coarser and less glossy, but of the same shape; bunches rather smaller; berries larger, with thinner skin. It is to be found mixed with the *Cabernet* in most of the Victorian vineyards where the latter is cultivated.

* **Carignane.** Synonyms: *Carignan, Bois dur* (signifies hard wood), *Crignane, Catalan,* and improperly *Mataro* in some parts of the south of France.

This is a rather common red variety. It is extensively cultivated in the south of France, where it gives very good results. Foex says that it is perhaps the one which combines in the highest degree both quality and quantity. It frequently gives crops of 1,500 gallons per acre in France.

It comes into leaf late and is thus able to escape spring frosts. It ripens during the third period. Unfortunately its greatest fault is its susceptibility to the attacks of fungoid diseases, especially oidium and anthracnosis, and its liability to set badly at flowering time.

It should only be cultivated in the dryer parts of the colony where these diseases are not very prevalent.

It requires a well-drained, free, clayey soil.

The *Carignane* is very well adapted for the gooseberry mode of training, being an erect grower and requiring short pruning. It may be described as follows :—Vigorous erect grower, wood strong and thick, of light-red colour, hard and brittle, short-jointed at the base ; buds dark in colour and rather large ; leaves large, wrinkly and uneven, five-lobed, the sinus being deep ; upper surface dark-green and smooth, under surface slightly downy ; the leaves assume a fine red colour at vintage time ; bunch large ; berries rather long, slightly oblong, juicy, not very good to eat. It is cultivated in Victoria.

* **Chasselas, Golden.** Synonyms: *Chasselas de Fontainebleau, Fendant, Valais Blanc, Sussling, Frauentraube, Gutedel, Marzemina Bianca, Chrupka*, &c., &c.

A white grape, respecting the value of which for wine-making purposes the most varied opinions prevail. It is recognised by all to be an excellent table grape.

Although many authorities condemn it as a wine grape, we are not of their opinion, and can confidently recommend it for the production of a clean light wine. It presents the peculiarity of giving a similar wine in countries subject to very different climates. In Switzerland it gives a good wine where most other varieties would only produce a crude sour wine, whilst in warm countries it never gives a very strong wine.

The cuttings of this variety should be selected with the greatest care, as one often finds certain vines in a block of Chasselas almost sterile. This is due to faulty selection of cuttings in the first place.

Although one of the first sorts to come into leaf, it does not suffer considerably from frost. It is one of the earliest sorts to ripen (first period).

It is rather liable to fungus diseases, but not excessively so.

Although thriving in any soil, it seems to give the best results in a free well-drained loam, with clay subsoil.

It is well adapted to either long or short pruning, but does not thrive if trained on the gooseberry-bush system.

The *Chasselas* may be described as follows :—Rather vigorous grower, wood of a reddish brown colour, often short-jointed near the old wood; leaves about as broad as long, five-lobed, but not deeply indented; teeth broad, obtuse, and almost even; upper surface smooth, but not glossy, of a yellowish-green colour; under surface without down and similar to the upper, only paler. The young leaves are conspicuous by their deep yellowish bronze tint. Bunch above the average size, conical, shouldered, more or less compact. Berries rather large, thick-skinned, with small seeds, and of delicious flavour. When grown in the shade they are of pale-green semi-transparent colour, but if exposed to the sun of a golden bronze. It is rather largely grown in Victoria.

The *Chasselas Violet*, *Chasselas Rose*, and *Chasselas de Falloux* are only of value as table grapes, the latter is somewhat similar to the *Chasselas Rose;* they differ from the golden chiefly in the colour of the fruit.

Chasselas Musqué is another sort, differing chiefly in the Muscat flavour of its fruit.

Cinsaut.
Synonyms: *Bourdalès, Boudalès, Espagnin, Salerne,* and sometimes, but erroneously, *Picardan Noir* and *Ulliade Noir.*

A good red variety, largely cultivated in the south of France, on drier soils. It yields as much as 400 gallons per acre of a good, light, red wine. It comes into leaf late, and ripens early in the second period. It is similar in many respects to the *Oeillade*, but is a more spreading grower, with more slender shoots. Leaves smaller, more deeply indented, and more downy underneath than those of the *Oeillade.* Berries also larger. It is a good variety for table purposes.

Clairette.
Synonyms: *Blanquette, Cotticour.*

A white variety from which some excellent French wines are made. It is very long-lived, but suffers from a peculiar form of anthracnosis, termed punctuated anthracnosis.

The average crop it gives is about 250 gallons per acre. It is very well suited for table purposes.

Corinth (Currant).

A small berried seedless variety of *Muscat*, of value for the production of currants with a fine flavour. It is very similar to the *Muscats*, and, as a rule, less hardy than the *Zante*.

* **Dolcetto Nero**. Synonyms: *Nebbiolo, Bignona, Uva d'Acqui.*

A good red grape, largely cultivated in the north of Italy. It is better suited for the second region of the colony than either of the others, and fears drought more than moisture. It is cultivated to some extent in the Bendigo district is a good bearer, ripens very early; the wine made from it is light, clean, pleasant, and of good colour. It will thrive in almost any soil suitable for vine culture, and should be pruned long.

This sort is in many respects very similar to the Malbec.

The *Dolcetto* is rather a vigorous grower, with filbert-coloured short-jointed shoots, buds large and whitish before bursting. Leaves of medium size, smooth and almost glossy above, downy underneath, three or five lobed, sinus round and rather deep, pointed teeth; the young leaves are of a reddish colour, covered with down, and become red before falling off. Bunch of medium size, pyramidal, long, rather close, with a brown stalk. Berries medium, round, bluish-black, covered with bloom, with thin skin and juicy pulp. They fall off pretty easily when ripe.

† **Doradillo.** Synonyms: *Jaen Blanc, Plateado* or *Plateadillo, White Syrian* (?).

A very prolific, white Spanish grape, capable of yielding very heavy crops of light wine. It is admirably suited for the third or warm region of the colony. The fruit is suitable for table as well as wine purposes.

* **Espart.** See *Mataro.*

† **Folle.** Synonyms: *Enrageat, Plant Madame, Grosse Chalosse, Picpouille Blanc, Plant de Grèce,* &c.

La Folle is the white grape from which all the celebrated brandies of the Cognac district were made before the invasion of the phylloxera. In some parts it is used for blending with red grapes, as it greatly improves the wine made from them, rendering it lighter and more agreeable. Wine made from it alone is usually of little value.

The average crop it gives is about 250 gallons per acre. As it comes into leaf rather early it fears late frosts; it ripens during the second period.

It is not very liable to fungoid diseases, and will thrive in most soils. In France it is pruned short.

La Folle is not a very vigorous grower. Shoots thick and short-jointed, of a light-reddish tint. Leaves five-lobed sinus, of limited depth, especially the upper lateral ones ; upper surface of a peculiar dull green colour, rather flabby, reminding somewhat of the *Isabella* (*Vitis Labrusca*), free from down, with veins of a reddish tint, under surface rather downy; bunch medium size, close; berries rather large, round. With one exception it is not cultivated in Victoria.

*Gamay, Petit (Small). Synonyms : *Gamay Noir, Plant d'Arcenant, Gamay Nicholas.*

A good red variety extensively cultivated in the Beaujolais district of France.

It is admirably adapted for the first or cool region of the colony, although rather liable to frosts, as it comes into leaf early; it ripens during the second period, and is a heavy bearer. It is rather susceptible to the attacks of the oidium. The wine made from it varies more than that of most of the proceding sorts with the character of the soil. In a granite or porphyry soil it produces the excellent wines of Beaujolais, whilst in the Burgundy district, where the soil is rich in lime, it yields a very inferior wine, although the climate of both places is practically the same.

It ought to be pruned short, and is a moderately vigorous upright grower, with shoots of medium size ; leaves medium, five lobed, teeth short and irregular, upper-surface light-green, under-surface almost free from down ; bunch medium, close ; berries medium, slightly oval, black, covered with bloom.

The *Gros Gamay*, also called *Gamay Rond* or *Gamay d'Orleans*, differs little from it, but is, if anything, a heavier bearer, although the wine made from it is of inferior quality; it differs chiefly from the preceding one by the berries being round instead of oval. It is only to be found in a few Victorian vineyards.

*Gouais. Synonyms : *Burger Blanc* (white), *Elbling*, &c., &c.

The Gouais has been confounded with La Folle, from which, however, it is totally distinct.

It deserves mention, as it is cultivated to some extent in Victoria, but is, at the best, an inferior sort, the wine made from it being weak, flat, poor in tannin, and not keeping well. It is a very heavy bearer and yields, under favorable circumstances, 800 gallons per acre. It may be planted to a limited extent in a vineyard if blended with other sorts at vintage time, and would prove of value for brandy making. It is rather subject to oidium, and the fruit does not always set well. It is suited to long and short pruning. The Gouais is a vigorous erect grower, which can be recognised by the purple colour of its shoots during the summer. Leaves large, dark-green, almost entire; bunch of medium size, rather close; berries rather large, round, thin-skinned, liable to rot at vintage time.

* **Grenache.** Synonyms: *Roussilon, Alicante, Arragonais, Granaxa, Rivesaltes, Bois Jaune* (yellow-wood), *Redondal.*

A choice red variety, largely cultivated in the south of France and Spain, where some celebrated wines are made from it. It will give the best results in the second and third regions of the colony, where it has already been planted to some extent. It is especially suited for the production of wines of a Port character; the wine made from it has a good bouquet and considerable character, but its colour is not permanent; after a few years it assumes a tawny brown, or sometimes almost a yellowish tint similar to old Port. As a rule it is better to mix it with some other sorts, such as Carignane, Aramon, or Mataro at vintage time; it will improve the resulting wine by giving it more character and causing the wine to mature sooner. It should only be made into wine by itself for the production of a Port or liqueur wine, and should then be grown on pebbly soil, preferably on a granite formation. For blending purposes it should be cultivated on a richer soil.

It is fairly prolific, and gives crops of 350 gallons per acre. Not very subject to oidium, it suffers considerably from anthracnosis and mildew or peronospora, and should be pruned short.

The Grenache is a very vigorous semi-erect grower, with thick shoots of a yellowish colour, short-jointed with swoollen buds, the extremities often remain green in the winter; leaves medium size, smooth on both sides, very glossy on the upper; bunch large, close; berries medium, slightly oval, not very dark, covered with bloom, and thin-skinned. There is also a *White Grenache* similar in most respects to the red, and an excellent variety for the third region, especially for the production of a full-bodied wine.

* **Hermitage (Red).** See Shiraz.
* **Hermitage (White).** See Roussanne.

Maccabeo. Synonyms: *Ugni Blanc* (white), *Queue de Renard, Grédelin.*

A white variety not cultivated in Victoria, but of value for the production of fruity wines in the third region. A good bearer, which will adapt itself to almost any soil. It comes into leaf late, and ripens very late (at the end of the third period).

* **Malaga.**

An oval grape of a purple colour, well adapted for raisin-making, and, on account of its thick skin and good carrying qualities, of great value as a table grape. It ripens in the second period.

* **Malbeck.** Synonyms : *Cot, Baloutzat Gourdoux, Estrangey, Noir* (black) *de Pressac,* and many others, in Australia sometimes erroneously termed *Red Chasselas.*

A choice red variety, much cultivated in the Bordeaux district, where it helps to a considerable extent to make the best clarets. The wine made from it resembles in many respects that made from the *Cabernet Sauvignon,* but is lighter than it, and matures more rapidly. This sort is admirably suited for the second region of the colony, where it is already cultivated to some extent, and parts of the first, although it is liable to set its fruit very badly in cool moist localities. The wine made from it in the third region, being rather strong, would benefit by being blended with that of such kinds as *Mataro, Aramon,* &c. It is a pretty good bearer, and in well drained soil will give good crops. It comes into leaf rather early, and is liable to suffer from frost, but has the peculiarity of bearing fruit on shoots growing off the old wood if the normal fruit-bearing shoots are destroyed. It ripens towards the end of the first period.

It suffers but slightly from oidium, but is, on the other hand, very liable to anthracnosis.

It gives best results on soils rich in lime.

Although capable of bearing fruit when pruned short, long pruning suits it very much better. It is the sort grown in the part of France where the vines are grown on what is termed the "Chaintres" system, which gives the plant an enormous extension, as we shall see further on. The *Malbeck* is a vigorous grower, with wood of a brownish-fawn colour, rather short-jointed, with large buds; leaves above medium size, distinctly three-lobed, of a pinkish-white when they first come out ; upper surface smooth, but wrinkly and uneven, often of a reddish colour in parts, the remainder being of a pale-green colour; under-surface covered with flaky down; bunch large, branched, not very close; berries rather large, round, dark violet, covered with bloom; stems red, especially the extremities, to which the berries are fixed.

Malvoisie.

There are several sorts of *Malvoisie*, differing chiefly from each other in the colour of the fruit. They are suited for the production of sweet or liqueur wines in the third region and the warmer parts of the second. The grapes have a characteristic flavour comparable to that of the *Muscats*. They are, as a rule, very subject to oidium.

***Mataro.** Synonyms: *Espar, Esparte, Spar, Mourvedre, Balzac, Catalan, Charnet, Flouron,* &c.

A valuable red sort, largely cultivated in the south of France and in Spain, and admirably suited for the production of commercial wines in the second and third regions of the colony—it is not suitable for the first. The wine made from it, although somewhat rough, is light and of good colour and keeping qualities, and is admirably suited for blending with other sorts such as the Aspiran or Shiraz, and many others. It yields, under favorable circumstances, as much as 1,000 gallons per acre.

It comes into leaf late and ripens during the third period.

It is very hardy, and will grow in almost any soil, but gives the best results in a limestone formation. It is not subject to fungus diseases of any kind. It should be pruned short, and is well adapted for the gooseberry method of training on account of its upright growth.

The *Mataro* is a vigorous erect grower, with short-jointed wood of a reddish-brown colour and large buds. Leaves medium size, five-lobed, but not deeply indented, petiolar sinus open, two series of rather sharp teeth, upper-surface dark-green, rather rough, under-surface downy and whitish—leaf-stalk and veins dark reddish-brown; bunch medium, close, with small shoulders and woody stalk; berries of medium size, round, black, covered with bloom, not agreeable to eat.

†**Merlot.** Synonyms: *Vitraille, Bigney, Crabutet, Plant Medoc.*

A choice red variety, cultivated to some extent in the best Bordeaux vineyards. The wine made from it is lighter, and has less bouquet than that of the *Cabernet Sauvignon*, but it matures faster. It is an excellent sort for the first or cool region.

It is a prolific sort, comes into leaf rather late, and ripens during the second period. The soil which suits it best is the same as for the *Cabernet Sauvignon*. It may be pruned short, but gives better results with long pruning.

The *Merlot* is a vigorous semi-erect grower, with wood of a greyish-fawn colour, short-jointed, ribbed; leaves broader than long, of medium size, five-lobed, with petiolar sinus open as well as the others; teeth sharp and uneven; upper-surface smooth, uneven; under-surface downy; bunch long, conical, ramified; berries small, round, uneven, of a blue-black colour, covered with much bloom.

Mission Grape.

A variety extensively cultivated in California, where it was probably imported from Morocco. It is considered by the American authors as a common sort, giving large crops of strong coarse wine, of little value.

Mondeuse. Synonyms: *Mouteuse, Molette, Persaigne, Savoyanne, Maldoux.*

A good variety for the first region of Victoria, being a heavy bearer, giving as much as 800 gallons per acre in Savoy and the adjoining departments of France, where it is extensively cultivated. The wine made from it becomes of high quality with age, and keeps well.

It is a very hardy variety, will do well in almost any soil, and gives good results with either long or short pruning, the former being preferable. It comes into leaf late, and ripens at the end of the second period.

The Mondeuse is a vigorous spreading grower, with long-jointed shoots of a greyish-yellow colour; leaves rather large, longer than broad, three-lobed, smooth above, downy beneath; bunch large and loose; berries of medium size, slightly oval, of a somewhat acid and astringent flavour.

† Morrastel. Synonyms: *Mourrastel, Perpignan,* and sometimes, but erroneously, *Mataro.*

A valuable variety, in many respects similar to the *Mataro*, from which it may be distinguished by its wood being of a darker and redder colour; its leaves are paler, and with rounder lobes. The young leaves are reddish, whilst those of the *Mataro* are whitish.

It bears as much as the *Mataro*, of a somewhat higher class wine.

† **Morrillon.** Synonyms: *Gros Plant Doré, Maitre Noir.*
Seems to be a variety of *Pinot,* with large bunches and large berries. It is better suited for the table than for wine-making. It must not be confounded with the *Morillon Blanc* or ordinary white *Pinot.*

* **Muscats.**
There are many different *Muscats,* which it is useless for us to enumerate here. We shall endeavour to describe one or two of the principal ones, to which the others all bear considerable resemblance.

The character common to them all is the strongly perfumed flavour of their fruit, which renders them only suitable for the production of liqueur wines, raisins, or table grapes. The strong Muscat flavour renders them unsuitable for blending with other sorts to make a light wine. We shall give a description of some of the leading sorts.

* **Muscat de Frontignan.**
This is the best Muscat variety for wine-making purposes. It is admirably suited for the production of high class liqueur wines in the third region of the colony, and is a fairly good bearer. It comes into leaf early, and ripens at the end of the second period. It is very subject to oidium, anthracnosis, and all fungoid diseases.

Either long or short pruning suits it. The flavour of the fruit is superior with the former. It is a vigorous rather spreading grower, with thick, short-jointed shoots of a reddish-brown colour; leaves medium size, five-lobed, but not very deeply indented as a rule, two series of long sharp teeth, upper-surface smooth and even, under-surface almost devoid of down; bunch cylindrical, close, not much shouldered; berries round, medium size, of a beautiful amber colour on the White Frontignan, but of a reddish-brown on the Brown Frontignan. These two only differ in the colour of their fruit.

* **Muscat Gordo Blanco.**
This is the best raisin grape we have, and is extensively cultivated in the third region of Victoria. In its general characters it pretty closely resembles the former, but is more vigorous and a better bearer, whilst its berries are oval. Considerable difference of opinion exists as to its identity with the *White Muscat of Alexandria;* although many authorities say that they are the same sort, it is not

probable that this is the case. This Muscat is an excellent table grape, but for wine-making purposes is inferior to the Frontignan.

† Oeillade. Synonyms : *Ulliade, Ouillade.*

One of the choice red varieties of the south of France which, although not cultivated to any extent in Victoria, would prove of value in the third region. Its wine is very clean, delicate, and light in colour, and would be very suitable for blending with that of such kinds as the Mataro, as it would reduce the roughness of the resulting wine. It is a good bearer, and thrives best in deep, well-drained soils. In schistose formations it gives very good results. It is subject to oïdium and anthracnosis in moist places. It comes into leaf early, ripens during the second period, and requires short pruning. It is a semi-erect moderately vigorous grower, with thick short-jointed reddish wood and large buds. Leaves medium, rather longer than broad, five-lobed, teeth large and sharp, upper-surface dark-green and rather rough, under-surface rather downy; bunch large, loose; shouldered; berries large, oval, black, covered with bloom, juicy. There is also a *White Oeillade* very similar to the red in its general characters and producing a very good wine.

* Pinots.

The Pinots are a group of sorts, all of which are of great value and admirably suited for the cool region of this colony. They are the sorts cultivated in the Burgundy, Chablis, and Champagne districts, and only give very high-class wines on a limestone formation (p. 27). As the type of the group, we will first consider the

* Pinot Noir (Black). Synonyms : *Smooth-leaved Burgundy, Burgundy, Black Cluster, Noirien, Franc Pinot, Morillon Noir, Auvergnat Noir, Salvagnin Noir, Blauer Klavuer,* &c., &c.

This choice red variety is cultivated, to the exclusion of other kinds, in the best vineyards of Burgundy, such as Chambertin, Clos Vougeot, &c. In the cool region of Victoria, on limestone soils, it would give an excellent wine. Unfortunately, it is a poor bearer; its average yield in the Burgundy district is only about 200 gallons per acre. It is very free from fungus diseases, but does not always set its fruit well. It is usually pruned short, but gives far better results if pruned long.

It is one of the first to come into leaf, and also one of the first sorts to ripen (early in the first period).

It is a spreading grower of less than medium vigour, with slender long-jointed shoots of a slightly purple-grey colour. Leaves medium, five-lobed, not unlike those of the *Cabernet*, but not so deeply indented, petiolar sinus open, teeth short, blunt, and even, upper-surface almost glossy, under-surface slightly downy; bunch small, cylindrical, very close; berries small, rather thick-skinned, not perfectly round, often deformed from being very close in the bunch, very black, covered with bloom, and very juicy.

* **Pinot Meunier.** Synonyms: *Miller's Burgundy, Meunier, Blanche Feuille, Morillon Taconné,* &c.

Similar to the *Pinot Noir* in almost every respect, but differing from it by the leaves being covered both above and below with a considerable amount of flaky down, giving it the appearance of having been dusted with flour, whence its name. The red wine made from it resembles that of the *Pinot Noir*, but it is lighter, and does not keep so well. In the Champagne district it is the most extensively cultivated sort, and is one of the few cases in which white wine is made from red grapes on a large scale.

† **Pinot Gris.** Synonyms: *Beurot, Fromentot, Auxoit, Auvergnat Gris, Gris Cordelier, Malvoisie* (improperly) *Levraut, Edel Clavner.*

A choice pink variety, yielding an excellent white wine. It is from this grape that the highest class Champagne is made. It is very similar to the *Miller's Burgundy*, although leaves are not so downy, and the fruit, instead of being black, is of a beautiful greyish-pink colour.

* **Pinot Blanc (White).** Synonym: *White Burgundy.*

Very similar to the others, only with white fruit. There are several white Pinots, differing slightly from each other. The Aucarot is probably one of them. They are valuable sorts, and give good results in all the three regions; in the warmer parts they produce excellent liqueur wines.

† **Pinot Blanc Chardonay.** Synonyms: *Morillon Blanc, Epineth, Beaunois, Plant Doré, Auvergnat,* &c.

This is the best of the white Pinots, and is the one from which the best Chablis wines of France are made. It is somewhat different from the other Pinots, especially in its leaves, which are less deeply indented, and of a more yellowish colour. It also does best in a limestone soil.

* Pedro Ximenes. Synonyms: *Pero Ximen, Pedro Jimenez, Boutelon.*

One of the choice Spanish white varieties which enters to a great extent into the composition of the best sherries, and is somewhat extensively cultivated in the warmer parts of Victoria, where it is well suited for the production of full-bodied wines. It is a good bearer, but is rather subject to oidium. It comes into leaf rather late, and ripens during the third period. It gives the best results in a sandy or pebbly schistose soil. It is a spreading grower of medium vigour, with shoots of a reddish-grey colour and a considerable number of laterals. Leaves rather large, distinctly five-lobed, dark-green and smooth above, very cottony underneath; bunch medium size, with tender stem; berries medium size, slightly oblong, soft, and thin-skinned.

† Pulsart. Synonyms: *Poulsart, Blussart, Plant d'Arbois, Mescle.*

A choice red sort, not cultivated to any extent in Victoria, but which could with advantage be planted in the first and the cooler part of the second region. It gives an excellent wine, especially in limestone soils, and is a good bearer on condition that it be pruned long.

It ripens during the second period.

The *Pulsart* is a vigorous grower, with short-jointed wood of medium thickness. Leaves small, five-lobed, with U shaped petiolar sinus very open; they are free from down on both sides, and of a light green. Bunch medium size, long, loose, and shouldered; berries of medium size, oval, thin-skinned, and juicy.

* Riesling. Synonyms: *Rossling, Gentil Aromatique,* &c.

A choice white variety, already extensively cultivated in Victoria. This is one of the best white varieties for cultivation in the first and the cooler part of the second region, and gives good results even in the third. It is the grape cultivated on the Rhine, and from which the celebrated Hocks are made.

It is a good bearer, and can give crops of 500 gallons per acre, but does not always set well at flowering, and is subject to oidium.

It gives best results in a granitic or schistose formation, but will thrive in almost any well-drained soil.

It comes into leaf somewhat late and ripens during the second period.

Long pruning is indispensable for it. If pruned short it gives very poor crops.

The *Riesling* is a spreading grower, of medium vigour, with rather long-jointed wood of a glossy grey colour. Leaves medium, thick, round, five lobes (sometimes three-lobed), rather deeply indented sinus, rounded, teeth almost even, upper-surface dark green, very wrinkly, free from down, under-surface covered with short down, veins very thick and covered with stiff short hairs; bunch small and close; berries small, round, of a greenish colour, covered with bloom, with several hard black specks adhering to the skin. They may be recognised by the peculiar aromatic taste they leave on the palate. What is commonly termed *Shepherd's Riesling* is a variety of the above. It is a better bearer and has larger berries, but the wine is not of such high quality as that of the little Riesling.

* **Roussanne.** Synonyms : *White Hermitage, Bergeron, Fromonteau, Plant de Seyssel.*

A choice white sort, from which are made the best White Hermitage wines of France. There is some difference of opinion as to whether our White Hermitage is the Marsanne or the Roussanne. The following properties of the *Roussanne* enable it to be said with almost certainty that it is our White Hermitage:—

It is very subject to oidium, whilst the *Marsanne* is only slightly so; its berries are smaller, the skin thicker, and the seeds larger than those of the *Marsanne*; its berries become browner when exposed to the sun than those of the *Marsanne*.

If pruned long it will yield crops of 300 gallons per acre. The wine made from it is of excellent quality. It is rather alcoholic, sound, and has a beautiful bouquet, keeps well, and improves for a long time. The *Roussanne* is best suited for the first region, but will also give good results in the second. It gives the best results in a granitic soil, but will thrive in most other sorts.

It is more subject to oidium than most other fungoid pests. Comes into leaf late, and ripens towards the end of the second period. It is a vigorous somewhat spreading grower. Shoots rather thick, long-jointed, of a yellowish-grey colour, with rather small buds. Leaves rather large, five-lobed, teeth blunt and irregular, upper-surface of dark green, glossy and bulgy, under-surface downy; bunch medium, and close; berries small, round, thick-skinned, of a golden colour when ripe, brownish where exposed to the sun.

* **Sauvignon (Red).** See *Cabernet.*

† **Sauvignon (White).** Synonyms: *Surin Fié, Blanc Fumé, Feigentraube.*

One of the choicest of all the white varieties. It, together with the Semillon, yields the celebrated Chateau Yquem wine, and most of the other renowned vineyards of Sauternes. In the first region it would give excellent results. It thrives in most soils, but gives the best results in a well-drained friable pebbly clay soil.

The *Sauvignon* is hardy, little subject to fungus diseases, but is a poor bearer.

It is a vigorous spreading grower, with medium-size yellowish-brown wood. Leaves small, thick, three-lobed, broader than long, teeth short, blunt, and uneven, upper-surface smooth, under-surface downy; bunch small and close; berries medium size, slightly oval, transparent, thin-skinned when ripe, of a delicious flavour.

Semillon. Synonyms: *Colombier, Goulu Blanc, Chevrier,* and sometimes, erroneously, *Malaga.*

This is another "Sauternes" variety, the wine made from it is similar to that of the *Sauvignon* in most respects, although not quite so perfumed. It is a better bearer than the *Sauvignon*, which it resembles to some extent, differing from it by the colour of the wood, which is dark-brown (mahogany). Leaves large, three or five-lobed; bunch large, rather close; berries large, almost round, of a golden colour, with thin skin.

* **Shiraz.** Synonyms: *Red Hermitage, Schiras, Sirac, Syra, Sirrah, Serine, Candive.*

An excellent red variety, perhaps more extensively cultivated than any other in Victoria.

It forms the base of the celebrated Hermitage vineyards of France, where it was first planted by a monk, who, returning from Shiraz, in Persia, brought the cuttings with him. So goes the story, and it explains the two most common names by which it is known.

It does best in a granitic soil, but will grow in almost any that is fit for viticulture. It is a good bearer and yields crops of as much as 700 gallons if pruned long. It gives good results if pruned short.

The wine made from it possesses many excellent qualities, it is perhaps rather strong when grown it the third region, and is better when grown in either the first or second.

Although liable to oidium, it resists mildew (peronospora), and does not suffer much from anthracnosis.

It comes into leaf early, and ripens during the second period.

The *Shiraz* is a vigorous spreading grower. Shoots thick, long-jointed, of a characteristic grey colour; leaves, rather large, five-lobed, but not deeply divided, teeth blunt and even, upper-surface of a fine, bright, but dark-green, not glossy, with a few traces of flaky down; the colour is so characteristic that a block of this kind may easily be recognised at a distance; under-surface, cottony; bunch rather large, long, conical, sometimes rather loose; berries below the average size, oblong, black, covered with bloom, thin-skinned, and juicy.

* **Sultana.** Synonyms: *Kechmish, Sultanieh, Conforogo.*

This is the seedless grape from which the well-known Sultana raisins are made. It is also a good table grape, and produces a good light white wine. It should be pruned long.

* **Sweet Water.** Synonyms: *Listan,* (?) *White Nice.* (?)

Like the *Chasselas*, this sort is considered to be only of use as a table variety, but this is not the case in the second and third regions. Some excellent white wines are made from this grape, which is superior to *Gouais* in these conditions. It may be easily distinguished by its thick, dark-green, five-lobed leaves; the lower indentations of which are the deepest. The leaves are smooth and glossy above and downy beneath. Bunches large, and berries medium size, round. Very agreeable to eat.

† **Tinto.** Synonyms: *Teinturier, Gros Noir Oporto, Tinto Francisca, Rome Noir,* &c.

The *Tinto* is one of the few grapes which have red juice. In most other red grapes the colouring matter is contained in the skin, but the juice of the *Tinto* is of a deep red colour as well. The wine made from it is of a remarkable colour. This is, in fact, its only quality; in other respects it is flat, and does not keep wel.. It is neither a vigorous grower nor a good bearer, but may, however, be useful in a bad year, and in a cold district, to increase the colour of other wines, and for this reason a few acres of it may be added to vineyards in cooler parts of the first region if the soil is not colour-promoting.

It may be described as follows :—Plant not vigorous, resembling the *Pinots*; leaves, five-lobed, and deeply indented, the two lower indentations being the deepest, they are slightly cottony on both sides, but more so on the under one; at vintage-time they can easily be recognised by their magnificent red colour; bunch small, close; berries, small, round, and with crimson juice.

* Tokay.

It is difficult to say what grape our *Tokay* really is; it does not seem to be identical with the *Furmint*, which is the chief grape grown in the celebrated Tokay vineyards of Hungary; nor does it answer to the description of the *Balafant*, another Hungarian sort. It is, however, a very good grape and gives abundant crops of excellent wine. It generally sets well at blossoming, and although very subject to oidium, is not attacked by the anthracnosis. The fruit ripens pretty early, and is very liable to rot if the vintage be a wet one. The wine does not ferment regularly as a rule, and requires careful treatment when young, still it may be recommended as a very good variety for the first and second regions, for which, perhaps, it is too strong by itself. It cannot be recommended for the third. The *Tokay* is a rather vigorous erect grower, with short-jointed shoots of a pale reddish-yellow. Leaves large, three-lobed, longer than broad, with deep, sharp, and uneven teeth, upper-surface uneven, of a yellowish-green, without down, under-surface rather downy; bunches above medium size, shouldered; berries medium, round, thin-skinned. The Tokay will give good crops when pruned short, but will do better with long pruning.

† Verdot.

This is another of the red varieties largely cultivated in the Bordeaux district for the production of clarets. The wine made from it is very good, although rather hard at first. In this respect it resembles the *Cabernet*, although it is inferior to it in bouquet. It is also a better bearer than it. It is, as a rule, cultivated in Bordeaux in the rich soils, termed palus, along the river. If injured by frost, new shoots often come out at the base of those destroyed.

The leaves are medium sized, longer than broad, when young covered with a characteristic silvery white down, when full-grown three or five-lobed, teeth uneven, indentations rather open and not very deep—upper surface smooth, uneven, of a paler green than Cabernet, under side downy; bunch somewhat similar to Cabernet but more shouldered and smaller; berries rather small, round, with thick skin, and large seeds; it ripens in the third period.

* **Verdeilho.** Synonym: *Gouveio.*

The *Verdeilho* is the principal white variety grown in Madeira, where an excellent wine is made from it. It is best suited for making a wine of Madeira type in the second and third regions of the colony. It also gives good results in the cool regions in situations where it ripens properly, but it is better suited for the others.

May be described as follows :—Plant moderately vigorous, shoots slender, rather closely knotted, and of a reddish tint. Leaves not very large, almost entire, upper side dark-green, smooth and rather shiny, under surface slightly downy, teeth even, short, and blunt; bunch medium size, rather close; berries medium size, oval, even. regular, thick skin.

This variety is very subject to oidium; should be pruned long.

* **Zante (Currant).** Synonym: *Passolina.*

Is the grape from which the currant of commerce is made. It is said by some to be identical with the Corinth, but this does not appear to be the case. It is a vigroous grower and must be pruned very long. It gives the best crops on high, overhead trellises, and does not come into full bearing for seven or eight years under ordinary circumstances. Its leaves are easily recognised, they are large, five-lobed, and with large (very), even, rather sharp teeth on the margin, different to most vines many of the leaves on a plant have seven instead of five principal veins, which separate from the juncture with the petiole; the upper-surface is dark-green with a few flakes of cotton, especially on the veins, whilst the under-surface is downy and of a whitish colour; bunches large; berries very small and seedless. There are three sorts, the fruit of each are respectively white, red, and black.

Zinfandel. Synonym: *Zierfahnder Rother*.

An Austrian red variety much cultivated in the United States. The wine made from it is light and agreeable.

It is a heavy bearer and requires short pruning. It is not, as yet, cultivated in Victoria.

AMERICAN VINES.

We saw that the European vines all belong to one species (*Vitis Vinifera*). The American ones may be resolved into several distinct species, each of which in turn comprises a greater or lesser number of varieties. Many of these, being of no practical interest, need not be described. We shall confine ourselves to such as have been proved to be worth propagating, or which, being frequently met with, deserve mention.

The chief character of the American vines, and the one which has caused them to come into so much favour in Europe of late years, is the remarkable resistance they oppose to the attacks of the phylloxera. With a few exceptions, they can all thrive with this terrible insect living on them. Their roots are, as we have seen, tougher than those of the European vines. The injuries caused by them heal quickly, and are insignificant compared with the destruction of the more succulent roots of European sorts brought about by the bite of the insect—destruction which invariably results in the death of the plant after a more or less considerable period of time, usually about three years.

Not only are the American sorts able to resist, but they are less exposed to the ravages of the phylloxera, which lives chiefly on their leaves, whilst, with European sorts, the roots are the usual habitat of the insect. Even in infested vineyards (planted with European sorts) it is exceedingly uncommon to find insects on the leaves.

The American vines are not phylloxera-proof, in the sense that the phylloxera is never to be found on them. They are phylloxera-resistant, as the insect can and does live on them without causing any considerable injury. These vines having existed for many centuries with the phylloxera living on them, have, by natural selection, become able to resist their ravages. The phylloxera and the American vines have, so to speak, been brought up together in nature's nursery. The Vitis Vinifera never having had to cope with this natural enemy, and being unprepared by nature to resist it, falls an easy prey to its ravages.

It must not be thought that the phylloxera and the American vines are indissolubly linked together. Once free from the insect and transported to a clean district they will remain so. Under such circumstances it would be just as impossible for the phylloxera to suddenly appear on them without having been brought from elsewhere as it would for it to suddenly come into existence on a European vine (*Vitis Vinifera*). Although it has been conclusively proved that they are to blame for the presence of the pest in Europe (where they were imported in the shape of rooted vines, no precautions having been taken, since the very existence of the pest was then unknown), the American sorts may with perfect safety be introduced into any clean district, provided they are absolutely free from all traces of the insect. Too much caution cannot be observed in their introduction into this colony; only seeds or cuttings from vines which have been growing in a clean district side by side with European vines for some years, without detrimental effect upon the latter, should be tolerated for this purpose. It must be remembered that a single insect might suffice to start an invasion, which it would be most difficult, if not impossible, to check. Many American varieties have been introduced into Victoria; they are at the present moment growing perfectly free from this dreaded insect, and could be reproduced with perfect confidence.

With few exceptions, this immunity from phylloxera is the only thing to recommend their cultivation, although in some cases, if employed as stocks, they improve the yield of some European sorts grafted on them. They have many faults and are inferior in almost every respect to the European sorts. With the exception of the varieties of *Vitis Æstivalis*, their fruit possesses a peculiar taste, reminding of black currants, termed in America "Foxy taste," or they are acrid or otherwise unfit for wine-making purposes. Many of them are but poor bearers, and in addition to this they suffer more than the others from unsuitable descriptions of soil, being liable to chlorosis, and are often very difficult to propagate by cuttings.

Although we shall describe such American sorts as are of interest in detail, it may be of service to vine-growers to have some simple rule by which they may distinguish between an American sort and a *Vitis Vinifera*.

The following rule is given by L. Portes and F. Ruyssen, and will be found to hold good in the majority of cases, although some American sorts are very similar to a Vitis Vinifera, and *vice versâ*. Fig. 7 represents a typical leaf of Vitis Vinifera, and Fig. 8 one of Vitis Labrusca (an American species), which may to some extent serve as a type for them all.*

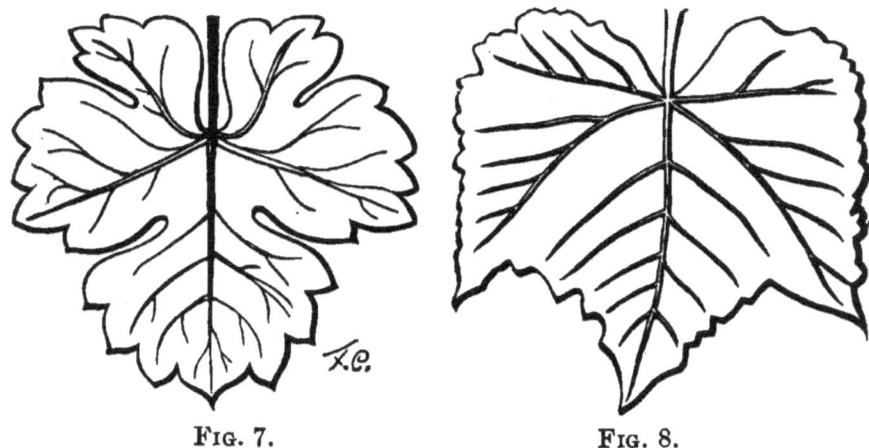

FIG. 7.   FIG. 8.

The most characteristic difference between the two and the only one presenting any degree of fixity is in the petiolar sinus or main indentation, where the petiole or leaf stalk joins the limb or flat part of the leaf. In the *Vitis Vinifera* the edges, after separating at first, tend to join again higher up, giving the opening the form of a U which has been closed in at the top; in the *Vitis Labrusca*, on the other hand, it is more similar to a V which has been widened above so that the extremities point outward. The portion of the leaf above the insertion of the petiole is far more considerable in the *Vitis Vinifera* than in the *Vitis Labrusca*, or the insertion of the petiole is much nearer the centre of the leaf in the former variety. The texture of the leaves presents a somewhat characteristic difference. Those of the American sorts appear to be more or less flabby, whilst the leaves of *Vitis Vinifera* have a more crisp appearance.

---

* It must be borne in mind that the general form of the leaf is not always as in the cuts; for example, V. Vinifera frequently has three-lobed and V. Labrusca five-lobed leaves. The two examples given are the most common forms of each species.

The only American species of interest are the following :—*V. Æstivalis, V. Arizonica, V. Berlandieri, V. Californica, V. Candicans, V. Cinerea, V. Cordifolia, V. Labrusca, V. Riparia, V. Rotundifolia*, and *Vitis Rupestris;* in addition to these there are many others of purely botanical interest.

VITIS ÆSTIVALIS.

The *summer grape* of North America. This is the only species from which are derived direct producers, that is varieties yielding grapes capable of being made into wine, similar to that of *V. Vinifera*. Almost all the sorts belonging to the other species are only used as grafting stocks.

The grapes of the *V. Æstivalis*, however, are more similar to those of *V. Vinifera*, being free from foxy or other foreign taste. Unfortunately most of the varieties derived from it are poor bearers.

The species, as a whole, may be described as follows :—

Plant of medium vigour, with long thick climbing shoots, usually dark and covered with bloom ; tendrils large, discontinuous ; buds and young leaves of a brilliant carmine ; leaves at first covered on both sides with down, but when full grown without down on the upper side ; ordinarily lobed, but sometimes almost entire ; bunch variable ; berries small, thin-skinned, covered with bloom. This species is divided into a northern and southern group. The former have leaves almost entire and rusty-coloured down on the veins. All the varieties belonging to this species resist the phylloxera.

The chief "cepages" are as follows :—

Cunningham. Synonym : *Long.*

A pink variety, somewhat extensively cultivated in France, although a poor bearer. It ripens very late and is to be preferred for making white wine on account of the very light colour of that fermented with the skins.

It is difficult to propagate by cuttings, and is not a good stock to graft on.

The leaves are large, three-lobed, or almost entire, smooth and dark-green above, downy beneath.

Cynthiana. Synonyms: *Norton's Virginia, Red River, Norton.*

A good red variety, producing a very good wine, but being a rather poor bearer, and requiring a rich soil.

It requires long pruning, resists fungus diseases very well, but does not strike well from cuttings.

†**Devereux.** Synonyms: *Black July, Lincoln, Thurmond, Hart, Tuley, McLean,* sometimes erroneously termed *Lenoir.*

A good red-wine grape. It is hardy, vigorous, and will grow in most soils, but is only a poor bearer.

Some authors consider it to be a hybrid between *V. Æstivalis* and *V. Vinifera*. The leaves are of medium size, three-lobed, with obtuse lobes not deeply separated; upper-surface dark-green, glossy, very uneven, with a few silky hairs; under-surface pale-green, with numerous hairs on the veins,

†**Elsinburgh.** Synonyms: *Missouri Birdseye, Smarts.*

A red grape belonging to the northern group, producing a good wine, but not extensively cultivated on account of its very small yield.

Herbemont. Synonyms: *Warren, Warrenton, Neil's Grape, Herbemont's Madeira.*

A good red grape, belonging to the southern group, perhaps one of the best American direct producers. It is a fair bearer; its wine is of good quality, although light in colour. It does not come into full bearing till rather late, and is liable to chlorosis unless planted in well-drained soils of a dark colour. It is a vigorous spreading grower, with wood of a pale-pink colour; leaves large, three, five, and rarely seven lobed, lightish-green above, pale-green below; two series of blunt teeth; bunch rather small, close; berries small, round, thin-skinned, dark-red or black, covered with bloom.

†**Jacquez.** Synonyms: *Lenoir, Jack, Cigar, Box Grape, McCandless, Black Spanish, Longworth's Ohio.*

A red grape, belonging to the southern group, perhaps the best of all the American direct producers; also suitable as a resistant stock to graft on, although inferior in this respect to certain varieties of *V. Riparia* and *V. Rupestris.*

It is a good bearer, and yields a wine of magnificent colour, similar to that made from *Mataro, Carignane,* &c., although slightly inferior to them, and of a bluish tint if the grapes are over ripe.

It is a hardy variety, and thrives in most soils, although it is, unfortunately, very liable to fungus diseases, especially anthracnosis and mildew.

It is a vigorous semi-erect grower, with brownish-purple wood, even when green; leaves longer than broad, large, usually five-lobed, bright green, and smooth above, paler beneath, and with some silky down; bunch large, long, loose; berries rather small, round, purplish-black, covered with bloom, hard, with tough skin and red juice.

Pauline. Synonyms: *Burgundy of Georgia, Red Lenoir.*

A pink variety of little value, being a poor bearer and very subject to a peculiar form of anthracnosis, termed in French "Anthracnose deformante."

VITIS ARIZONICA.

A hardy vine, thoroughly phylloxera-resistant, which, although not used as yet, would give very good results as a stock to graft European varieties on. It does not grow readily from cuttings.

It is a medium vigorous spreading grower, with smooth adherent bark. Leaves small, usually heart shaped, upper-surface dark-green and shiny, under-surface paler and with stiff hairs on the veins; berries small, of agreeable taste; seeds small.

It is similar to the *V. Californica* and *V. Cordifolia.* No cultivated varieties of it are known as yet.

VITIS BERLANDIERI.

Synonyms: *Surret Mountain, Little Sweet Mountain.*

This species deserves mention as it is the one recommended by Pierre Viala as a stock to graft *Vinifera* on in the chalky soils of the Department des Charentes, where the other American sorts will not grow. Its chief drawback is the difficulty with which it is propagated by cuttings.

It is a vigorous spreading grower, with long slender shoots of polygonal section towards the extremities. Leaves small, usually heart shaped, glossy above, under-surface either smooth or covered with grey down; bunches small and close; berries small, round, black, without foreign taste.

It is not used as a direct producer.

VITIS CALIFORNICA.

Deserves mention as it is held in some esteem in America. It is a vigorous grower, with slender, ramified, slightly downy shoots. Leaves small, usually entire, with blunt teeth, upper-surface glossy, under-surface paler, with tufts of hairs on the veins; small black berries. This species is not esteemed in France, where it is said to be subject to chlorosis, and fungus diseases. It resists phylloxera, but its very small yield unfits it or a direct producer. It is a good stock to graft on, but is difficult to propagate by cuttings.

VITIS CANDICANS.

Commonly termed the *Mustang grape* in America.

Like many others, it would form an excellent stock for grafting, as it is very vigorous and phylloxera-resistant, but can only be propagated with difficulty from cuttings. The fruit is so acid as to render it unfit for a direct producer. It is a heavy bearer.

It is a most vigorous grower, with medium, long-jointed shoots; leaves rather small, either heart-shaped or lobate, upper-surface bright green and smooth, under-surface covered with a very close white down; bunches small, but very numerous; berries large, black, and of an acrid taste; seeds large.

VITIS CINEREA.

This species seems to be allied to *Vitis Æstivalis* and *V. Berlandieri*. Like the latter, it thrives in chalky soils, but is also difficult to propagate.

It is a vigorous spreading grower, with small leaves, either entire or subdivided, of a whitish-green above and below, the veins on the under side are hairy; bunch small; berries very small, black, without bloom, acid, but without foxy taste.

VITIS CORDIFOLIA.

Called in America *Winter Grape*, *Frost Grape*, or *Chicken Grape*.

It is similar to the last in most respects, such as its adaptability to chalky soils and the difficulty with which it can be propagated.

Its leaves are somewhat similar to those of *V. Riparia*, although they differ from it by opening out flat. The leaves of *V. Riparia* remain folded for some time after first coming out. The acid taste of its grapes renders it unfit for a direct producer.

VITIS LABRUSCA.

This species, usually termed in America *Fox Grape*, or *Northern Fox Grape*, is perhaps the one which has been submitted to cultural methods with the object of improving the fruit for the greatest number of years, and for this reason there are many varieties derived from it, few of which, however, are considered to be of practical use from a European stand-point. In the first place they are not all, strictly speaking, phylloxera proof. Although they resist it far better than the *V. Vinifera* varieties, many of them suffer from the attacks of the insect, some even succumbing to it after a few years. In addition to this the fruit has a strong foxy taste, rendering these vines unsuitable for cultivation as direct producers, and many of them are subject to chlorosis if the soil be light in colour and not properly drained. We must describe a few varieties on account of the frequency with which one meets with them in gardens, &c. One or two of them possess the above-named defects in so small a degree that they may be considered as being of value.

The general characteristics of the species are as follows :—Spreading growers of medium vigour, with long thick shoots, sometimes hairy near the knots in the green state. The tendrils are continuous, that is, there is a tendril (or bunch) opposite to every leaf. This is the principal characteristic of the species, and distinguishes it from all others, which have discontinuous tendrils. Leaves rather three than five lobed, upper-surface of a dull dark-green colour, under-surface covered with thick close down, usually white, brownish on the veins; bunch rather large; berries large, either round or oval, with pulpy flesh and foxy taste; skin thick; seeds large. As a rule varieties belonging to this species ripen early.

The following are some of the varieties derived from this species :—

† **Adironda.**
An early black grape of little value.

† **Anna.**
A hardy white sort, probably a seedling of Catawba, not of much value.

† **Canby's August.** Synonyms: *York's Madeira, Black German, Hyde's Eliza, Monteith.*

Canby's August is usually considered to be a hybrid, but it is more closely connected with *V. Labrusca* than any other species.

It resists the phylloxera, and, as it is very hardy and capable of doing well in almost any soil, it forms an excellent stock to graft on, although, perhaps, inferior to *V. Rupestris* and some varieties of *V. Riparia*. It cannot be employed as a direct producer on account of the very foxy taste of its fruit and its being a poor bearer.

† **Catawba.** Synonyms: *Red Muncy, Catawba, Tokay, Singleton.*

A purple variety, considered to be very good for wine-making purposes in America, as it is freer from foxy taste than most *V. Labrusca* varieties. A kind of champagne, known as Sparkling Catawba is made from it in America. It is almost adapted for cultivation as a direct producer, although a rather poor bearer. It is of no value as a stock, as it cannot be said with certainty to be phylloxera-resistant.

Concord.

This variety is much esteemed in the eastern states of America, where the foxy taste is not so much disliked as in France or the western states. It is a good bearer, and is phylloxera-resistant, but the fruit has a foxy taste. It will not thrive in very warm dry districts, nor in any but dark well-drained soils, being very subject to chlorosis.

† **Diana.**

A rather good white variety.

† **Isabella.** Synonyms: *Woodward, Payne's Early, Samboton.*

This is, perhaps, the best known American sort in Australia. It is a hardy black grape, and a rather good bearer, but is not phylloxera-resistant, and its fruit has a marked foxy taste, so it is not to be recommended.

† **Israella.**

Very similar to Isabella, of which it is probably a seedling.

† **Ives' Seedling.** Synonyms: *Ives, Ives' Madeira, Kittredge.*

A vigorous prolific black variety, easily recognised by its very handsome leaves, dark-green above, white beneath. It is of little value as a grafting stock, and cannot be used as a direct producer on account of the taste of its fruit.

† **Logan.**
A prolific black variety.

† **Maxatawney.**
A white sort, rather suited for table purposes.

† **Martha.**
A white sort, with less foxy taste than many of the others.

† **Miles:**
An early black grape, somewhat free from foxy taste.

† **Perkins.**
A pale lilac early grape, with very pronounced foxy taste.

† **Rebecca.**
A beautiful white grape, but of little value.

† **Tokaylon.** Synonyms : *Wyman, Spofford Seedling.*
A robust, vigorous, rather late, black variety, almost free from foxy taste.

VITIS RIPARIA.

The *Sand* or *River grape* of the Americans.

The varieties derived from *V. Riparia* are of great value as stocks to graft on, being thoroughly phylloxera-proof, and thriving in most sorts of soils. They cannot be employed as direct producers on account of the flavour of their fruit, which is rather acrid than foxy. Some of them only bear male flowers, and are necessarily sterile.

The following are the main characteristics of the species :—Very spreading slender grower, but capable of covering large surfaces; long-jointed wood; leaves at first folded along the midrib, but after opening out flat, they are usually heart-shaped or three-lobed, with sharp teeth, upper surface smooth, and often very glossy, under-surface duller in colour, smooth, or with a few hairs on the veins (when the leaves first come out they are sometimes very downy); bunch usually small; berries small, with a less pronounced foxy taste than those of *V. Labrusca*; seeds small. The sorts derived from *V. Riparia* come into leaf, blossom, and ripen very early.

† **Clinton.** Synonym : *Worthington.*
This red variety is extensively grown in America as a direct producer, as it is a fair bearer, and its wine is of good colour and body.

It cannot, however, be recommended as such, as its fruit has the foxy taste. It is an excellent stock in good, free soils, and grows easily from cuttings. The leaves have some hairs on the under side of the veins.

Solonis. Synonyms: *Cordifolia Solonis, Long's Arkansas, La Souys.*

Some authors consider this sort to be rather a *V. Cordifolia* than a *V. Riparia*. It is a very constant type, so much so that it can be reproduced by seed without much variation.

It resists phylloxera in a remarkable manner, and does well in almost any soil, for which reasons it is probably the best stock for grafting purposes lthough it is of no value as a direct producer.

The young leaves are downy, but when full-grown smooth on both sides, with the exception of a few hairs on the under side of the veins.

† **Taylor.** Synonyms: *Bullet, Taylor's Bullit.*

A white grape, in other respects similar to the *Clinton*. It is a good stock for grafting on, although inferior to the *Solonis* and *Wild Riparias*. It is a thick stock, and therefore most suitable for vigorous growing varieties. It is without value as a direct producer on account of its small yield, although the fruit is almost free from foxy taste.

† **Wild Riparia.**

There are several *Wild Riparias* cultivated somewhat extensively in France as stocks. They are excellent for this purpose, being very hardy and absolutely phylloxera-resistant. They ought to be grafted very young, as the graft takes better under these conditions.

VITIS ROTUNDIFOLIA.

Synonym: *Vitis Vulpina.* Known in America by the names of *Muscadine, Bullace,* and *Bullet Grape.*

This species deserves mention, as it differs greatly from all the foregoing kinds.

It can be readily distinguished by its bark, which, instead of being like that of the vines we are accustomed to see, is smooth, and covered with small lenticels, and, in a general way, similar to that of a mulberry.

The leaves are small, entire, heart-shaped, and glossy on both sides. Bunches very small, made up of a very few large berries, with very large seeds. The fruit do not ripen simultaneously, as is the case with other vines, but successively, and fall off as soon as ripe. They are very poor in sugar, and can only produce a drinkable wine in a hot climate, where this species might be cultivated with advantage, as it is an exceedingly vigorous grower, one vine being capable of covering over an acre of ground. Although phylloxera-resistant, they do not make good stocks, on account of the difficulty with which European sorts can be grafted on them.

The following are the best known varieties :—

† **Flowers.** Synonym: *Black Muscadine.*

A late variety, esteemed in Georgia, Alabama, and South Carolina, where it is said to yield a good red wine.

† **Scuppernong.** Synonyms: *Yellow Muscadine. White Muscadine. Bullace. Roanoke.*

A very hardy white sort, from which wine is made in the Southern States of North America.

† **Thomas.**

A reddish grape similar to the others in most respects.

† VITIS RUPESTRIS.

This species is also termed *Rock Grape* and *Sugar Grape* in America. No cultivated varieties have, as yet, been derived from it. It is a a very poor bearer, most of the flowers being sterile, and is therefore unsuitable as a direct producer. It is, on the other hand, an excellent stock for grafting European sorts on, as it is thoroughly phylloxera-resistant, and very hardy, doing well in almost any but chalky soils.

HYBRIDS.

There are, as might be expected, many hybrids between the different species, some of which deserve mention ; these are—

† **Allen's Hybrid.**

Chasselas × *Isabella.* A good early white table grape, but not phylloxera-resistant.

† **Alvey.** Synonym: *Hagar.*

This is a *V. Vinifera* × *V. Æstivalis* hybrid. A good red variety, producing a good wine. It is phylloxera-resistant, but the fruit sets very badly, and it is subject to what is termed in French "*anthracnose deformante.*"

† Delaware.
Is a *V. Vinifera* × *V. Labrusca.*. A white grape of little value, although it seems to resist the phylloxera.

Elvira.
A hybrid of *Taylor* × *Sphinx*. A white or pink phylloxera-resistant variety. It is a good bearer, and although its fruit has a foxy taste, it seems to yield upon distillation an excellent brandy.

† Goethe.
Is a hybrid between *V. Vinifera* and *V. Labrusca*. It is a good white grape, but a poor bearer, and does not seem to be phylloxera-resistant.

† Lindley.
A brick-red table grape derived from *V. Vinifera* × *V. Labrusca* × *V. Riparia*.

† Salem.
A *V. Labrusca* × *V. Vinifera* (Bl. Hamburg). A variety of little value.

Vialla. Synonym : *Clinton-Vialla*.
One of the most valuable hybrids as a stock to graft on, but useless as a direct producer, on account of the foxy taste of its fruit and the small number of flowers which set. It is a *V. Riparia* × *V. Labrusca*.

† Wilder.
A *V. Vinifera* × *V. Labrusca* × *V. Riparia*, said to be a good purple table grape.

AUSTRALIAN VINES.

This chapter would not be complete without a brief mention of some of our indigenous Australian varieties. Although at present they are considered as being without value, and have never been cultivated with a view of improving the fruit, it is quite possible that something might be done in this direction.

They differ from vines one is accustomed to see in being evergreen, with bark similar to that of *V. Rotundifolia*, and oblong serrated leaves, comparable to those of the laurel or camellia. The flowers are more similar to those of the Ampelopsis or Virginia creeper than a vitis. The petals open above, and in appearance are similar to Fig. 4.

The following species are described as follows by Baron von Mueller in his work "Select Extra Tropical Plants":—

Vitis Acetosa.

"Carpentaria and Arnheim's land.—Stems rather herbaceous than shrubby ; erect. The whole plant is pervaded with acidity, thus the foliage proved valuable in cases of scurvy. The berries are edible, and very white, purple, and black. This species, if planted in countries with a mild temperate clime, would probably spring afresh from the roots annually. Mr. Alfred Giles made from this grape some wine of fair quality, reminding of claret."

Vitis Baudiniana (F. v. Mueller). Synonyms : *Cissus Antarctica, Vitis Antarctica.*

"East Australia.—With V. Hypoglauca, the most southern of all species of grapes, none extending to New Zealand. It is evergreen, and a vigorous plant for bowers, but suffers even from slight frosts. The berries are freely produced and edible, though not large."

Vitis Hypoglauca (F. v. Mueller).

"East Australia, as far south as Gippsland.—An evergreen climber of enormous length, forming a very stout stem in age. The black berries attain the size of small cherries. This species, also, may perhaps be vastly changed in its fruit by continued culture; bears slight frost, but it is best in cool climes to keep seedlings for two or three years under shelter, so that sufficient increment and induration of the woody stem takes place for its resisting subsequently some frost."

Vitis Opaca (F. v. Mueller). Synonym : *Cissus Opaca* or *Burdekin Vine.*

A Queensland species, which is, like the others, a hardy evergreen climber.

* * * * *

In addition to these there are several Asiatic and African species, which, however, need not be described here.

CHAPTER V.

SELECTION OF SITE AND CHOICE OF SUITABLE VARIETIES.

The selection of a suitable site for a vineyard is of the greatest importance, and cannot receive too serious consideration at the hands of the intending planter.

When it is remembered that the important factors—climate, aspect, soil, &c.—depend upon the site chosen, the importance of a judicious choice becomes manifest.

When selecting a site the main thing the future vinegrower must keep in view is the kind of wine he wishes to make. Choice or abundant, light or strong, dry or sweet, red or white, all depends upon these points, and they should receive the fullest consideration, more especially from any one who has not as yet purchased his land, but wishes to know which will be the most profitable district for him to settle in. It is a delicate matter to say that any district is best situated for this purpose, such a course would expose one to much unfavorable criticism from residents of all the other districts, who might consider that they were slighted and their land depreciated.

We shall briefly enumerate the different advantages of such and such a climate and soil, and leave it to the intending planter to choose between them.

Most wine-growing districts of Victoria, and a good many districts where no vines have as yet been planted, have some distinct advantage to recommend them, such as freedom from excessive moisture, and consequent immunity from fungus pests; prolificacy of the vine in them; excellent quality of the wine; freedom from frosts; suitability to such and such a variety.

It would be well to here warn the intending planter against devoting himself to the production of abundant crops of small value instead of smaller yield of superior wine. It pays a man better to obtain 100 gallons per acre of wine for which he can obtain 4s per gallon than 400 gallons per acre of wine only worth 1s. per gallon.

The absolute return per acre will be the same in both cases, but the smaller yield, entailing less expense in gathering, vintaging, and casks, leaves a larger margin for profit.

At present the production of Victorian wine is so limited that it has not come to be looked upon as a regular article of commerce in the markets of Europe. The demand for it is small, and, consequently, in the absence of competition, wines in reality of very dissimilar values often sell for the same price. With the largely-increased production, which is sure to result from the extensive planting of the last year or two, a re-arrangement of prices is bound to come, tending to raise the price of superior wines and lower that of wines of ordinary quality.

The successful wine-grower of the future will be the one who devotes himself to the production of high-class wines. At present it may be more remunerative to produce larger quantities of an inferior article, but a time will come when the producer who sacrifices quality to quantity will find difficulty in getting rid of his wine, whilst for a superior article there will always be a demand.

The strength of the wine to be produced is the next point requiring consideration. In Europe strong wines are going out of fashion every day and giving place to lighter ones; people preferring a claret of which they can drink a bottle without inconvenience to a strong wine of a port or sherry type, which does not quench the thirst, and of which only a couple of glasses may be taken with impunity. In Australia the taste for strong wines still continues, although lighter ones are coming more into favour every day.

A light wine is the one for which there is, and always will be, the greatest demand. It is destined to be the universal drink for all classes, being more beneficial, cheering, and invigorating than any other. The great bulk of strong wines now produced will be devoted chiefly to blending purposes, and will not probably command a high price in the near future, with the exception of a limited number of high-class strong wines, which will always command good prices as liqueur wines or ports.

Sweet wines may be included in the same category as strong wines. A wine cannot remain sweet unless it is sufficiently rich in alcohol to prevent the fermentation of the unchanged sugar. Such wines, often termed ladies' wines, liqueur, or fruity wines, are perhaps more sought after in the colonial market than dry, strong wines. They are often of excellent quality when made in certain privileged situations, but their production ought not to be encouraged.

Red wines are in greater demand than white, although wines of the type of Chablis or Hock meet with a ready sale. In short the wine the future grower will find the most profitable to make is a dry red wine—the lighter the better. As for producing what is commonly called a claret, it will not do to imitate what one is in the habit of tasting as such. It must be remembered that only a small proportion of what comes out here as French wine was ever grown in France at all. Wines of a delicate character, liable to be mistaken by true connoisseurs for the celebrated wines of France and Germany, such as Bordeaux, Burgundies, Hocks, &c., can only be produced in the first or cool region of the colony. The second region is capable of producing excellent wines of a somewhat stronger description, but which are still light wines, provided proper care be observed in the selection of sorts. Whilst the third is best adapted for the production of good commercial or blending wines, but in greater abundance, as well as some high-class strong wines. In France it is only the central portions which produce Clarets, Burgundies, and other light wines; no wines in the south of France or any part of Spain, Portugal, or Italy are similar to a first-class Bordeaux. It is a surprising thing that the first region of Victoria, which is so very favorably situated for the production of light wines, and in which it is not impossible that some privileged spots may be found capable of producing wines equal to the celebrated Chateau Latour, Margaux,' and Lafitte of Bordeaux, has been so greatly neglected by persons devoting themselves to viticulture. The greater part of north-eastern Gippsland comes within this region, yet there are not twenty acres of this vast district planted with vines.

This is a word of advice *en passant* to any one who has not as yet decided in which district to plant. The greater number of persons have already purchased the land, and wish to know if it be suitable for viticulture or not. It is unnecessary to say that the most reliable information in this direction will be given by the vine itself, and intending planters cannot do better than study the established vineyards in the district, and ascertain from the owners the advantages or disadvantages they labour under.

The principal points respecting which information should be sought in either of the three regions are :—

1st. Suitability of the soil, both from a physical and a chemical point of view, as already set forth (page 23).

2nd. Suitable rainfall. In an approximate manner it may be said that localities with an annual rainfall of under 10, or over 40 inches, are unfavorable for vine-growing purposes. If recourse can be had to irrigation, of course vines can be profitably cultivated in districts where the rainfall is even less than 10 inches. A good deal depends upon the distribution of this water. If it be spread evenly over all the months of the year a lesser rainfall will be necessary than would otherwise be the case. The following table, giving the annual rainfall of some of the best known wine districts of France, may be of interest to intending planters :—

Champagne	18·71
Burgundy	29·35
Beaujolais	37·27
Bordeaux	23·09
Bas Languedoc	25·65
Avignon	23·42
Arles	16·67
Marseille	20·17

Champagne is situated in the north of France; Burgundy, Beaujolais, and Bordeaux in the central portion; whilst the Bas Languedoc, Avignon, Arles, and Marseille are in the south. It will be seen that Victoria and France are very similarly situated as regards rainfall.

3rd. Liability to late spring frosts occurring after the vines have come into leaf.

4th. Liability to violent winds occurring in the very early summer, at which time the shoots, being neither long enough to be tied up nor strong enough to resist the action of the wind, sustain considerable damage.

5th. Frequency of injurious hailstorms. These are of very local occurrence, and concern the site of the vineyard itself rather than a whole district, especially in hilly country; they are often confined to certain ranges and valleys. It is common to observe two places only a mile or so apart, one of which is devastated by hail nearly every year, whilst the other enjoys comparative immunity from it. The injury done to vines by this scourge is very great. A single storm is capable of annihilating in a few minutes an entire crop.

6th. Several other points ought to be considered, such as the visitation of locusts. In order to be as little exposed as possible, the shelter of some natural obstacle, such as a creek, river, belts of timber, or a high range of hills should be taken advantage of where practicable.

Other considerations, such as distance from market, facility of obtaining labour, &c., &c., should receive due consideration, but need not be mentioned here.

The above conditions must be fulfilled in any vineyard, no matter how or where situated. There are others which vary with the climatic region in which the vineyard may be situated, so must be considered separately for each.

First Region.

The great advantages of this region have been mentioned ; it is not, however, without its drawbacks. The vine, growing with less vigour than in the warmer districts, necessitates closer planting, which, without increasing the crops, renders cultivation more expensive, there being more vines per acre to prune, disbud, tie up, sulphur, &c., &c., whilst the work of ploughing and scarifying is also rendered more difficult.

In addition to this, the frequent summer rains promote the growth of weeds, or cause the flowers to set badly and facilitate the developments of fungus diseases; whilst in the colder parts unfavorable weather towards vintage time may interefere with the proper ripening of the grapes. On account of these many drawbacks a site requires to be chosen with great care in this region. Contrarily to what we will find to be the case for the other two regions, the vineyard should be so situated as to promote the production of alcohol, otherwise the wine would be too weak. Hill sides with a N. or N.E. aspect should alone be selected, unless the ground be almost level, as on the summit of a rise, when the direction of the slope is of no consequence. Low-lying flats are most unsuitable, and should never be selected. A slope steeper than 1 in 7 is not to be recommended, as considerable quantities of soil would be carried away by the rush of the water during the winter. The soil must be friable, easily cultivated, preferably pebbly, and of such a nature as to insure thorough drainage. If these conditions are fulfilled a pale-coloured surface will promote the ripening of the fruit. If the drainage be not thorough a darker soil is to be preferred. Rich soils, especially black or peaty ones containing much organic matter, should never be planted with vines.

The " cepages " which give the best results vary according to the chemical character of the soil and the temperature of the spring and autumn.

In a limestone soil with fine spring but early autumn, the best red wine will be produced by the Pinots, either the ordinary Pinot Noir or the Millers Burgundy (Pinot Meunier); under similar conditions this sort yields the celebrated Burgundies of France. The Pulsart ano ther sort which would do well under these circumstances. It is also a better bearer, and does not suffer from frost to any considerable extent. If the autumn be fine, the Mondeuse would prove a valuable red sort, as it gives large yields of good wine, it ripens later than either Pinots or Pulsart. The Malbeck is also to be recommended, although it frequently sets badly at flowering time.

For white wine the different white Pinots, the Pinot Gris, and Aucarot will give the best results. The Chasselas may be added to these.

In granitic and schistose soils the most suitable red sorts are Shiraz or Red Hermitage, and Gamay, whilst for white, Roussanne or White Hermitage, Riesling, and Tokay.

On a clayey subsoil, covered with a more or less sandy or loamy surface soil, most of the above-mentioned sorts thrive. Those, however, which give the best results are the Bordeaux varieties, Cabernet, Carmenet, Verdot, Merlot, and Malbeck, more especially if the soil be sandy, or rich in quartz pebbles. The Shiraz (Red Hermitage) also gives very good results in it, whilst it is a better bearer than most of the above.

For white wine, the Semillon and Sauvignon (white) will give excellent results, as also will Riesling, White Hermitage, and Chasselas. The latter will serve to blend with either of the former varieties, although they must not be blended with each other. The Tokay and Pinot Gris also give good results in such a soil.

Second Region.

This is, perhaps, the region in which the greatest facilities are offered to the grower, he having few of the drawbacks which are to be met with in the cool region to contend with. The vine growing in a more luxurious manner enables larger crops to be obtained from vines planted farther apart. The wine, however, although in many cases excellent, is of a rather different character, and not so delicate as that of the last region. It is, if anything, too strong; so, in selecting a site, unless with a view of making liqueur wines, raisins, or currants, the chief preoccupation of the intending planter must be to aim at diminishing the percentage of alcohol. The most favorable aspect for this purpose will be S.E., or W. Level ground, with sufficient slope to allow surplus water to drain off, will give very good results. A sandy soil should also be sought for; wines in such soils being considerably lighter than those grown in stiffer ones. Limestone soils should be reserved for the production of strong wines, and should be avoided for the production of those of lighter character. In this region several of the sorts mentioned above will give excellent results in the same descriptions of soil as suits them in the first region. These are Aucarot, Pulsart, Shiraz (Red Hermitage), Gamay, Roussanne, Riesling, Merlot, Verdot, and Malbeck. The latter gives excellent results, being far less liable to set badly than in the cooler part. These sorts should not be planted exclusively in a vineyard, as the wine made from them would be too strong; they should be used to give bouquet and other qualities to the wine, whilst other sorts producing lighter wine form the basis of the vineyard, of these several will thrive in any soil. They are the Dolcetto, Black Hambro, Black Prince, Black St. Peter, Mataro, Morrastel, and Carignane, whilst a certain percentage of juice of La Folle grapes would greatly improve the quality. The Oeillade and Grenache may be added to this number; they give the best results in schistose and granitic soils. For dry white wines the sorts to be recommended are—Riesling, Chasselas, Doradillo, and Tokay, although the latter does not give such satisfactory results as in the first region. To these may be added the Sweet Water, which produces large crops of good light wine well adapted for reducing the strength of the other wines.

The Gouais is a sort which should not be too extensively planted. Good wines of a strong character may be made on stony hill sides, with N. or N.E. aspect from the following sorts :—For red, Cabernet Sauvignon, Carmenet, Grenache, and Pinots. For white, Pedro Ximenes, in granitic or schistose formations, where also the Roussanne will give a strong wine. Verdeilho, which, perhaps, is superior to any other for the production of a wine of a Madeira type; and, lastly, the Muscats, which yield excellent liqueur wines of well-known character.

Third Region.

This region cannot produce wines as light as those of the two former ones. The object of the grower in this region being to make a wine containing as little alcohol as possible, the same precautions should be observed as mentioned for the last region, such as S. or S.W. aspect, and sandy soils. Under these conditions excellent dry wines, containing less than 25 per cent. of alcohol, may be grown in abundance, well suited for commercial purposes, and which should successfully compete with wines of similar character imported largely into France from Spain and other warm countries. For this purpose only a limited number of sorts mentioned as suitable for the first region should be tolerated; in fact they are Shiraz and Malbeck, and they should be only sparingly planted. Such sorts as Aramon, Carignane, Cincaut, Grenache, Mataro, Aspiran, Morrastel, and Oeillade are, without doubt, the most suitable ones. The three last-named would produce a lighter wine of very good quality without any other admixture. The Grenache is better suited for the production of liqueur wines, as also are Muscats, Malvoisies, Roussanne, Verdeilho, Pedro Ximenes, Aucarot, Maccabeo, &c., whilst for the production of a light white wine, Chasselas, Riesling, Doradillo, La Folle, and perhaps also Sweet Water and Gouais may be named.

It is needless to mention that this region is better suited than the others for the cultivation of raisin and currant varieties.

CHAPTER VI.

PREPARATION OF SOIL.

Having selected the site for the vineyard, the next thing to do is to prepare the soil for planting.

The vine being a deep-rooted plant, the greater the ease with which its roots can penetrate to a considerable depth the more vigorous and healthy will it be, the longer will it live, and the better will it be able to stand severe drought during the summer months. No means facilitates the penetration of the ground by the roots more than deep preliminary cultivation, which is, therefore, not only beneficial but necessary. Many persons are in the habit of saying that deep cultivation is unnecessary, and that they have observed vines doing better on land which was simply ploughed to a depth of a few inches than on that which was subsoiled. This may be the case for the first few years, but once the vines have attained their full development, the difference between the yield of the two soon becomes manifest, the advantage, of course, being on the side of the properly cultivated vines, which will continue to thrive for many years without becoming exhausted. Although good results are often obtained on land which has received only a simple ploughing, far better results would have been obtained had it been more deeply worked. The longevity of vineyards in the old country, where vines have frequently been cultivated for centuries on the same land, is, in a great measure, to be attributed to proper preparation of the soil. Although a stiff soil naturally benefits more by deep cultivation than a free one, it has been found in France, at Aigue Mortes, where vines are planted in almost pure sand in order to enable them to resist the attacks of the phylloxera, that, contrary to expectation, trenching to a considerable depth (2 or 3 feet) had a most beneficial effect on the growth of the vine, and increased the yield to a considerable extent.

The stirring of the soil does not only act mechanically, in rendering it penetrable for the roots, but by aerating it renders certain substances more readily assimilable. In addition to this it improves the drainage and enables rain to be absorbed more readily, as well as a proper amount of moisture to be retained.

Gaillardon is of opinion that deep cultivation diminishes the aromatic taste to be met with in some Algerian wines, which he considers to be due to the presence of débris of aromatic plants in the surface soil. It is quite possible that the same rule might apply in Australia, where the débris of Eucalyptus leaves which have been collecting on the ground for thousands of years may be responsible for the "Australian taste" with which many of our wines are sometimes reproached by European connoisseurs. The freedom from peculiar taste of wines grown on sandhills where no Eucalypti exist tends to confirm this theory. The depth of the preliminary cultivation depends upon the climate. The warmer and drier this is the deeper ought it to be. Vines growing in a warm climate attaining a far greater development than is the case in a cold one, the roots, which spread more or less equally in every direction, require a deep soil. In addition to this, it may be mentioned that the deeper the soil is worked the lighter will the resulting wine be.

If we examine what is usually done in France we will find that in the northern parts the preliminary cultivation is extremely shallow, whilst in the warmer and drier south it is very deep, except in certain parts where a thin layer of soil rests on broken limestone, easily penetrable by the roots of the vine. Such soils, called "*Garrigues,*" prevail in Languedoc and part of the Herault and Pyrenees Orientales, and this accounts for the small depth to which they break up the soil in these places. The following are the ordinary depths to which the soil is broken in some of the leading wine countries of Europe :—

Provence (southern France)	30in. to 39in.
Hermitage ,, ...	50in.
Douro (Portugal)	39in. to 59in.
Cyprus (island of)	28in. to 32in.
Bordeaux (medium climate of France) ...	24in.
Beaujolais ,, ...	24in.
Burgundy (cooler part of France) ...	14in.
Champagne ,, ...	12in. to 24in.
Canton de Vaud (Switzerland) ...	36in. to 39in.

In Australia it would never pay to subsoil land to such depths, on account of the high price of labour, and the following will be found quite sufficient for each region.

First or cool region from 12 to 18 inches; second region, 18 to 24 inches; and third region, 24 to 30 inches.

There are three ways of breaking up the ground—1. Subsoiling or breaking up the soil to the required depth, but leaving the different layers in their natural position; 2. Trenching or breaking up the soil in such a way as to bring the subsoil to the surface and bury the surface soil at the bottom of the trench; 3. Mixing the surface and subsoil to the required depth. This last method necessitates the employment of hand labour, and being, therefore, too expensive for application in Australia, need not be considered here. We have thus to decide between subsoiling and trenching.

This is one of the vexed questions of viticulture, many persons holding different opinions about it. In the evidence given before the Royal Commission on Vegetable Products, the majority of witnesses are in favour of subsoiling (see Appendix A), and, in fact, this method is the one which will give the best results in the great majority of cases. In Australia, the most common description of soil is a more or less free surface, resting on a rather stiff subsoil; in such a case trenching would prove injurious, as by bringing the subsoil to the top the surface would be rendered stiff and difficult to cultivate. It would hinder the absorbtion of water during rain, and by the facility with which it would cake and crack, would promote in an undue manner the evaporation of the necessary moisture during the summer, besides rendering the proper aeration of the soil very difficult.

Trenching is only to be recommended in the somewhat exceptional case when the subsoil, or at least the soil situated at the depth of a foot or so be looser than the surface soil, or capable of becoming so by exposure to the action of the air. In places where the soil continues identical or practically so to the depth of 3 or 4 feet, it is indifferent which method be employed, although perhaps trenching is to be preferred, as the well-aerated surface soil, being buried whilst fresh layers were exposed to the action of the air, would have a most beneficial effect upon its fertility.

Partial subsoiling, or only subsoiling a foot or so on each side of the row in which the vines are planted, is not a judicious operation, as it places the roots in a sort of drain, where they are liable to suffer from too much moisture. The advantages to be gained from such a course would in any case be small, as it must be remembered that the roots of the vine spread in every direction, and not only immediately under the plant itself.

The best time to subsoil land for viticultural purposes is at the end of the autumn, when the first rains have sufficiently softened the soil to render the operation possible. This presents the great advantage of exposing the newly-broken land to the action of air, rain, frost, &c., during the whole of the winter preceding the planting, thus rendering it loose and sweetening it in a considerable degree.

Before proceeding to subsoil, the land should be thoroughly cleared, all trees and bushes being removed, and roots run to the depth of at least 18 inches or 2 feet. Any live trees should be ring-barked during the early summer; they will be dead by the time subsoiling is to be commenced, and will send up no suckers. They may be pulled out with a Forest Devil, or one of the numerous appliances used for this purpose, after the soil round the roots has been loosened. All rubbish should be burned on the ground itself, the ashes, containing a considerable amount of potash, forming a valuable manure.

The best way to subsoil land is with a double-furrow plough specially made for the purpose, the second or front mouldboard of which has been removed and replaced by the subsoiler which consists of a curved bar of iron so arranged as to be capable of being raised or lowered by a lever, and carrying an ordinary plough-share at its lower extremity or terminating in a broad point like the chisel tooth of a scarifier. An ordinary plough opens up a furrow to the depth of 8 inches or so, then the subsoil plough can be started, the subsoiler engaging in the furrow already opened, and stirring the soil to the required depth, whilst the shear and mouldboard open up a fresh one in which the subsoiler will work on the second round, and so on.

In moderately stiff soils five horses ought to be able to subsoil an acre per day to a depth of 18 inches.

If the ground has not been thoroughly freed from roots, or there are stones which interfere with the progress of the plough, it will be better to substitute for the above two single ones, which follow each other in the same furrow, the second one being without a mouldboard. Any stoppage of one of them will not interfere with the working of the other.

In order to trench the soil, the best way is to employ an ordinary plough to go first and open the furrow to as great a depth as possible, and follow up in the same furrow with a trench plough with a high mouldboard capable of raising the soil to the surface.

If the trench plough be sufficiently strong, and a good team of bullocks be available, it will be possible to turn the soil to a depth of 15 inches in a single operation. The ground, after having been subsoiled or trenched, as the case may be, and left exposed during the winter, will have settled down considerably and be almost level. It should then receive a light ploughing and harrowing, when it will be in a fit state for planting.

Any parts which are sour and swampy (especially in the first region) should be drained. Places of this character should be carefully marked when observed, and properly drained before being planted with vines.

The most suitable system of drainage consists of a series of small drains running into larger ones, which in turn empty themselves into main drains situated in suitable positions.

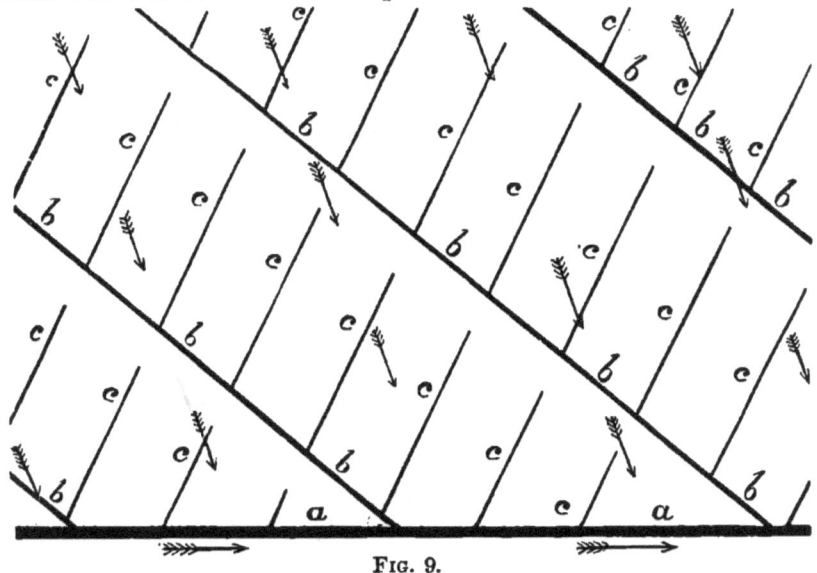

FIG. 9.

A glance at Fig. 9 will show the disposition of these drains. The small arrows indicate the direction of the greatest fall. *a a*, the main drain, which may be situated along a gully, in which case it can be left open. *b b b* are the secondary and *c c c* the small drains. All the drains should be so placed as to make as great an angle as possible with the line of greatest slope. This presents the double advantage of not giving too much fall, in which case the scour might be too great, and rendering the drainage more effective. A drain often acts as beneficially by intercepting the water from above and preventing it from entering the parts requiring drainage as another one would by carrying off the water which is already there.

The main drains should, if closed, be made of stone, slabs, or earthenware pipes, and should be of sufficient size to enable them to carry off all the water brought to them by the others. The secondary drains may be made of slabs or stones, but more economical and quite as effective ones may be made of vine-cuttings or scrub, the former being preferable.

These drains should be dug to a depth of 2 to 3 feet, or until the good clay subsoil be reached; they may be from 9 inches to 1 foot in width at the top, tapering down to 6 inches at the bottom. They are then filled in with vine cuttings, which must be put in carefully in order that no vacant places are left where the water lodging would cause the whole drain to collapse and become useless. They should not be put in bundles, but by small quantities at a time, starting from the top of the slope and working down, so that the layers are arranged the reverse order to that which slates are fixed on the roof of a house. They should be rammed tight, and filled in with earth. A layer of straw or weeds will prevent any loose earth from falling through, and will thus keep them more open than would otherwise be possible. Drains of this class may be made of a maximum length of 200 to 300 yards, they last for upwards of twelve years, and even when quite decomposed leave sufficient spaces to insure an escape for surplus water, whilst the decomposed cuttings make an excellent manure for the vines growing in proximity to them. The small drains need not be so deep as the secondary ones in Fig. 10. The secondary drains are 300 yards in length, and the small ones being 80 yards long and 40 yards apart; in this case we have a gradual slope, for which reason the angle between the small and secondary drains is acute, in order to insure a sufficient fall for the water; on a steeper slope the angle might be made obtuse, an advantage, as it would enable less drains to be made per acre. It is not always on ground without much slope that drains are wanted; it frequently occurs that on steep hillsides there are sour wet spots which must be drained; in such cases the whole block would not require to be systematically treated, and the vigneron must use his judgment and only drain what is necessary, as the process is expensive, and should not be applied unless where required.

CHAPTER VII.

LAYING-OUT OF VINEYARD.

A vineyard should be methodically laid out and planted in such a manner as to enable a maximum of yield to be obtained with the employment of a minimum of labour, the high price of which in Australia renders many methods often applied in Europe impracticable with us.

As in the case with most other vineyard operations, no fixed rule can be given, the laying-out depending essentially on the climate, soil, and sorts grown; so much is this so that a perfectly laid out vineyard on the Murray would be most unsuitably so in one of the cooler districts of the colony.

In laying out the vineyard we have to consider—
1. Distance apart of the vines.
2. Arrangement of the vines.
3. Extent and form of the blocks.

The distance apart of the vines, having considerable influence upon the disposition and form of the blocks, must be considered first.

Perhaps no question concerning viticulture has given rise to more discussion than this, the most conflicting opinions being held by practical vignerons.

It is impossible to lay down any hard-and-fast rule for the distance which vines ought to occupy relatively to each other. The vigneron must be guided by practical experience and by climatic and economical considerations.

It was mentioned (p. 10) that plants exhale a considerable amount of water through their leaves. If the ground contains too much moisture, close planting, by giving more leaves per acre, enables more water to be got rid of than would be the case if the vines were planted far apart. In the warmer districts the reverse is the case, the amount of moisture is insufficient, and, if recourse cannot be had to irrigation, the vines will suffer if not planted at such a distance that each vine has a sufficient store of water at its disposal. This necessity for planting vines far apart in a warm climate is much intensified by the great augmentation in the vigour of the plant under the influence of the increase of light and heat to which it is there subjected. We saw (p. 9) that the less grapes there are on a vine the richer the must will be in glucose, and consequently the stronger will the wine be—the vigour of very closely-planted vines being small, the crop on each vine is lessened, and the resulting wine is stronger than would otherwise be the case, an advantage in a cool district where grapes sometimes ripen with difficulty, but a drawback in a hot climate where under normal conditions the wine is too strong, and the object of the vigneron is to reduce it as much as possible by natural means.

In France the number of vines per acre varies very greatly; the following figures give some idea of the ordinary distances in some of the leading districts:—

Champagne	...	1ft. 3in. × 1ft. 3in.
Burgundy	...	1ft. 10in × 1ft. 10in.
Beaujolais	...	2ft. 4in. × 2ft. 4in.
Hermitage	...	3ft. 3in. × 3ft. 3in.
Cognac	...	3ft. 3in. × 4ft. 10in.
Bordeaux	...	3ft. 3in. × 3ft. 6in.
Sauternes	...	2ft. 8in. × 4ft. 4in. to 2ft. 8in. × 6ft. 6in.
Herault	...	4ft. 6in. × 4ft. 6in. to 5ft. 3in. × 5ft. 3in.

It will be seen from this table that the distance between the vines gradually increases as one goes from the north to the south of France.

In Australia, where the high price of manual labour makes it imperative that the vineyard should be so arranged as to substitute by horse labour wherever possible, the majority of the above distances would be totally unsuitable. At 3ft. × 3ft. the ground must be worked by hand, and at 4ft. × 4ft. it can only be worked with difficulty by horse labour during the summer months, unless the vines be tied closely to stakes or wires.

It does not do to rush to extremes, and, except in exceptional cases, such distances as 12ft. × 12ft. are not to be recommended, as the diminution of the yield per acre would not be compensated by the greater facility with which the soil can be worked. As proof of this, let us suppose two plots of ground of one acre each, one planted 5ft. × 5ft., which we shall call A, and one planted 10ft. × 10ft., which we shall call B. A will contain 1,742 vines per acre, whereas

B will only contain 435; if the individual vines bear the same crop in each block, A will give 400 gallons to B's 100 gallons; therefore, for each block to pay equally well, the cost of cultivation must be £2 for B if it be £8 for A.

If the individual vines of B bear twice as much as those of A, the yield would be as follows:—A 400 gallons and B 200 gallons; in such a case B would be the most remunerative block, although a third one planted at, say, 7ft. × 7ft. would probably give the best results.

There is for each locality, with the same conditions of soil and climate, a certain distance, which we may call the optimum, at which vines will give the best results; if this distance be increased they will not improve, and if it be diminished they will deteriorate. Unless this be a distance which cannot conveniently be worked by horse labour it would evidently be a waste of land to plant wider, and would entail the cultivation of unnecessary soil. It would be just as foolish to plant closer than this distance, as it would necessitate unnecessary pruning, disbudding, tying-up, &c.; that is, if the climate be such that grapes will ripen satisfactorily in it.

In the first or cool region, the optimum distance is $4\frac{1}{2}$ft. × $4\frac{1}{2}$ft. or 5ft. × 5ft., but vines may be planted as far apart as 6ft. × 6ft., on account of the greater facilities afforded for cultivation. In other words, the number of vines per acre should be from 1,200 to 2,000.

In the second region it will be found more advantageous to plant vines farther apart, say 7ft. × 7ft., 8ft. × 8ft., or 8ft. × 5ft., or from 680 to 1,100 vines per acre.

In the third or warm region they should be planted still farther apart, 10ft. × 10ft., or about 400 vines per acre, being a very suitable distance. These distances may be varied to some extent by circumstances. Vigorous varieties should be planted farther apart than weak ones. Vines in rich soils, growing more vigorously than in poorer ones, must also be planted farther apart.

Arrangement of the Vines.

There are three methods of arranging vines. These are the square, the quincunx or equilateral triangle, and the rectangular rows.

The square system is so simple as to require no description. The following table gives the number of vines per acre for different distances apart:—

Distance apart.	Vines per acre.	Distance apart.	Vines per acre.
1 ft. x 1 ft.	... 43,500	7 ft. x 7 ft.	... 889
1½ ft. x 1½ ft.	... 19,360	7½ ft. x 7½ ft.	... 774
2 ft. x 2 ft.	... 10,890	8 ft. x 8 ft.	... 680
2½ ft. x 2½ ft.	... 6,970	8½ ft. x 8½ ft.	... 603
3 ft. x 3 ft.	... 4,840	9 ft. x 9 ft.	... 537
3½ ft. x 3½ ft.	... 3,556	9½ ft. x 9½ ft.	... 482
4 ft. x 4 ft.	... 2,722	10 ft. x 10 ft.	... 435
4½ ft. x 4½ ft.	... 2,151	11 ft. x 11 ft.	... 360
5 ft. x 5 ft.	... 1,742	12 ft. x 12 ft.	... 302
5½ ft. x 5½ ft.	... 1,440	13 ft. x 13 ft.	... 257
6 ft. x 6 ft.	... 1,210	14 ft. x 14 ft.	... 222
6½ ft. x 6½ ft.	... 1,031	15 ft. x 15 ft.	... 193

In the cool region, with vines planted 5ft. x 5ft., there is ample room to work implements in two perpendicular directions. At 6ft. x 6ft. they may be worked in four different directions. At distances stated for the other regions implements may at any time be worked in four directions.

The quincunx system will be readily understood by reference to Fig. 10. It presents the advantage of enabling the ground to be worked in three directions, but is somewhat inconvenient, as the oblique rows towards the outside of the blocks are all of different lengths.

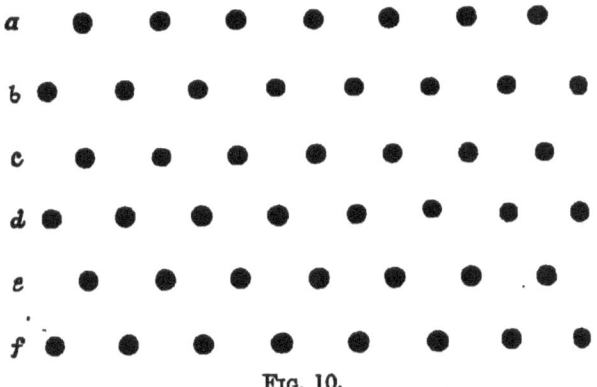

FIG. 10.

Each vine is opposite to a space, thus offering facilities for working, it being possible to move the scarifier to avoid projecting branches. The vines are so situated that one is always equidistant from six others, for which reason it is sometimes termed the septuple system. The following table gives the number of vines per acre and distance between the rows for different distances of the vines from each other:—

Distance between vines.	Distance between rows.	Number of vines per acre.
4ft.	3ft. 5in.	3,205
5ft.	4ft. 4in.	2,025
6ft.	5ft. 2in.	1,392
7ft.	6ft. 1in.	1,038
8ft.	6ft. 11⅛in.	785
9ft.	7ft. 9½in.	619
10ft.	8ft. 8in.	505
11ft.	9ft. 6¼in.	420
12ft.	10ft. 4¾in.	330

Planting in rectangular rows is to be recommended where vines are trained on wires; in any other case either of the two former systems is to be preferred. If the vines be placed at less than 4 feet from each other in the rows it prevents cross cultivation by horse labour, thus presenting all the drawbacks of the trellis system without any of its advantages.

In the third region, where vines must not be planted close, it may be advantageous to plant wider in one direction than another, even if the vines are to be staked or trained gooseberry-bush style. For example, 10ft. x 6ft. is more convenient than 8ft. x 8ft., as it enables a dray to be driven to any part of the block, whilst it does not entail any considerable augmentation in the number of vines per acre. The number of vines per acre for different distances apart are as follows:—

Distances apart.	Vines per acre.	Distances apart.	Vines per acre.
4ft. x 3ft.	3,632	8ft. x 6ft.	908
5ft. x 3ft.	2,904	8ft. x 7ft.	778
6ft. x 3ft.	2,420	10ft. x 6ft.	726
6ft. x 4ft.	1,816	10ft. x 7ft.	622
6ft. x 5ft.	1,452	10ft. x 8ft.	545
7ft. x 4ft.	1,556	10ft. x 9ft.	465
8ft. x 4ft.	1,360	10ft. x 11ft.	395
8ft. x 5ft.	1,090	10ft. x 12ft.	363

If the vines are to be trellised the wires should run in the direction in which the vines are closest. This will leave more room for cultivating, and entail less manual labour per acre than would be the case if the rows were placed close together.

There are several ways of marking out a vineyard before planting. If it be intended to plant in squares or rectangular rows this is a very simple matter. The sides of the blocks should be marked off at the required intervals with pegs or vine-stakes, and lines drawn across the block joining these marks. A chain, specially made for the purpose, with links of specified length, will be found very convenient. The chain being stretched across the block where a row is to be situated, the junction of each link indicates the position for a vine. If such a chain cannot be obtained, an ordinary piece of fencing-wire, or a gardener's line, may be substituted for it. This should be tightly stretched along the row. With a piece of wood of the required length for measure, the position of each vine will be easily ascertained.

Persons having a really first-class ploughman in their employ will find it more economical to run furrows across the field at the required distance apart, two vine-stakes, or other easily-distinguished marks, one considerably behind and in a line with the other, being placed at the opposite side of the field to the one the plough is started from, to enable the implement to be guided with precision. The ploughman must be careful to always keep these in a line. If the ground be in very good condition the plough may be replaced by a wheelbarrow, the same precautions being taken in order to obtain straight lines.

Marking-out land for plantation according to the quincunx system is slightly more complicated, as the lines cut each other at an angle of 60 degrees. If a theodolite or suitable instrument cannot be obtained, a convenient method is to only mark out every second line. Referring to Fig. 10, for example, rows 1, 3, and 5 would be marked out and rows 2, 4, and 6 inserted afterwards, each vine being inserted in the rectangle formed by four vines first marked. For example, if the vines are to be planted 6 feet apart, mark out the block as if for the rectangular system, the rows being 10ft. 4in. apart and the vines in these rows 6 feet from each other. By joining them diagonally the position of each vine in the intermediate rows will easily be obtained.

The direction in which the lines are planted is not of very great importance if the vines are planted on the square or quincunx systems. If planted on wires, it deserves consideration.

It is often recommended to direct the rows north and south, one side receiving the morning and the other the evening sun; the fruit is more likely to ripen evenly. Other considerations, however, may be of greater importance than this. If spring frosts are of frequent occurrence plant east and west, as the vines sheltering one another from the first rays of the sun will be less liable to sustain injury. If very strong winds or hail storms are to be feared their direction should be noted, and the rows directed accordingly.

In steep ground care must be taken not to let the rows follow the line of greatest slope, especially if the vines are to be trained on wires, as the rush of water down the furrows in winter would be liable to carry off considerable quantities of soil.

Provision should also be made for irrigation in localities where this may prove beneficial.

Extent and disposition of blocks.—A vineyard should be laid out in blocks separated by roads, which serve as a means of communication with the pickers at vintage time, for the removal of cuttings, for the cartage of sulphur, manures, &c., as may be required, and to give turning room to ploughs, scarifiers, and other implements. The number and extent of roads must be varied according to circumstances. The distance apart greatly modifies their distribution. If the vines be planted 10 feet apart, few of them will be required, there being room for a dray to pass freely between the rows. In such a case all that is necessary is a head-land at certain intervals on which implements may be turned.

Care must be taken to lay the vineyard out in such a way as to enable the different cultural operations to be executed with as little turning as possible ; every time a plough or scarifier is turned it entails a much greater waste of time than might be expected. The blocks should, therefore, be laid out in such a way that the rows of one correspond with those of the next one, so that the implements can work for a clear distance of, say, half-a-mile or so, without stopping at roads ; if this can be done in two directions, so much the better. If it be proposed to train part of the vines on wires, let the rows in this part be so directed as not to interfere with the above conditions.

In more closely-planted vineyards, say anything less than 8ft. x 8ft., the distribution of roads is of far greater importance, and some definite system should be adopted. Dr. Guyot recommends to divide the vineyard into 2½-acre blocks, 50 yards wide by 200 yards long ; the roads, 200 yards apart, being 10 feet wide, whilst the others are 16ft. 3in. in width. Under these conditions 11·5 per cent. of the whole vineyard would be taken up by roads.

In Victoria it will be preferable to have the main roads wider, say, 25 feet, and the smaller ones not less than 12 feet. If the vines be staked or trained gooseberry style, they should be divided into 5-acre blocks, say 5 x 10 chains; if trained on wires, these blocks might, with advantage, be divided into two by a narrow road running lengthways. This greatly facilitates work at vintage time, and enables lighter straining posts to be used for the wire, the expansion and contraction of which is also less on a short length.

The division of a vineyard into blocks of the same size is to be recommended ; it greatly facilitates observation and comparisons, and is a great advantage if part of the vineyard is to be worked by contract.

The roads should be made deeper than the rest of the vineyard, in order that they may, to a certain extent, act as drains. If properly formed, with a water-table on each side, they will be just as firm and maintain themselves in as good order as if raised above the surface of the rest of the vineyard, whilst, at the same time, they greatly benefit it by carrying off the surplus water.

The practice frequently adopted in Europe of cultivating other plants, such as wheat, asparagus, fruit trees, &c., between rows of vines is strongly to be condemned, especially in a dry climate, where the vine requires all the moisture there is in the soil, especially when it is young and not deep-rooted and cannot obtain moisture from the lower layers of the soil. For similar reasons different sorts ought not to be mixed together in the same block, but kept separate. Their grapes can easily be blended at vintage time, and the grower will have the advantage of knowing in what proportion they are blended, as well as all particulars of yield per acre, &c., of such and such a sort, details of which he would otherwise be totally ignorant.

The above are the principal points which require attention, and should be fulfilled by any one going in for viticulture in a thorough manner. Such conditions as shape of land to be planted or excessive steepness of portions of it may render it impossible to observe them in every detail, but nevertheless they should receive attention wherever practicable.

CHAPTER VIII.

PROPAGATION OF THE VINE.

The vine may be propagated in three ways—
> By seed,
> By cuttings,
> By layers.

PROPAGATION BY SEED

is only resorted to for the production of new varieties, as the vines grown in this way often differ considerably from the parent stock, even if the seeds were not the result of hybridisation.

Certain American sorts may be raised in this way if they are intended to form stocks to graft on. Such are the V. Solonis, some of the wild varieties of V. Riparia and V. Rupestris, and some of the other species which cannot easily be grown from cuttings, although these give more constant results. The seeds should be only taken from perfectly ripe grapes, and preferably from the finest berries of the bunch. They should be steeped in water for a few days, sown in October, and covered with about an inch or two of rich, loose soil. It takes about a month for them to appear above ground, and they will not commence to produce fruit till the fourth or fifth year.

Although seeds are the means provided by nature for the reproduction of the vine, and plants grown in this way are remarkably well constituted, it cannot be recommended to the practical vigneron.

PROPAGATION BY CUTTINGS

is the usual, and one may almost say the only, method employed on a large scale. It is our intention to here consider cuttings and rooted vines together   In the following chapter we shall discuss the relative advantages of each.

Any fragment of a vine shoot less than twelve months[*] old, and comprising one or more buds, may be looked upon as a cutting, and is capable of producing a new vine.

---

[*] It may be of interest to mention that of late years vines have been largely propagated in France from what are termed herbaceous cuttings; that is, the green fragments such as are broken off the vine when disbudding. They require great care on account of the facility with which they dry up, but otherwise strike easily. According to Fox, the softer the tissue the greater are the facilities for the emission of roots.

Selection of cuttings.—As a rule, when purchasing cuttings one is obliged to take what one can get, and hope for the best, but whenever it can be done they should be selected with the greatest care.

The vine the cuttings are taken from has in many cases a marked influence on the character of the young vine. In a block planted exclusively with one variety there will often be differences between some of the individual vines. These differences bear upon such qualities as the size of the fruit or prolificacy of the vine, the latter being the more important. Some vines identical to the others in every other respect are almost completely sterile, whilst others are remarkably heavy bearers, and this may be observed on the same vines year after year. Cuttings taken from such vines would perpetuate the characteristic of the parent, and be either almost sterile or remarkably prolific, as the case may be. During the summer or autumn, before the cuttings are taken, all vines in the vineyard which are remarkable for the quantity or quality of their fruit should be carefully marked, and cuttings only taken from them. The sorts which require most care in this direction are the Chasselas, red and white Hermitage, and Pulsart.

The portion of the vine the cuttings are taken from must also receive attention. Only such shoots as have borne or have been capable of bearing fruit should be selected for this purpose. The wood which fulfils this condition is that which, instead of growing directly off the old stem, grows off the wood of the previous year. Shoots growing off the old stem are termed in French "gourmands;" they, as well as suckers, should never be employed for cuttings; in certain cases the vines they give rise to are sterile.

The age of the vine the cuttings are taken from is not of any consequence provided it be older than three years.

There are two sorts of cuttings, viz., ordinary cuttings, which consist of any part of the shoot; and those which formed the lower end of the shoot, and have a small piece of two-year-old wood at their base. These, known in French as "*crossettes*," present the advantage of enabling the purchaser to see that they fulfil the condition of having been capable of bearing fruit, and are principally to be recommended on this account. They also strike more easily, as at the junction with the older wood there is a ring of buds, which facilitate the emission of roots. A cutting off any other part of the same shoot would ultimately produce as good a vine, although, perhaps, less liable to strike at first.

The piece of old wood at the base of these cuttings should be removed before planting, as it is incapable of giving rise to roots. Care should be taken not to injure the above-mentioned ring of buds when doing so.

Fig. 12.

Fig. 12a represents an ordinary cutting; Fig. 12b one with a piece of old wood at its base; and Fig. 12c the same, with the old wood removed, all but the strip of bark which is in contact with the above-mentioned buds.

Medium-sized, short-jointed cuttings give far better results than either very thick ones or thin, slender, and long-jointed ones. The wood must be well ripened, that is, it should have its regular winter appearance, and no trace of green at the extremities of the shoots. It must also be free from diseases of any kind, more especially anthracnosis or black spot. Cuttings which have been attacked by oidium, and which have brown or black marks on them in consequence, are not to be recommended as a rule, although if the injuries are only on the surface of the bark, and do not extend into the green part or cambium layer, no ill effects may result from their employment.

The length of cuttings has given rise to much discussion. It may be said, in a general way, that the shorter it is the better will the resulting vine be, as the more similar will the conditions be to those of a vine grown in the natural way, which is from seed. In the wild state the seed would doubtless germinate very near the ground, and send down roots penetrating the soil in all directions. The portion of stem of such a vine below ground would be exceedingly short. The more the cultivated vine resembles the wild one the more favorable will the circumstances be in which it is growing. As we have already seen, the complete root-system of the vine consists of tap-roots and laterals. If either of these develop themselves exclusively at the expense of the others the vine will not thrive. A long cutting produces a crown of lateral roots at each knot, and no tap-roots; it is thus very differently situated from that produced by a short cutting, which is much more similar to a seedling vine.

Fig. 13 represents the vine resulting from a short cutting, Fig. 14 that resulting from a very long one.

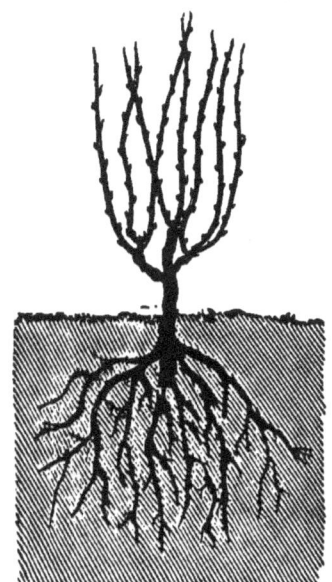

FIG. 13.

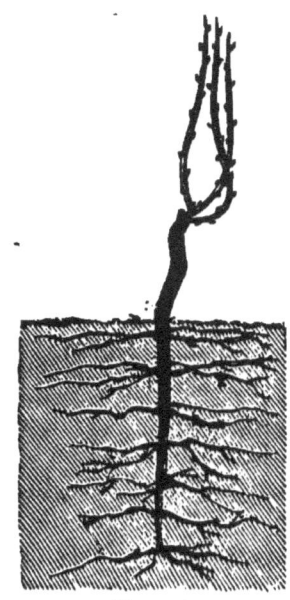

FIG. 14.

Although vine roots must penetrate deeply into the soil, their junction with the stem should be as near the surface as possible.

So great is the advantage of short cuttings over long ones that it has been recommended by many authorities to plant what are termed single-eye cuttings (Fig. 15).

These are sown in drills like seeds, and covered with an inch or so of soil. They give excellent results, and are of great value for reproducing rare sorts, as every eye will, under favorable circumstances, give rise to a plant. Some of the American sorts, which do not as a rule strike easily, are propagated

FIG. 15.

in this way, being forced under glass. The resulting vines are excellent, and are, of course, as nearly as possible in the same conditions as if grown from seed. In spite of these advantages, the system cannot be recommended in practice, on account of the great care which must at all times be bestowed on the young plants in the way of watering, &c., in order to bring them to a successful issue.

It is evident from all this that a short cutting gives the best vine, but in practice it must be of sufficient length to permit it to reach layers of soil sufficiently moist to enable it to stand through the warm summer months until its own roots are capable of doing so.

In dry climates, especially if the soil be porous, one will have to go to a more considerable depth in order to fulfil these conditions than in a cool district. This may be expressed in the following words—the drier the climate the longer the cutting must be, and the shorter the cutting the better will the resulting vine be.

The vigneron must carefully consider these points, and, using his judgment, fix upon a suitable length of cutting. As a general rule the following lengths will be found to suit the different regions:—

First region	8in. to 10in.
Second region	12in. to 15in.
Third region	15in. to 18in.

If recourse can be had to irrigation, it is needless to say that the length of the cutting in the third region may be considerably reduced. In soils which retain moisture for a considerable time, the length may also be sensibly reduced.

Preservation of cuttings.—Although the vitality of the vine is very great, and fragments of shoots which have been exposed to atmospheric influences for a considerable time may grow when planted, this is by no means to be relied on, and the greatest care should be taken of cuttings after they have been removed from the vine in order to protect them from the drying influence of the air. Want of care in this respect is frequently the cause of failures in young plantations. The careless way in which cuttings are often sent by rail is strongly to be condemned. One frequently sees bundles of them lying for days at a time in an exposed state on railway platforms or in goods sheds, with the result, often blamed to other causes, that only 20 to 30 per cent. of them strike when planted. Had they been wrapped in damp straw before being sent to the railway station, although perhaps entailing a little more expense, the far greater percentage of strikes would amply repay the extra cost.

Cuttings must therefore be carefully protected from the desiccating action of the air and sun from the time of their removal from the vine until the planting season; the longer this interval is the greater is the necessity for proper preservation.

Cuttings are preserved in different ways, but none is more efficacious than burial in soil. They may be buried in a vertical or horizontal manner. Some persons advise to place them in heaps, with the lower extremities turned uppermost, and cover them over with soil; but this does not seem to give better results than if they were buried in an upright position. If cuttings have only to be preserved for a few weeks before planting out the bundles may be partially buried, that is, the lower extremities stuck in the ground to a depth of 9 inches or so. Before planting it is well to soak them in water for a day or two.

Stratification of cuttings is the French term for their burial in a horizontal manner, as indicated (Fig. 16). This is more to be recom-

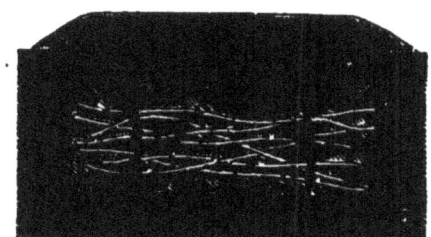

FIG. 16.

mended than the vertical position, and will in the great majority of cases give the best results.

The soil in which cuttings are stratified should be loose and, preferably, sandy. It should be sufficiently moist to prevent loss of moisture, but not wet, as this would render them liable to become mouldy or even to rot.

A trench, about 18 inches deep and as wide as the cuttings are long, should be dug in such a position as to ensure thorough drainage. The cuttings should then be placed in bundles of 50 each, the earth replaced over them and well trampled.

The advantages of this system are obvious; it gives the vigneron a much longer time to plant his cuttings in, and at the same time causes them to strike far more readily, as the process serves as a preparation for the emission of roots, which takes place immediately after they are planted out. Cuttings may with perfect safety be left for several months in this way, provided the soil contain neither a deficiency nor an excess of moisture.

Several means of facilitating the emission of roots have been suggested, such as removing narrow strips of the outer bark before planting; poundin them with a mallet, the bruises and splits thus caused, although promoting the formation of roots, often act injuriously by facilitating the penetration of too much water, which often causes the young vine to partially rot. Twisting the lower extremity has the same effect, and is less injurious. Soaking the cuttings in running water promotes their striking, but it should not be continued for too long a time, as it presents serious drawbacks if too prolonged.

Several other methods have been also suggested, but they may be said to be quite unnecessary for the V. Vinifera or European sorts, which all strike with ease; they may give good results with some of the American sorts.

PROPAGATION BY LAYERS.

Layering, although not a general operation for the production of young vines, may be extremely useful for the propagation of such sorts as do not strike easily from cuttings. Its principal utility, however, is for the replacement of one vine by another or the filling up of a vacant place with as little loss of time as possible.

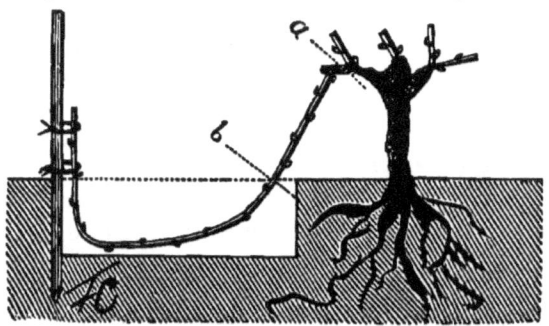

FIG. 17.

Ordinary layering, as represented in Fig. 17, is so simple as to require little description. A trench, varying in depth from 1 to 2 feet, according to the climate,* is opened from the foot of the old vine to the place which the new one is to occupy. A shoot of not more

---

* The warmer the climate the deeper should the trench be.

than one year old is brought down and buried in this, the extremity being turned up so as to leave two buds free above ground.

The underground part emits roots, and is at the same time nourished by the parent vine until severed from it, usually two years after the operation was performed ; by this time the roots of the young plant are sufficiently developed to enable it to dispense with the parent stock.

Although fruit is often obtained the first year, thus saving considerable loss of time, vines produced in this way are not well constituted; the laterals are greatly developed at the expense of the tap-roots, which are usually absent. We have, in fact, a vine such as is illustrated in Fig. 14, only still less desirably constituted, as the main underground stem, instead of penetrating deeply into the soil, runs along at a small distance from the surface. In a warm, dry climate such a vine would be unable to procure the requisite moisture from the deeper layers of the soil, and might suffer considerably.

In a cold climate, where there is seldom or never any deficiency of moisture, and where grapes ripen with difficulty, this may be an advantage, as the weakening of the vine increases the strength of the wine.

For this reason the practice is common in colder parts of Europe, such as Burgundy, where vines are "*provigné*," as this operation is termed, every six or seven years, a certain number of vines being treated each year.

Ordinary layering is also employed to obtain young rooted vines in some parts of France, but is not to be recommended.

Complete burying of a vine is adopted when it is wished to replace an old vine by one or more young vines. This process will be readily

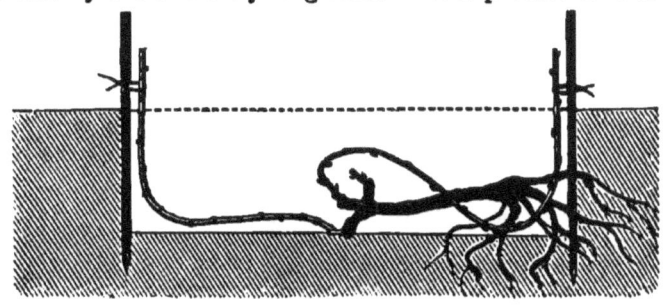

FIG. 18.

understood by reference to Fig. 18. It presents the same disadvantages as the previous method, and is only to be recommended in a cool climate. In Champagne this has become a regular cultural operation; the totality of the vines of a vineyard are thus buried every year, one shoot, cut back to three eyes above ground, replacing the vine of the previous year.

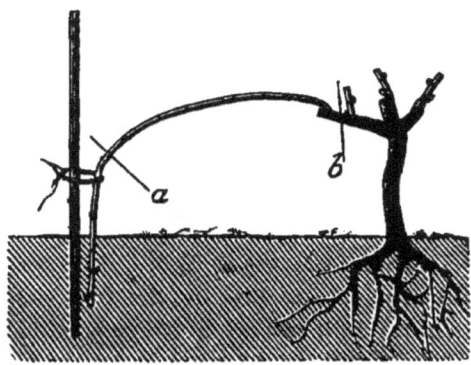

FIG. 19.

Reversed layering (Fig. 19) gives more vigorous vines than either of the other methods, the root-system being well constituted and identical to that of a vine raised from a cutting. Strange though it may seem, no ill effects result from the turning upside down of the stem of the young vine which this process entails.

The buds on the long rod should be brushed off when they commence to grow, with the exception of the three or four nearest the ground. The young vine may be severed from its parent during the winter following the operation.

It is unnecessary to insist that the part of the shoot buried in the ground should be much longer in a warm than in a cold climate, where 6 or 7 inches would suffice. Varieties which only strike with difficulty may be propagated in this way. The only disadvantage of reversed layering is to prevent cross cultivation during the summer months.

Multiple layering is made use of for the propagation of such sorts as do not grow readily from cuttings. It is doubtful whether it would pay to have recourse to it on a large scale under ordinary circumstances, although the plants obtained in this way are excellent in every respect. Small vine-growers having only an acre or so per year to plant would derive great benefit by adopting it.

Fig. 20.

A glance at Fig. 20 will enable the process to be readily understood. A small gutter is excavated at the foot of the vine which it is desired to propagate, and a rod from the vine is pegged down in it. The layer is covered with about 1 inch of soil, and the gutter is otherwise left open until the young shoots have attained a length of 8 or 10 inches, when it is carefully filled. In the following winter it will be found that each shoot has formed a nice bunch of roots at its base, so that when separated from each other with the secateur each of the shoots a, b, c, d, e, f, and g constitutes an excellent young rooted vine, ready to be planted out. In a warm climate the layer should receive several waterings during the summer.

*   *   *   *   *

From what we have seen, it is evident that the most practical and economical means of propagating the vine is by cuttings, although in certain cases some of the other methods may deserve consideration.

CHAPTER IX.

PLANTING.

The subject of planting brings us face to face with the serious question: *Are cuttings or rooted vines to be preferred?*

This is another of the questions upon which authorities differ—in point of fact there is much to be said on both sides.

The opinions of the witnesses examined by the Royal Commission on Vegetable Products, as will be seen in the Abstract appended hereto, are divided, although the majority admit that cuttings ultimately produce a better vine. This opinion is also shared by some of the best European authorities; others again consider that the difference between the vigour of plants grown in either way is insignificant.

Other considerations than the vigour of the resulting vine are of greater importance in deciding which ought to be used.

In very dry climates or poor soils rooted vines strike more readily than even very long cuttings, and, as they can for this reason be made considerably shorter, they ensure the resulting vines having a better root-system (p. 91). At the same time they present the disadvantage of being more expensive, whether if purchased as such or if raised by the vigneron himself in a nursery, as the extra handling would be rather considerable.

Unless it be possible to irrigate, or the season be exceedingly favorable for transplanting, the time gained by the employment of rooted vines is so small as not to constitute a strong argument in their favour.

As a general rule, we may say that the employment of cuttings will prove most economical in all cases where they strike with ease (not less than 70 per cent.). If the number of misses reach 50 per cent. it will pay better to employ rooted vines.

In this chapter we have to consider—1st, planting of cuttings in the vineyard; 2nd, planting of cuttings in the nursery; 3rd, planting of rooted vines in the vineyard.

PLANTING OF CUTTINGS IN THE VINEYARD.

The depth at which cuttings should be planted is determined by their length. This has already been discussed in the previous chapter (p. 90). They should be planted at such a depth that two eyes alone are left above ground ; one only is necessary, but it is better to have "two strings to one's bow," and if two shoots develop themselves they will each grow less vigorously than if either existed alone, and consequently be less liable to be broken by strong winds. The lower of these eyes should be level with, or half an inch or so below, the surface of the ground.

The time for planting depends to some extent upon the climate; the warmer this is the earlier ought vines to be planted.

In the great majority of cases our Victorian vignerons plant their vines far earlier than is necessary or even beneficial. Cuttings properly stratified, as directed in the previous chapter, need not be planted o until the buds are on the point of bursting, as at this moment they will find the soil in the best condition for the continuation of their growth. In a warm climate this will, of course, take place sooner than in a cold one; and if drought is to be feared they should be planted out as soon as the terminal buds show a tendency to swell.

The commencement of September is the most favorable time for planting in the third region, whilst the beginning of October would not be too late in the first. In many parts of France stratified cuttings are not planted out until the parent vines have already come into leaf ; it has been observed that the percentage of strikes is increased by such a course.

Inclination of cuttings.—In many parts of France it is customary to bend portion of the base of the cutting at right angles with the remainder in the hole in which it is planted, or to plant it slanting, sometimes so much so that it only makes a very small angle with the surface.

Except in a very cold climate, where it is desired to weaken the vine in order to facilitate the ripening of the grapes or where the roots must be kept near the surface to ensure their receiving sufficient heat, no advantage is to be derived from such a practice. As we have already seen, the shorter the cutting the better the resulting vine. Cuttings are only increased in length in order that the base may be situated in deep, moist soil. It is evident that the same cutting placed perpendicularly will reach deeper than one planted slanting.

For this reason perpendicular planting is to be recommended in Victoria—at least in all the districts where the vine is cultivated as yet.

Method of planting.—Cuttings may be planted in several ways, but the principal ones are with the spade and with the bar.

In loose, friable soils, which are not liable to cake, the bar or dibble will give very good results.

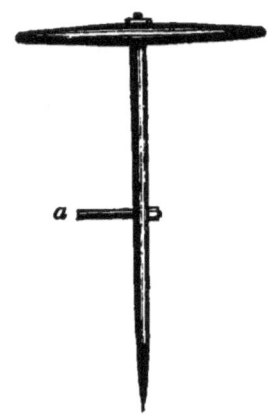

Fig. 21.

Such a one as represented in Fig. 21 is to be preferred, as the projecting piece of iron (*a*) insures all the holes made being of a uniform depth, and at the same time greatly facilitates the work, the vigneron being able to use his foot as well as his hands to force it into the soil. The bar, after being inserted into the ground to the required depth, is moved to and fro to enlarge the hole. The cutting, which will benefit by being dipped in a mixture of cowdung, clay, and water, is placed in the hole into which some soil (mixed with a little manure if it be very poor) is tightly rammed, the hole should be gradually filled, only small quantities of soil being introduced at a time, the soil near the surface should be left in a loose state to a depth of a couple of inches. It is essential that the contact between the cutting and the soil be as intimate as possible, especially at the base, care should therefore be taken not to put too much soil into the hole before ramming, but to fill gradually. A very good method to insure a perfect contact with the soil at the base of the cutting is to pour into the hole before its insertion about half a pannikinful or so of a mixture of soil, water, and manure of about the consistency of treacle, the remainder of the soil is then put in and well rammed.

In stiff soils planting with the bar often gives unsatisfactory results, as the soil becomes compressed on the sides of the hole and hardens it to such an extent that the young roots can only spread with difficulty. In such a case the hole should be made with a spade, and the soil, which will greatly benefit by the addition of a little manure, rammed in tightly with a rammer or with the foot. Should the soil be very stiff, better results will be obtained by filling the hole around the young plant with loose soil brought from elsewhere than with the soil taken out of the hole. If the soil be very sandy, the addition of a spadeful of good manure to the soil taken out of the hole will greatly facilitate the strike. When planting, it will be found advantageous to employ several men, each of whom has his special work to do. The best vigneron should ram the soil around the cuttings, this being the operation requiring most attention in order to insure a good strike.

Sometimes two cuttings are planted in each hole in case one does not strike. If both strike, one should be removed before it has attained considerable development so as not to allow its removal to interfere with the roots of the one which is to remain.

In very dry districts only one bud should be left above ground, which should be covered with a small heap of sand or very loose soil to protect it from atmospheric influences until the commencement of vegetation.

PLANTATION IN A NURSERY.

If it be intended to plant rooted vines a nursery should be formed.

The site for which must be selected with care ; a loose but not too sandy a soil is to be preferred for this purpose. If irrigation be possible so much the better. Above all, the land must be thoroughly drained. The cuttings to be planted in a nursery may be 2 or 3 inches shorter than would be necessary for those to be planted in the vineyard ; in other respects the same rules hold good. The cuttings should be planted perpendicularly, and rammed as tightly as possible, especially at their base.

The proper distance apart for cuttings in a nursery is 2ft. 6in. by 6in. or 3ft. by 6in., as it leaves room to cultivate ; they can, however, be planted as closely as 1ft. 6in. by 6in. without prejudice to the resulting plants.

It is often stated that to make a nursery all that is necessary is to open a plough furrow, place the cuttings upright in it, and turn the soil against them with a second furrow. This is by no means to be recommended, as the second furrow cannot establish a sufficient contact between the cutting and the soil. In a cool district a certain proportion may strike, but in the warm region the great majority, if not the totality, would miss.

To form a nursery properly a trench proportionate in depth to the length of the cutting should be opened up, preferably with the spade, although the plough may be employed for this purpose. In this the cuttings are placed as nearly vertical as possible (Fig. 22), the soil

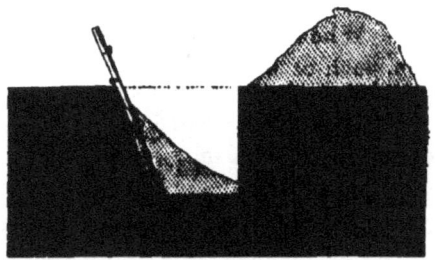

FIG. 22.

taken out of the trench is then carefully put back in small quantities at a time, and tightly rammed with the foot, with the exception of the surface, which should be kept nice and loose, and preferably heaped up against the cutting, as in Fig. 23.

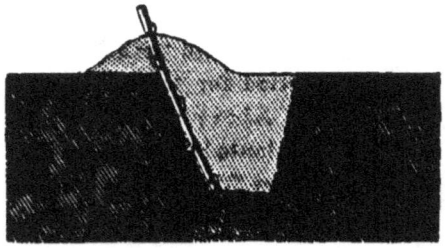

FIG. 23.

The proper time, &c., for planting cuttings in a nursery is the same as if they were to be planted in the vineyard.

The length of time vines should remain in the nursery depends upon the growth they make, as a rule two-year-old vines are the best in the colder districts, whilst one-year-old ones give excellent results in the warmer parts on account of the greater development they have acquired during the time—they are even to be preferred to two-year-old ones, which might have acquired so considerable a development that they could not be transplanted without injury to their roots.

Whilst in the nursery the young plants should receive every care; the soil should be continually kept in a loose state and free from weeds. If remaining more than a year in it they should be pruned, one or two of the best shoots only being left, which are cut back to one eye each.

Planting Rooted Vines in the Vineyard.

The rooted vines should be extracted from the nursery with care in order to break as few roots as possible; the broken extremities of these should be carefully trimmed with a sharp knife, and the shoots pruned before proceeding to plant them, which should be done as soon as possible after their removal from the nursery.

It is of the greatest importance that they should be planted out at exactly the same depth as they were in the nursery, the underground part being unsuited for exposure to the air.

A hole should be dug with the spade, into the bottom of which a little loose surface soil, and if possible a little quantity of manure, is thrown, the young vine is placed in it, the roots being carefully separated from each other, if entangled, and spread out in all directions; the remainder of the earth is put back by small portions at a time and pressed with the foot but not rammed tight, as should be done with the cuttings. Care should be taken to loosen the surface soil thoroughly before leaving the vine.

Young plants obtained by ordinary layering require the same treatment as those raised in the nursery. If the result of multiple layering (p. 96) they require rather more care, as their feeble depth at which they should be planted renders them very liable to suffer from drought. In fact this process can only be employed in the first and second regions (p. 21), or on a limited scale where it is possible to water them.

A hole is dug into which the greater part of the earth is put back, after having been thoroughly loosened in such a manner that it will form a sort of cone, the summit of which is almost level with the surface of the surrounding soil. On this cone the young plant is placed, the roots being carefully spread around. The soil, after being beaten with the spade, is then put back, and heaped up around the stem of the young plant in such a way as to afford it as much protection as possible.

Young vines should be staked, whether they be planted as cuttings or otherwise. This is a great advantage, as it enables them to be tied up, and thus escape the action of high winds and other causes of destruction, and insures the stem of the resulting vine being straighter than would otherwise be the case. The stakes used for this purpose may be small temporary ones, but it is far better to at once establish the permanent ones, which must be employed sooner or later.

CHAPTER X.

FORMING THE YOUNG VINE.

The form of the vine, depending, as it does, upon the mode of pruning adopted, ought perhaps, strictly speaking, to be treated in the chapter devoted to that subject. The importance of proper training from the first, however, and the fact that a good many owners of young vineyards may find it useful to have a few plain hints as to how to prune their vines for the first two or three years, or before they have mastered the different methods of pruning adult vines, has led us to devote this chapter to the purpose. Moreover, as with the exception of a few methods not to be recommended in Victoria, all the different forms of vines may be said to require the same preliminary training in a given climate.

If a vine be not properly formed from the first it is very difficult to get it into shape afterwards, and it must be borne in mind that the form exercises no inconsiderable influence upon the facility of cultivation as well as on the quality and quantity of the wine.

Vines trained according to any of the systems mentioned in this work consist of an upright stem or trunk, and an upper part or crown which may be of very variable form.

Height of vines.—The height of the vine above the ground, or, in other words, the length of the trunk, is not purely arbitrary, but should vary according to certain fixed laws.

Vines with low crowns are liable to spring frosts, but, receiving more reflected light and heat in the summer, the fruit contains more glucose and yields a stronger wine. The facility with which the grapes become covered with mud or dust is, however, a disadvantage, as the soil, which is always alkaline, neutralizing part of the natural acid of the fruit, causes the fermentation to proceed irregularly and favours the production of lactic acid, the great enemy of the winemaker in the warmer districts, where the grapes are often deficient in natural acid even under favorable circumstances. It has lately been suggested that the *goût de terroir*, or earthy taste, so common in our wines is caused by a certain amount of soil being present in the grapes during fermentation.

If the grapes are situated at some distance from the soil they are no longer exposed to these drawbacks, which are more serious in a warm than in a cold district, in which one is obliged to keep the fruit near the ground in order that the wine may not be too weak.

As a general rule the crowns of all the vines in the second, and especially in the third, regions of the colony are far too low. Were these higher, heavier crops of wines—lighter, more delicate, and better in every respect than those made at present—could be produced. The extra length of stakes or wires this would entail would be amply compensated by the increased facilities for working given by the men not having to stoop so much when pruning, disbudding, or gathering the grapes.

For raisin-growing, the crowns require to be lower than for wine grapes, as the object of the grower is to increase the proportion of glucose and lessen that of water as much as possible.

For wine grapes the following heights will give good results:—

First region	1ft.
Second region	1ft. 6in.
Third region	2ft.

For the production of liqueur wines these heights should be lessened in the second and third regions.

Forming the stem.—Having decided its length, the next thing is to form the stem. It is important that this should be thick and strong, so as to be able to support the vine, especially if it be grown gooseberry-style, and to allow the sap to circulate freely. It is evident that this is all the more necessary in the third region, where the vine attains a larger size than in the first, where its development is not considerable.

We have already seen (p. 4) that the more gradually the stem is formed the thicker will it be. In the third region, therefore, it must be brought up to its final height gradually, a small portion being added year by year until the desired height is reached.

In the first region we have already seen that more eyes may be left out of the ground than in the second or third; in fact, it is better to leave two than one, and even three will not be too many provided they be close together. When pruning time arrives the vigneron must use his judgment, and leave a spur, pruned to two or three eyes, according to the strength of the plant, upon whichever shoot is the strongest (Fig. 24). The following year, if it be the upper shoot which was left, the shoots resulting from the development of the

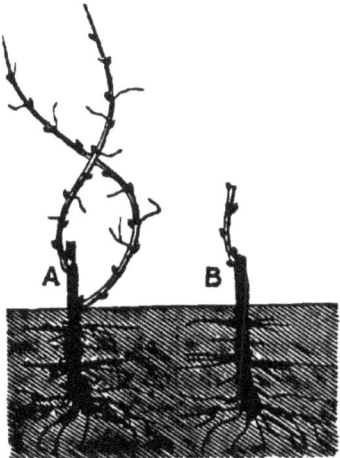

Fig. 24.

two lower buds should be removed, and the upper one cut back to one or two eyes, according to the vigour of the plant.

Fig. 25 shows the young vine now in its second year. The dotted lines indicate the mode of pruning. If the plant be very vigorous it

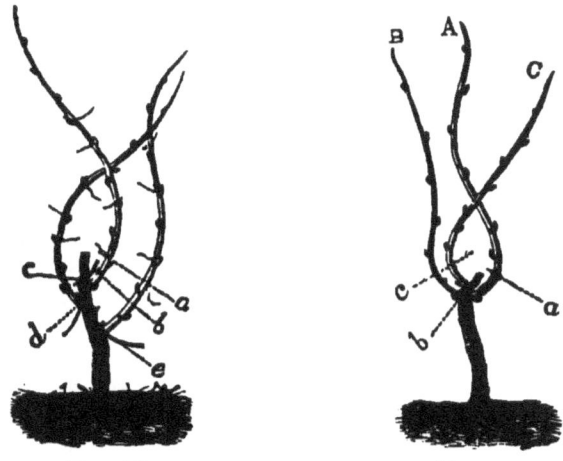

Fig. 25.   Fig. 26.

may be cut in *a*, otherwise it should be pruned to one eye in *b*. This rather close pruning will probably cause some of the buds at the base of the spur to develop, so that the third year the vigneron will be able to start forming the crown. The pruning in this case will be readily understood by reference to Fig. 26. The buds on *a* are capable of producing fruit during the ensuing season. The crown is now formed, and the vigneron will find the rules for subsequent pruning in another chapter.

In the second and third regions the stem requires to be thicker than in the first, for which reason no part of the original cutting should be employed to form it, as this, having lost part of its vigour through transplanting, is not capable of producing so stout a stem as a new shoot. If the two eyes left have developed themselves, the upper one should be entirely removed, as well as the portion of old cutting between it and the lower one, which is cut back to three eyes. At the second pruning (Fig. 27) the top shoot A is cut back to three eyes and the lower two, B and C, removed, as is also the case again at the third pruning, as will be seen by reference to Figs. 28 and 29, which

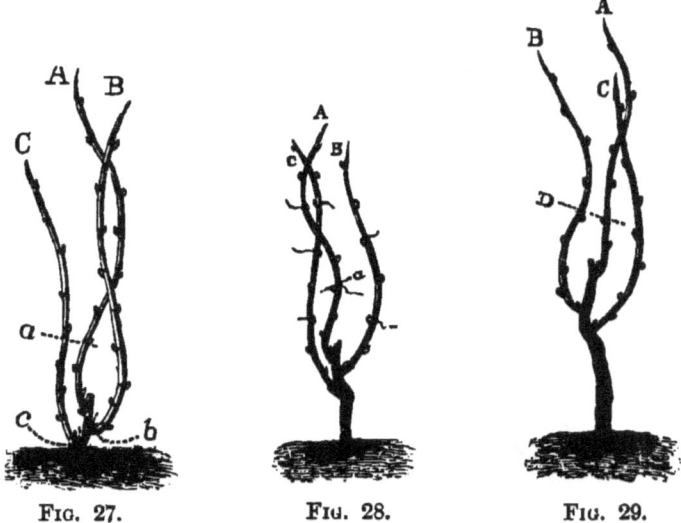

FIG. 27.   FIG. 28.   FIG. 29.

represent respectively the third and fourth prunings. At the third pruning (Fig. 28), the shoots B and C should be removed, and the shoot A cut back to three eyes in *a*. At the fourth pruning also (Fig. 29), the shoots C and B should be removed, and A cut back to three eyes in D. By this time the vine will produce some grapes; and at the fifth pruning two spurs, pruned to two eyes each, may be left, or, in other words, the crown may be formed in the same manner as was done for the first region. In this manner a good, straight stem will be obtained, and no more time lost than if the spurs were formed the second year, besides not presenting the danger of overcharging the young vine before it is fit to stand it. If by the fourth pruning the stem has not attained within 4 or 5 inches of what is to be its total length, it will be well to defer forming the crown till the fifth pruning, very little time being lost, since the vine is capable of bearing some six or seven bunches by this time on the shoots resulting from the development of the three eyes left.

These are the general indications which, as a rule, ought to be followed with vines of ordinary vigour; but the intelligent vine-grower must use his judgment, and make the best use of the vigour of the vine, if this be above the average, or make allowance for it if below it.

CHAPTER XI.

PRUNING.

The objects of pruning are to increase the yield, to improve the quality of the wine, to ensure a uniform product by giving the same development to each vine, and also, by giving them a definite symmetrical shape, to facilitate cultivation, and the instruction of the men who are to work in the vineyard.

The fruit of the vine, unlike that of most fruit trees, does not grow off the old wood, but upon the green shoots of the current year, and only on those resulting from the development of buds situated on a shoot of the previous year, which in turn grows off the two-year-old wood of the vine. Any green shoots which do not fulfil these conditions will in nearly every case bear no fruit. The wood constituting the spurs or rods left when pruning must be chosen with care; that growing off the wood of the previous year, which in turn grows off the two-year-old wood, is alone of use for this purpose.

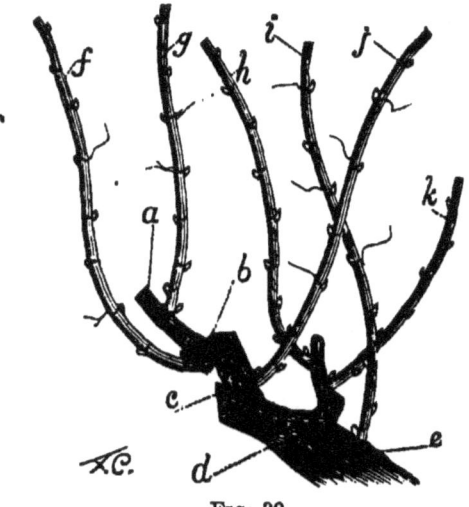

Fig. 30.

In Fig. 30 the shoots f, g, h, and k fulfil these conditions; i, which grows directly off the two-year-old wood, and j, growing directly off the old stock of the vine, are incapable of giving rise to fruit-producing shoots for at least two years; it is therefore useless to leave them when pruning, unless one or two eyes at their base be left in order to obtain wood for pruning on in a future season.

All the buds on a shoot will not give rise to equally prolific shoots; whilst some would give three bunches each, others might only give one, and others again might prove absolutely sterile. It is important to know what is the position of these prolific buds, as it is evidently useless to leave those which will not produce fruit.

This position of the prolific buds varies with the kind of vine. With some they are at the base of the shoot, with others at a certain distance from the base, and with others again all the buds of a shoot capable of bearing fruit are equally prolific.

Fig. 31 represents a vine of the second type. It will be seen that the shoots a and b have no fruit, whilst c, d, and e have two bunches each.

On a vine of the first type the reverse would be the case, a and b having fruit on them, whilst c, d, and e are sterile or almost so.

Fig. 31.

This leads us to the question of long or short pruning, these being the two great classes into which all the different methods are divided.

A vine is pruned short when the shoots of the year which are left to bear fruit or wood are cut back to two or three eyes each.

A vine is pruned long if one or more of these shoots are left, each of which has on it more than five buds.

It would be most foolish to short prune a vine having its prolific buds situated as represented in Fig. 31, as little or no fruit would be obtained. It would be just as foolish to long prune, or leave a long rod on a sort where the buds at the base were alone prolific. The others bearing no fruit would only develop themselves at the expense of the prolific ones, and thus be worse than useless.

With a vine of the third description (one on which all the buds are prolific) it is a matter of indifference which method of pruning be adopted, provided a sufficient number of buds is left on each vine. This is in turn regulated to a great extent by the climate.

Many erroneous ideas are held with reference to long pruning. From what has been said above, it will be seen that its adoption is chiefly regulated by the sorts of vine grown. In addition to this there are other considerations—such as the strength of the wine—which ought to influence the selection of the style to be adopted when one has to deal with sorts suited to either long or short pruning.

Before describing the different methods of pruning, it will be well to briefly recapitulate the laws which govern this most important operation, some of which we are already familiar with.

First. Within certain limits, the production of fruit is increased if the vigour of the plant be diminished (page 2).

Second. The activity of vegetation on any branch is always greatest on the part of that branch farthest from the parent stem (page 4).

Third. The activity of vegetation is greatest in a vertical shoot; the production of fruit greatest in a horizontal one.

Fourth. The greater the number of shoots the lesser will the individual development of each be, and the greater the number of shoots the lesser the production of fruit on each, and *vice versâ* (up to a certain limit).

Fifth. The greater the quantity of fruit on a vine the smaller the percentage of sugar will it contain.

Before pruning, a point must be mentioned which does not receive sufficient attention at the hands of our vignerons : this is to always cut a shoot through the bud above the highest one which it is intended to grow, as in Fig. 32, where the dotted line indicates where it should be cut. The natural partition is here taken advantage of to prevent the accumulation of water, &c., which might rot and split the shoot, and injure the bud below. As it may be rather difficult to cut exactly through this division, it is better to make the cut slightly above it and obliquely, so as to destroy the bud which it is not intended to keep.

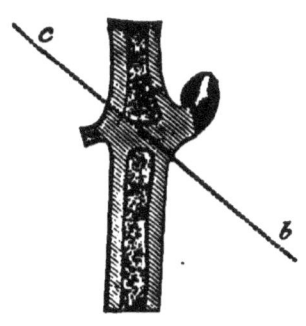

FIG. 32.

The vigneron having mastered these preliminary principles, we will proceed to describe the different methods of pruning.

SHORT SPUR PRUNING.

This system, being the simplest, is the one which must be considered first.

Vines pruned according to this method consist of a stem or trunk, and a crown composed of a variable number of short spurs radiating from the centre. These spurs consist of shoots of the year cut back to two or three eyes each. Care must be taken to leave the new spur in such a manner as to guard as much as possible against the excessive elongation of the arm which bears it.

 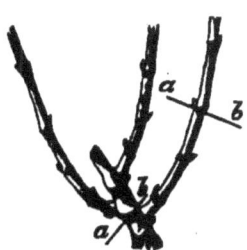

FIG. 33.

Fig. 33 represents in detail, before and after pruning, an arm and spur of a vine pruned according to this style. If either of the other shoots were made use of to form the new spur, it would entail the leaving of a fragment of two-year-old wood of appreciable length, and if this was continued year after year the arm would become so long as to seriously interfere with cultivation. Pruned as in Fig. 33, the length of two-year-old wood left is reduced to a minimum.

Several arms, each pruned in this way, are left every year, so that a complete vine will be as in Fig. 34. The same vine after pruning is represented in Fig. 35. The shoot b, growing off the old wood, has

FIG. 34.

FIG. 35.

not been entirely removed, but cut back to one eye. Although incapable of giving rise to fruit-bearing shoots, it will give a shoot which can be employed to form a new spur at the ensuing pruning, when the old arm (extending beyond it) which has become too long may be removed. In other words, the eye at *b* is left to provide for the replacement of an arm, which, through old age or faulty pruning, had become unduly elongated.

A properly pruned vine (pruned according to this system) should present spurs which radiate upwards and outwards, so that the young shoots springing from them do not get tangled and twisted together.

The number of these spurs to be left upon a vine depends upon the climate; if the climate be cold, three or four will be ample, whilst if it be warm it will be better to leave a considerable number—say, eight or nine.

This is as much on account of the extra size of the vine under the influence of the increase in light and heat as to regulate to some extent the strength of the wine. The greater the development and number of bunches on each vine the lighter will this be, as we have several times had occasion to see.

This method applies equally well to vines trained to stakes or gooseberry style; but should never be adopted for vines trained on wires, as no advantage is to be gained, whilst all the disadvantages of the wire will present themselves.

All vines which were said to require short pruning in Chapter IV. should be pruned according to this system. Those which will give good results with short or long pruning may also be pruned in this way in the cool parts of the first region. Those which were said to require long pruning should never be pruned in this way, although giving good results with either method.

The *Muscats* should be short pruned, and if grown for the production of raisins should, in addition to this, have their crowns near the ground, so as to enable large berries, with as high a percentage of glucose as possible, to be obtained.

Rod-Pruning,

Or, in other and general terms, long pruning, consists in leaving on the vine at pruning time one or more rods or leaders of wood of the current year having more than six buds or eyes on it. The shoot that has served during the previous year is removed and a new one brought down in its place, so that each leader only lasts a season.

Great care should be exercised in the choice of the leader. It is unnecessary to say that it should fulfil the conditions illustrated in Fig. 30 (page 110), as unless capable of bearing fruit it would be absolutely useless.

Care must also be taken to make provision for a new leader for the ensuing pruning. Except great care be exercised in the green pruning, as we shall see hereafter, none of the shoots growing off the rod or leader of the previous year are eligible for the ensuing one.

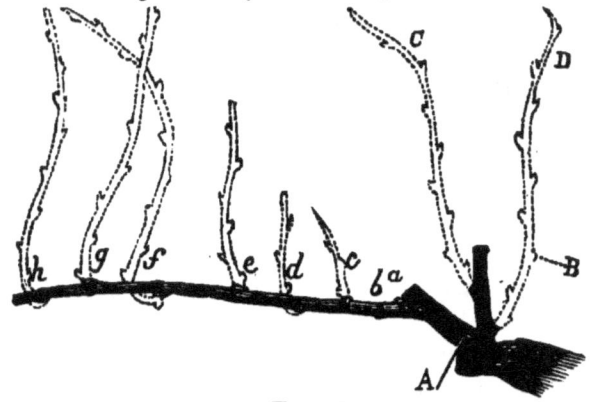

FIG. 36.

Fig. 36 illustrates this clearly. The leader left here had eight buds on it. Of these the first two, a and b, have not developed themselves; c and d have only grown slightly, the shoots resulting being too small to constitute a new leader. It would be necessary to go as far as f before obtaining a shoot of sufficient length and strength to form a new leader. If this were done, it is obvious that in a very few years the elongation of the arm of the vine bearing the leader would become so considerable as to seriously interfere with other operations. In order to obviate this difficulty a short spur is left at the base, which, by the development of the two eyes left on it, gives rise to the two shoots, c and d; the one resulting from the development of the lower one (D, Fig. 36) is cut back to two eyes, in B, and forms a new spur termed the wood spur, although also capable of bearing fruit. The shoot resulting from the upper bud (C, Fig. 36) forms the new rod, commonly termed the fruit rod. The old rod and fragment of two-year-old wood are removed by the cut marked A (Fig. 36), the two shoots resulting from the development of the buds on D (Fig. 36) will in turn provide for a new wood spur and fruit rod for the year succeeding their development, the rod formed by C being removed.

This is the main point to master in the rod system of pruning. If properly carried into effect, the elongation of the arm bearing the leader will not be more rapid than with the ordinary short spur system.

When choosing the rod a shoot of medium vigour should be preferred to a very thick long-jointed one, as it is likely to bear more fruit.

The simplest form of rod-pruning is that recommended by *Guyot*, which consists in leaving only one wood spur and fruit-rod on each vine. Figs. 37 and 38 represent a vine pruned according to this method respectively before and after pruning.

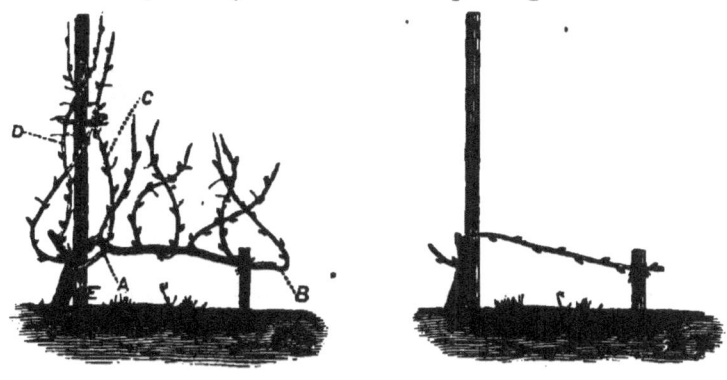

FIG. 37.   FIG. 38.

It will be observed that the crown of such a vine is rather near the surface of the soil; Dr. Guyot, living, as he did, in a cool district, was led to recommend such a course.

In Australia it will be found preferable to effect some slight modifications in this method, such as substituting wires for the large and small stake attached to each vine, and considerably raising the crown

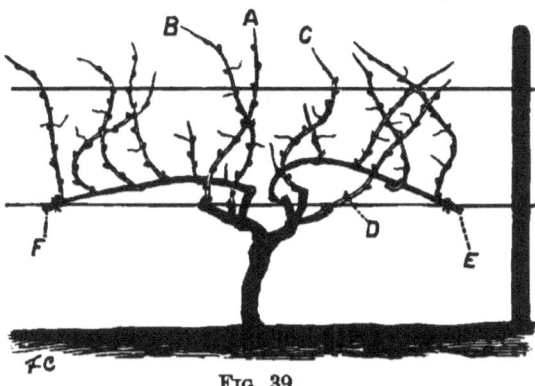

FIG. 39.

of the vine. In the second region of the colony it will be best to leave two leaders on each vine, as is represented in Figs. 39 and 40, which respectively show the vine before and after pruning. It is as well to leave a spare short spur or two on a vine pruned in this way.

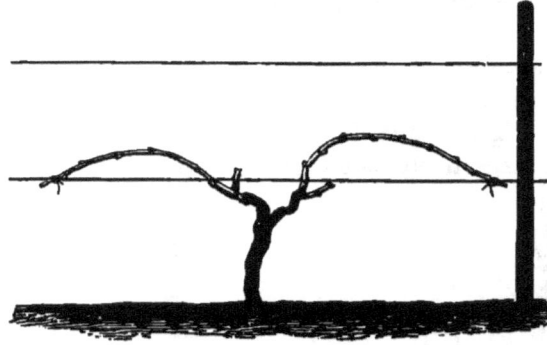

Fig. 40.

Should any accident happen to the arm bearing the leader, it may then be replaced without loss of time.

If the vines be staked, it is still possible to prune them long; the leader is then brought round the crown of the vine, and tied either to one of the other arms or to the main stem of the vine. (Fig. 41.)

Fig. 41.

This presents the advantage of enabling cultivation to be carried out in several directions, each vine not occupying a much greater space than would be necessary for an ordinary short pruned vine. It is not necessary to explain that the leader should be selected in the same way as for the former system.

This method, consisting of spurs and rod, may be termed the mixed system of pruning—it gives excellent results with such sorts as the *Shiraz* (*Red Hermitage*), *Tokay*, *Pinot*, and several others, which are suited for either long or short pruning, as stated in Chapter IV.

In warm climates with rich soils, where very large yields are to be expected, a more considerable development may be advantageously given to each vine, as is represented in Figs. 42 and 43, representing respectively the vine before and after pruning. It will be readily

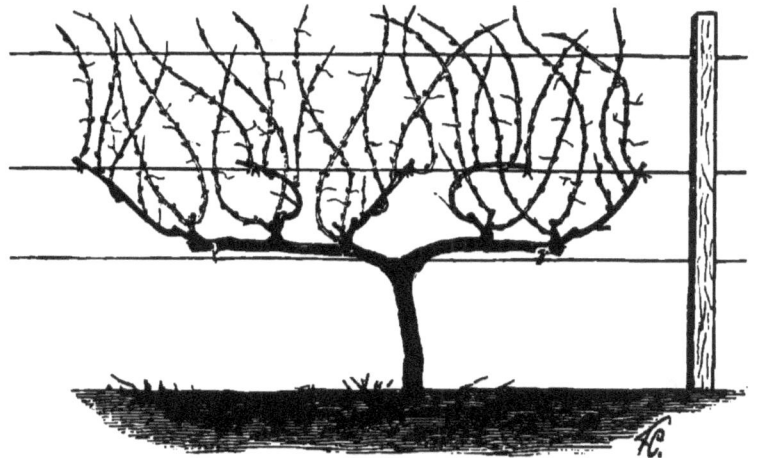

Fig. 42.

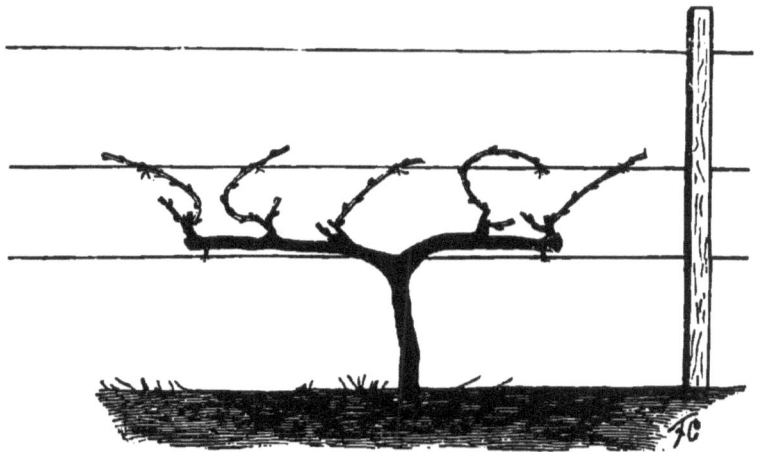

Fig. 43.

seen that this system consists of two *permanent* branches, from which protrude a variable number of arms, each constituted according to *Guyot's* method. The temporary leaders may be inclined upwards at an angle of about 45°, and tied to a second wire (the top one being reserved for the young shoots as they come out), or bent round and tied to the main branch of the vine. In forming such a vine care must be taken not to establish it too rapidly, but to only add, say, one arm bearing fruit-rod and spur each year until it has attained its full size ; in this way a vigorous long-lived vine may be obtained with a stout stem, which will be capable of yielding enormous crops for a considerable number of years.

These are the principal systems of training vines. There are many others—chiefly variations of these—which, although interesting, are not of sufficient practical importance to deserve a detailed description in an elementary work.

Once the above methods are thoroughly mastered, all other methods will be easily learned. Amongst the most important are the *Chaintres System*, consisting of a rather ramified stem bearing spurs and fruit-rods, which are propped on small forks driven into the ground. When it is desired to cultivate, the whole vine is thrown bodily over into the next row, the forks withdrawn, and the ground tilled; the forks are then replaced, and the vine thrown back upon them. The same thing is done to the next row, and so on till the block is cultivated. Although this system gives very heavy crops of light wine, and the shelter of the leaves, which entirely cover the ground, keeps the latter cool in a dry district, it is very doubtful if the system would give good results in Australia, on account of the extra labour rendered necessary.

Another system is training the vines on overhead trellises—this is very suitable for such sorts as the *Zante Currant* and others requiring great extension. It is established on the same lines as the other systems, and only requires notice " *en passant.*" The overhead part should be sufficiently high to enable a horse to pass underneath with the plough. Other systems, such as training vines on living or dead trees, are not practical, and therefore not to be recommended, especially the former.

Time for Pruning.—Vines must never be pruned before the wood of the year is ripe—that is when it has lost its green herbaceous appearance, and assumed its ordinary brown or grey winter state; once this has occurred, it is safe to prune. This change is marked by the cessation of bleeding or flowing of sap when a shoot is cut. It varies with the season and the sort of vine, and should be fixed accordingly. In a general way the middle of May is not too early to commence pruning, especially for early sorts, such as Pinots, Chasselas, &c.

In certain cases it may be an advantage to prune very late. If spring frosts are to be feared, by pruning the early sorts only when the buds are beginning to swell, their coming into leaf will be delayed for as much as a fortnight, a sufficient time in most cases to enable them to escape injury from this cause.

Again, late pruning is an excellent preventative of the non-setting of the grapes, to which some sorts are liable. The copious bleeding thus produced counteracts in a great measure the excess of sap in the vine, which we saw (p. 12) was in the majority of cases the cause of the abortion of a large number of flowers. It is well on this account to prune such sorts as are liable to set their fruit badly very late; these are chiefly the Cabernet, Malbeck, Riesling, as well as some others.

Instruments for Pruning.—In olden days the vine was pruned with a sort of hooked knife, termed a "serpette"; such an instrument was slow as well as dangerous, and has been replaced by the secateur, or pruning scissors, which is too well known to require description. A small garden-saw will also be found convenient for removing any old arms, &c., which cannot conveniently be cut with the secateur.

CHAPTER XII.

SUMMER PRUNING.

Under this heading we will consider all the different operations which have to be executed on the vine itself, from the time it begins to bud in the spring till vintage time. These comprise ordinary operations, such as disbudding, topping, and tying up, which are practised in most, if not all, of our Victorian vineyards, and some others which might with advantage be executed in special cases, if the augmentation in the crop due to them were sufficient to justify the employment of the extra labour necessary for their execution. Such operations as nipping off the tops of the young shoots, or making an annular incision round them, with the view of preventing the non-setting of the flowers, or stripping off the leaves to afford greater facilities for the ripening of the fruit, come under the latter heading.

Disbudding, as the name implies, consists in removing all unnecessary buds as soon as they have burst out into leaf. All shoots having no fruit on them, and which are not necessary to provide wood for the ensuing pruning, should be removed when they are from four to six inches long, or as soon as it can be ascertained with certainty that they bear no fruit, as at this time they can be removed with ease. If they have attained a considerable size before removal, this would entail a waste of energy to the plant, which ought to be avoided. It is also difficult to break them off without wounding to some extent the wood of the vine on which they grow. Sometimes two shoots grow out of the same bud. If this be a bud which was intended to produce a shoot to be utilized at the next dry pruning the weaker one of the two should be removed, otherwise they may both be left, that is, if both show fruit.

When disbudding, it is important to make provision for replacing arms which, by continual or faulty pruning, have become too long. With this object a few shoots (one or two) ought to be left at the base of such an arm, which may be cut back to one eye at pruning time, as has already been explained (p. 114).

The importance of disbudding varies with the climate and the kind of vine grown. As a rule, the colder the climate the greater the necessity for this operation. If we examine what is done in Europe we will find that, in the cold districts of Canton de Vaud (Switzerland), Burgundy, and Champagne, it is always carefully executed, whilst in many of the warm parts of Southern France (corresponding to our third and the warmer parts of our second region), it is entirely neglected even in well-managed vineyards. The question of the proper ripening of the fruit governs this operation. In a cold climate the extra shade is a drawback; in a warm one it is an advantage.

Certain sorts require disbudding far more than others. Those which send out shoots from all parts of the vine should be submitted to this treatment under any circumstances, whilst such sorts as only send out a limited number of shoots where no buds were left need only be disbudded in a cool climate. The Pinots (Burgundy), Gamay, Gouais, and many others, belong to the first type, and ought always to be disbudded, whilst such sorts as Shiraz (Red Hermitage), Chasselas, Tokay, &c., do not require so much care in this direction.

Certain conditions may modify the above directions. If strong winds are to be feared early in the season, it will be better not to disbud until the dangerous time has passed. If the winds occur later, it is better to leave the disbudding till the vines are fit to be tied up.

As disbudding weakens the vine it is a good preventative of the non-setting of the flowers, and ought to be rigorously carried out in districts where this is to be feared.

Topping consists in cutting or breaking off the shoots of the vine from time to time, in order to enable air to circulate freely among the vines, and to render summer cultivation possible. Although applied to vines trained in all manner of ways, those trained gooseberry-bush style are topped more than the others, as, having no support, they are more liable to spread in all directions, so as to hinder summer cultivation.

The operation is very simple, and consists in trimming the vine to the required size with a sickle or large knife. A broken scythe-blade, about twelve or fifteen inches in length, fitted to a handle, is very suitable for this purpose.

As is the case for disbudding, only in a far greater degree, topping is of more importance in a cold than in a warm climate. In the former all that is possible should be done to promote the ripening of the grapes, whilst in the latter they easily get over-ripe.

In the warmer parts of Victoria vines are extensively trained gooseberry style, and topped in an excessive manner, the idea of the vine-growers being that, by removing the extremities of the shoots, they strengthen the vine. No more fatal error could be made. As we saw (p. 11), the greater part of the solid substance of the vine is derived from the air by the green leaves; it stands to reason that by continually removing the fresh leaves the plant must eventually suffer considerable injury. Although vines topped even to a considerable extent may for the first year give excellent results, both as regards quantity and quality, they will gradually lose their vigour, and after a few years appear to be completely exhausted. The following passage from Dr. Guyot's work, "Culture de la Vigne et Vinification," amply proves this. He says :—" If one tops all the shoots of a vine evenly, without allowing any to extend as a long shoot, all the bunches succeed well, and the crop is abundant the first year, if the number of branches does not exceed that which the vine ought to bear; the second year the bunches are scarcer, looser, and smaller; the third year the vine has lost some of its vigour, and its buds are almost sterile. It remains in this state the following years, and only resumes its fertility when, by ceasing to top, it is allowed to renovate itself. The more vigourous the vine which is topped the more rapidly will it become sterile. It has occurred to me to see under these conditions the second buds develop with energy, and carry away the bunches in an exaggerated vegetation, in spite of a second topping executed on them; this topping which, when practised partially and only on one or two special branches of the vine, opposes itself to all non-setting of the fruit, becomes sometimes a cause of non-setting if applied to the entire vine, but in every case absolute and repeated topping becomes a cause of sterilization and final decline."

Dr. Guyot recommends topping to be only executed on the fruit branch left according to his system of pruning (Fig. 38 p. 117), the two shoots growing off the wood spur being tied to a stake, and allowed to fully develop themselves.

This would be impossible on vines trained gooseberry-bush style, for which reason the system is not to be recommended in the warm districts of the colony. The poor yield of our vineyards, compared to that obtained in Southern France, is probably due to the excessive topping practised, especially in the warmer parts.

I have observed many cases in which blocks of vines trained gooseberry style, which had almost ceased to be productive, and only produced miserable shoots scarcely worth leaving at pruning time, resumed their vigour and bore good crops when staked and the shoots allowed to grow.

In the south of France many vineyards are simply pruned in winter, and neither disbudded, topped, nor tied up to stakes or wires, but allowed to grow wild, so to speak, with the result that enormous crops of good wine are obtained from them. The shoots and leaves spreading in all directions protect the fruit from the burning rays of the sun, and at the same time shelter the soil and keep it cool, thereby hindering the excessive evaporation of moisture. In addition to these advantages, by forming a sort of network, the vines protect each other from the effects of high winds. The evidence given by witnesses before the Royal Commission on Vegetable Products also tends to prove this.

If the excessive growth of weeds is to be feared, it will be better to train the vines on stakes or wires, as this will render cultivation possible at any time.

In spite of these manifest disadvantages, the gooseberry system has something to recommend it, as it renders economy, both of labour and stakes, possible, so that in poorer soils, where the vines grow with medium vigour, it may be tolerated. Not more than one topping in a season should be given, and the shoots should be cut at least four leaves above the last bunch. Unless this is done there will not be enough leaves left upon the plant to provide for the necessary accumulation of reserve materials in the buds for the ensuing year after the elaboration of the crop of grapes. If care be observed in these points, the diminution in crop may be so small as to be compensated for by the greater facilities of cultivation, &c. It would be well to allow a portion of the vineyard to grow wild every year—say one-fifth—so that in five years the whole vineyard will have had time to completely regenerate itself. This reminds one of the precept in the Bible, Exodus xxiii. 10, 11, wherein it is ordained to cultivate the vineyard and olive ground for six years, and leave it alone the seventh.

Tying up must be had recourse to in all cases where the vines are not trained gooseberry style or let to grow wild; it necessitates the employment of some support to tie the vine to, which may consist of either wire or stakes. The suitability of either of these is decided, as we saw in the preceding chapter, by the mode of pruning adopted; the only method admitting of either sort of support being employed is that illustrated in Fig. 41, where it will be readily understood that, if the vines are staked, the rod or leader must be brought round and tied down to the crown, whilst if trained on wire it may be tied along it.

With this mode of pruning, it becomes a question of expense which method of training be adopted. The absolute cost of either depends upon a variety of circumstances, such as proximity to good timber, facilities for carting, wire, &c., &c. The relative cost, however, is more easily stated, and depends chiefly upon the distance apart at which the vines are planted. Under ordinary circumstances, with vines planted at 5 feet x 5 feet, stakes will cost almost twice as much as wire; at 7 feet x 7 feet, the expense will be almost the same in each case; whilst at 10 feet x 10 feet, wire will cost considerably more than stakes. The cost of cultivation with stakes is naturally less than would be the case with the wire. With the former this can be executed entirely by horse labour in two perpendicular directions, whilst with the latter there will always be a narrow band of soil between the rows, which must be cultivated by hand labour.

Whether tied to stakes or wire, the tying should be done as early as possible, so as to give the leaves time to grow in all directions and completely protect the berries from the sun. In warm climates great damage is done by postponing the tying until the fruit is of the size of large shot; the sudden exposure to the sun's rays causes them to be scorched, and thus injures both the quality and quantity of the crop. Vines should be tied up, especially in a warm climate, as soon as the flowering is over and the fruit properly set.

The material used for tying vines is not of great importance, the cheapest being the best. In districts where rushes are to be found growing on river flats they will be very useful, and may be cut, dried, and stacked away during the slack time after the vintage. The men may be employed to cut and trim them on wet days during the winter when no other work can be done. Before employing rushes to tie up vines they should be soaked in water for a day or two, in order to render them soft and pliable, as in the dry state they are very brittle, and snap off easily. If no rushes can be obtained, a good substitute will be found in rye-straw; an acre or so of rye, according to the size of the vineyard, may be sown for the purpose. New Zealand flax (*Phormium Tenax*) will also be found useful. A knife, with four or five blades about one-third of an inch apart, will enable a leaf to be cut into a large number of strips with ease.

After the vines are tied, the shoots will probably continue to grow—the extremities above the stakes may be cut off, although this should not be done too often. Good strong stakes should be employed, preferably made of split timber, not less than 2 inches square, and of sufficient height to allow a considerable amount of growth above the crown of the vine; if this be 2 feet above the surface, the stakes should not be less than 4ft. 6in. above the ground, which will necessitate their being 5ft. 6in. to 6 feet in length. Vine-stakes of stringybark, messmate, or box timber of the above dimensions, tarred or charred at the lower extremity before being driven into the soil, ought to last in good condition for fourteen or sixteen years. In France it is customary to draw and stack the stakes during the winter, but of course expense of labour renders such a course impracticable in Australia. Tying to wire is practically the same as tying to stakes, and needs no detailed description; the shoots are tied together in two or more small bundles, and not tied separately.

Nipping off the terminal bud of a shoot—or *Pincement*, as it is termed in French—resembles ordinary topping in many respects, but differs from it chiefly in being executed before the flowering; it is executed in many parts of France upon the fruit-bearing shoots as a preventative of the non-setting of the blossom. It is also had recourse

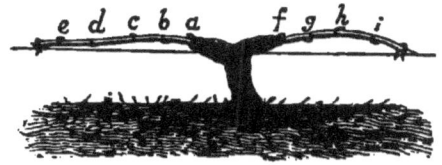

FIG. 44.

to as a supplement to the system of pruning employed in the Bordeaux district, which will be readily understood by reference to Fig. 44.

This is similar to the mode of pruning illustrated in Figs. 39, 40, but differs from it in there being no short or wood spur left at the base of the long or fruit rod; the shoots resulting from the development of *a* and *f* will provide fresh fruit rods for the ensuing year. As we saw (p. 116), under ordinary circumstances these buds would not develop themselves; only those in *c*, *d*, *e*, *h*, and *i* would produce shoots fit to form leaders. By carefully nipping these before flowering time their growth is slightly checked, and the buds *a* and *f*, which would otherwise have remained latent, are caused to give rise to two shoots which will constitute leaders for the next year. This system gives good results in France, but the difficulty of executing this nipping at a proper time and manner on a large scale in a country where skilled vignerons are scarce renders it unsuitable for Australia. The nipping of fruit shoots on vines trained on wire in the ordinary way might with advantage be practised on sorts which are liable to set badly at flowering time, a week or so before this important function takes place, should the benefit derived from it justify the extra expense it would entail.

Annular Incision.—Although this cannot be recommended as one of the ordinary vineyard operations, it deserves mention, and might in certain cases be employed with advantage. Its object is to prevent the non-setting of the flowers, and it consists in removing a ring of bark, as narrow as possible, from the base of a fruit-bearing shoot, just before flowering; or in removing a similar ring of bark before the end of the winter from near the base of the leader which is to bear the fruit-growing shoots. It seems to act, like most other operations which tend to diminish the non-setting, by weakening the vine, and should not be too extensively practised. It presents the disadvantage of rendering shoots thus treated very liable to break off under the influence of wind.

Although the operation may be performed with a small pruning-knife, special instruments are manufactured for the purpose, with which it is possible to treat many vines in a short time. On the whole, although good results have resulted from this operation, it is not employed anywhere on a large scale.

Stripping the leaves of the vine before vintage time, so as to facilitate the ripening of the grapes, is never necessary in either the second or third regions of the colony; in the cooler parts of the first it may, in exceptional cases, be employed with advantage. The leaves should only be removed a few days before the complete maturity of the fruit, otherwise it will be very liable to be hardened and burnt by the sun. Foex recommends to only tear off the limb or flat part of the leaf, leaving the petiole or leaf stalk in its place, in order to allow the fruit to profit by the materials contained in it, as well as to prevent wounding the shoot bearing the fruit, which may be required for pruning. In no case in Australia would it be beneficial to remove more than one-half or two-thirds of the leaves on a vine.

CHAPTER XIII.

CULTIVATION.

The surface of a vineyard must be kept in a thoroughly loose condition; we have already seen that the ground must be properly loosened to a considerable depth before planting; it must also be kept in a loose state as much as possible, and no agent is more powerful in this direction than thorough cultivation of the surface. If the surface be kept loose, the lower layers will not settle down to the same extent as would otherwise be the case. In addition to this, cultivation is necessary in order to destroy the weeds, which grow with great ease in most vineyards, with detrimental influence to the vines near them.

The different cultural operations which should be performed in a vineyard may be grouped as summer and winter cultivations.

The winter cultivation is the most important, and has for its primary object the proper aeration of the soil. This acts beneficially in a variety of ways, but chiefly in rendering many mineral substances more soluble, and therefore more readily assimilable than would otherwise be the case; this cultivation should preferably be executed with the plough, as by turning the soil upside down greater facilities are afforded for its thorough aeration.

The depth of this ploughing should not be too considerable, as it would be liable to injure the tender absorbent rootlets of the vine; as these do not, and should not, come so near the surface in a dry as in a moist climate, it follows that the winter cultivation should be deeper in the former than in the latter case. In a general way it should vary between 4 and 6 inches—4 inches in a cold, and 6 inches in a warm dry district. The best means of executing this ploughing varies according to circumstances. If excessive moisture during the winter is to be feared, the ground should be gathered up to the vines on each side, so as to leave a furrow down the centre of the row by which the surface water may run off. If too much moisture is not to be feared, this will not be necessary, and the soil may be ploughed in whatever way is most convenient. In many parts of France it is customary to gather the soil in the centre of the rows towards the latter part of the winter, the band of soil left along the row between the vines being drawn into the centre with hoes or other hand implements. This baring of the stems of the vines exposes larvæ of insects to the action of frost, &c., and enables all suckers or weeds to be removed with ease. As it must be done by hand labour, it is not to be recommended in Australia, more especially as the advantages to be derived from it would not be likely to repay the extra cost.

It is unnecessary to enlarge upon the different rules to be observed in ploughing, such as only moving the soil when in a fit condition, and not when wet and liable to form into lumps. These points are well known to practical farmers, and as for those who are as yet inexperienced, they will obtain better information from a practical ploughman on the subject than could be expressed in many pages of a book.

As far as implements are concerned, much the same thing may be said. In stiff soils ploughs with a long mould-board, capable of completely turning the sod, will be found to give the best results, whilst in loose or sandy soils short mould-boards may be used with advantage. It is unnecessary to say that wherever possible two or preferably three furrow ploughs should be employed.

Summer Cultivation.—The object of summer cultivation is twofold. First, to keep the vines clear of weeds; and second, by keeping the surface in a thoroughly loose condition, to insure the retention of a sufficient amount of moisture in the soil during the dry weather. The effect of a loose surface in checking evaporation is enormous. If the surface becomes compact and hard, it in reality consists of an innumerable number of small interstices, communicating with each other so as to form fine channels, which acting by capillary attraction, like the wick of a lamp, draw the moisture up from the lower layers of soil, and allow it to freely evaporate into the air. Surface cultivation breaks up these fine continuous channels, and checks the loss of moisture. Mulching or covering with sand or gravel acts in a similar manner. It is a well-known fact that soil under a small heap of straw is always cool and moist. Mulching with straw has many disadvantages; amongst others it presents a harbour for a host of noxious insects and interferes with ploughing, which, as we have seen, is necessary for the aeration of the soil. It is, therefore, best to mulch with soil, or in other words, to thoroughly cultivate the surface, unless in the case mentioned in the previous chapter, where the vines are allowed to grow wild during the summer, and where the large number of leaves protecting the surface of the soil and keeping it cool prevent excessive evaporation.

In all other cases thorough cultivation must be resorted to. More especially is this the case if vines be irrigated. As with other plants, a thorough surface cultivation must follow every application of water, without which no good results can follow from it.

The summer cultivations should always be executed with scarifiers, grubbers, or cultivators, of which there are an immense variety of types, some more suitable than others for certain descriptions of soils. It is unnecessary for us here to describe any of these implements; those which break the ground most thoroughly and leave it in the finest state of division are the best. As the summer cultivations only require to be superficial—not exceeding 3 inches or so in depth—the implements should be chosen accordingly.

The first of these cultivations should take place early in the spring, before the buds begin to burst, and should level all the ridges caused by the winter ploughing. If the vines are not trellised, but planted either on the square or quincunx system more than 5 feet apart, a very simple way of levelling will be to run a light single-furrow plough without a wheel at right angles (or at 60° if it be the quincunx system) to the direction of the winter ploughing; this furrow, in the centre of the row, will allow the wheel and front tooth of the scarifier to pass evenly along, whilst the other teeth tear and level the soil completely in all directions.

If the vines are trained on wires, it will be advisable to level the soil to some extent with a couple of furrows in each row, run in whichever direction may be required before proceeding to employ the scarifier. Of course the band of soil along the wires must be broken up by hand labour, either with spade or hoe, the latter being preferable. The number of summer cultivations necessary is very variable, and, as a rule, is regulated to a great extent by the growth of weeds; the amount of cultivation required to keep these down is usually more than would be absolutely necessary for the maintenance of the surface in a proper state. Persons who are so fortunate as not to be troubled with weeds will find it greatly to their advantage to give two or three good scarifyings during the course of the summer.

Cultivation may be proceeded with at any time when the soil is in a fit state, except when late frosts are to be feared, or at flowering time. The stirring of the soil reducing the temperature of the air, is liable to be attended with unfavorable results at these times.

CHAPTER XIV.

GRAFTING.

Although grafting is an operation which, it might seem, ought not to be required on a properly laid-out young vineyard, yet this handbook would be incomplete without a brief chapter devoted to the subject, more especially as it may often be found very useful to graft a few vines of a vineyard.

It is naturally better that the most suitable sorts should be planted in the first place, so that it will subsequently prove unnecessary to change them, but this is not always an easy matter, especially in a new district where the vine has not been cultivated before, and where, under the peculiar circumstances of the locality, one sort may prove so far superior to the others as to render it advantageous to replace them either completely or partially by it. Grafting enables this to be done without the loss of three or four years' crop, which rooting out and replanting would necessarily entail.

Another case in which grafting is employed must also be mentioned, but it is to be hoped that we may never be obliged to have recourse to it on this account. This is the grafting of European sorts on phylloxera-resistant American stocks. The American vines, although phylloxera resistant, with very few exceptions produce wine of totally different character to the different "*cepages*" of the V. Vinifera (European sorts). By grafting the latter upon the former we have a solution to the difficulty, which has already enabled European vine-growers to reconstitute to a great extent the millions of acres which were destroyed by the pest.

In addition to these cases, grafting often has a truly beneficial effect in making a vine bear more regularly and in diminishing the non-setting of the fruit, chiefly because the joint, presenting a certain opposition to the flow of the sap, weakens the vine to some extent in the same manner as late pruning, the annular incision, &c., which, as we have already seen, are means of combating the non-setting of the fruit.

I, myself, have had practical experience of some vines of Cabernet-Sauvignon grafted on Miller's Burgundy (*Pinot Meunier*) stocks, which set their fruit far better than similar vines growing on their own roots. Some authors go so far as to say that Cabernet grafted on Cabernet, or any sort on a stock of the same sort as itself, will bear better than growing on its own roots.

It has been found that the Malbec, which, as we have already seen, is very liable to set its fruit badly, gives far better crops when grafted on some American sorts, especially the Solonis (a variety of V. Riparia).

The above are examples in which grafting is attended with beneficial results, but this is not always the case. If the stock and scion do not suit each other the results may be disastrous. As an example, a case may be mentioned which came under my notice of some Shiraz (Red Hermitage) grafted, through a mistake of the vigneron, upon some vines of Pinot Blanc. Although the grafts took perfectly, the resulting vines were absolutely sterile, and never had a single bunch upon them, even ten years after the execution of the operation, besides which they did not ripen their wood till two months later than the other vines of the vineyard, the extremities of the shoots sometimes remaining herbaceous throughout the whole winter. Some Chasselas grafted on similar stocks in the same block were very successful, bore large crops of grapes, and ripened their wood thoroughly every year. A general rule often given by practical vignerons is to graft red sorts upon red, and white upon white. It will be observed that the case mentioned above was a departure from this rule.

The enumeration of the different American stocks suitable for grafting with such-and-such a European sort would lead us too far. It will suffice to say that the scion and stock should as much as possible be growers of similar vigour, a weak grafted on an extremely vigorous one, or *vice versâ*, being most liable to give unsatisfactory results.

The different methods of grafting vines are extremely numerous and varied. Want of space renders it impossible for us to describe them all; we shall limit ourselves to two methods which are applicable in different cases. Whatever be the method of grafting adopted, it is absolutely indispensable that the cambium, or generative, layer, situated between the bark and the wood of both scion and stock, should coincide in at least one point; the greater the length through which this contact takes place the better. If this condition be not properly fulfilled the graft will not take.

First. Ordinary cleft graft, applicable when the diameters of stock and scion are different.

Second. English cleft graft, which can only be employed when the stock and scion are of the same diameter, as would be the case when grafting young-rooted American vines with European scions.

Ordinary cleft graft.—This is the most common and simplest method of grafting, and is so well known as to scarcely need description. Reference to Fig. 45 will enable the process to be readily

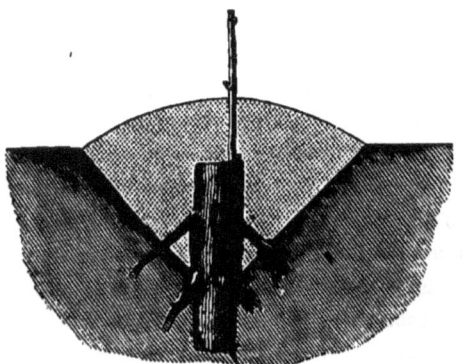

FIG. 45.

understood. The stock is cut off horizontally, and in as clean a manner as possible, 4 inches* or so below the surface, with a small saw. A clean cleft is made with a chisel or pruning knife, which should preferably not extend right across the diameter of the stem. The sides are cut clean with a sharp knife, and a small slip of wood may be removed in order to allow the scion to be properly placed with ease, and the cleft is kept open with a wedge made for the purpose. The scion, consisting of a well-ripened shoot of the year,

---

* If a V. Vinifera is to be grafted on an American stock in a phylloxera-infested district the stock should be cut off as near the surface as possible, so as to prevent the scion forming roots of its own later on, which would expose it to suffer from the attacks of the insect.

cut to three eyes, should be cut at its base, as illustrated in Fig. 46; that is, wedge-shaped, with the inner side narrower than the outer one. It is inserted into the cleft, care being taken that the cambium layers coincide, and the wedge carefully withdrawn; the stock will then hold the scion tightly, and all that will be necessary will be to surround it with grafting wax or clay. Should the cleft have been made too deep, or the stock be rather weak, this will have to be tied, so as to insure the scion being held firmly in its place. The operation properly accomplished, the soil which was removed should be replaced and preferably heaped up round the scion, as represented in Fig. 45.

In order to insure contact between the cambium layers of the stock and scion it is recommended to slightly incline the latter, so that there may be a certainty of their cutting each other, and thus being in contact in two points, one on each side of the cleft.

FIG. 46.

It is evident that this system of grafting may also be made use of if stock and scion are both of the same size. In such a case the cleft should be made right across the stock, and the scion cut to a wedge of the same thickness on each side, but, as a rule, *the English cleft or splice graft* will give more satisfactory results in such a case.

This method of grafting will be understood by reference to Fig. 47. Both stock and scion are cut obliquely at the same angle, and a longitudinal slit is made very slightly above the centre of the first section, so that with a slight pressure one can be made to slide into the other, as represented in Fig. 47. The stock and scion should be carefully fitted together, so as to render the binding of the joint with string or other substance unnecessary. In order that this should be the case both stock and scion must be cut in exactly similar manner, so that when put together no spaces where there is not contact between the two may be found.

This is the mode of grafting most extensively employed for grafting European sorts on phylloxera-proof American stocks. It gives excellent results. The cambium layers of stock and scion meeting in several places, a thorough joint

FIG. 47.

is made, which only weakens the resulting vine to an insignificant extent.

In France whole nurseries of cuttings are sometimes planted out already grafted, the cuttings striking and the graft taking simultaneously. Although a convenient process—as it may be executed during wet weather in a shed or other sheltered place—on an average only about 25 per cent. of these grafted cuttings strike; and, even to obtain these, great care must be taken, frequent waterings and weeding being necessary.

The best time for grafting is in early spring, just when the sap has started to rise with vigour and the first leaves have come out. This time varies according to the climate, but, as a rule, may be said to be about the month of October. In the drier parts of the colony it will be well to graft somewhat earlier, to avoid the desiccation of the scion, which might otherwise ensue. In the cooler parts it will be better to postpone the operation for a couple of weeks, to avoid the risk of decay through excessive moisture.

As a rule, it is best to graft a late on an early variety, as the rise of sap of the former causes the union between the two to effect itself before any leaves have made their appearance. The vessels of the stem are given time to prepare themselves for the supply of the sap rendered necessary by the transpiration of the leaves.

As this is not always possible, and it may even be necessary to graft an early on a late sort, it is advisable to stratify the cuttings intended to be used as scions in the same way as ordinary cuttings until the time for grafting has arrived.

It will be superfluous to insist that scions should always be chosen with as much, if not more, care than ordinary cuttings. The same rules are to be observed in the selection of each.

During the summer following the operation care should be taken to remove any suckers growing from the stock, or, if grafting on phylloxera-resistant stocks, any roots growing from the base of the scion.

The value of different stocks is a subject upon which much has been said, and opinions vary greatly. The following extract from the "Cour Complet de Viticulture," the valuable work of Foex, the director of the Agricultural College of Montpellier (France), will throw some light upon the question. He says:—" All the American 'cepages' are not of the same value as regards the chances of their successful grafting. The one of which the greatest number of grafts take is the Vialla; next to it come York Madeira, Jacquez, and Taylor; then Vitis Rupestris, and the wild V. Riparias. The latter, after being planted out for two years, are refractory to graft. Lastly, the Solonis, which is the most difficult of those usually employed. The question of the accommodation of different stocks to different 'cepages' used to graft on them is as yet very imperfectly known, and only seems to be of slight interest from a practical point of view. The majority of stocks employed so far seem to unite equally well with the different types grafted upon them, and to nourish them equally well. Some people believe to have observed that the Aramon succeeds particularly well on the Clinton, and the Bouschet Hybrids upon the Jacquez."

APPENDIX A.

ABSTRACT of Evidence taken by the Royal Commission on Vegetable Products, giving the opinions of the witnesses upon some debatable points relating to Viticulture.

IRRIGATION OF VINEYARDS.
IN FAVOUR OF IRRIGATION.

The Hon. Peter Laurence Van der Byl, Cape Colony.

279. Irrigation does not interfere with the quality of the wine, whilst crops of 2,000 gallons per acre are obtained with its aid.

Adolf W. Fox, Emu Creek.

2958. Irrigation would double the yield in the Bendigo district, and improve the quality. Would gladly give £2 per acre for irrigation.

Wm. Graham, Rutherglen.

6923. Would gladly irrigate if water was available. It would improve the quality, as natural rainfall is sometimes deficient.

Henry Petersen, Emu Creek.

2939. Irrigation would enable much land to be devoted to viticulture which is now lying idle.

G. S. Smith, Wahgunyah.

7447. Intends to try irrigation on his vineyard.

NOT IN FAVOUR OF IRRIGATION.

Angelo G. D. Bernacchi, Maria Island.

10097. Irrigation is practised in some Italian vineyards, but is not to be recommended. The yield is largely increased, but the quality deteriorated, even if the water is only applied in winter.

Jas. Bladier.

3020. Emphatically condemns irrigation of vineyards. Says no vines are irrigated in France. Mentions case of Frenchman at Wahgunyah who irrigated vines, but lost most of the crop through oïdium and black spot.

Alfred Büsse, Barnawatha.
6473. Does not believe in irrigation for vines.
Robert Turner, Rutherglen.
7109. Does not irrigate his vines, but irrigates other crops.

SUBSOILING OR TRENCHING.
In Favour of Subsoiling.
Hubert de Castella, St. Huberts, Lillydale.
4276. The land ought to be subsoiled before being planted. If it be very loose, a simple ploughing may give good results, but it is better to subsoil. The subsoil must not be brought to the surface.
G. B. Federli.
10418. Considers that soil should be deeply worked, but subsoil left where it is.
Hugh Fraser, Brown's Plains.
6811. Subsoiled his land before planting.
Wm. Graham, Rutherglen.
6853. Subsoils the land with two ploughs, the second one only loosening the subsoil without turning it over. If the subsoil be brought to the surface the vines do not come to maturity so soon. The soil is made cold, and cuttings are more liable to miss.
C. H. Morris, Brown's Plains.
6750. Brought the subsoil to the surface when planting his vineyard, but is of opinion that it is better to simply stir it, leaving it where it is.
Thos. A. Rattray, Tahbilk.
7538. Subsoils the land with two ploughs following each other, but does not bring the subsoil to the surface.

In Favour of Trenching.
Alfred Büsse, Barnawatha.
6452. Trenches the land from 18 to 20 inches with a trench plough.
Hon. Peter Laurence Van der Byl, Cape Colony.
329. Trenches the ground by hand to a depth of 2 feet if the soil be poor; if it be rich, simply ploughs it.
Robert Caughey, Gooramadda.
7300. Believes in bringing the subsoil to the surface; it keeps the vineyard cleaner for the time, and vines do better.

F. G. Docker, Bontherambo.

8617. Hand-trenched one portion of the vineyard and plough-trenched the other.

J. P. H. Gherig, Barnawatha.

6539. Prefers hand-trenching, but it does not pay. Two ploughs do very well ; bringing the subsoil to the top is the best, although in some sorts of soil it might make the ground sour.

Hans Larsen, Gannawarra.

5260. Necessity for trenching through clay till sandy subsoil is reached.

J. H. Smith, North Barnawatha.

6654. Trenches to depth of 15 to 18 inches, bringing subsoil to the top with a specially made double-furrow plough.

Robert Turner, Rutherglen.

7084. Plough-trenches the ground intended for vines.

The following witnesses consider both subsoiling and trenching unnecessary :—

D. G. Hamilton, Rutherglen.

7411. Is of opinion that a simple ploughing 7 or 8 inches deep is sufficient preparation. His soil is a clayey loam with ironstone pebbles.

Thos. Hardy, South Australia.

17. Of late has abandoned trenching, finding it to be unnecessary; simply ploughs to depth of 6 inches. The soil is of a loose character.

G. S. Smith, Wahgunyah.

7482. Simply ploughed the ground to a depth of 10 inches. The soil is sandy.

DISTANCE APART OF VINES.

The following distances apart were recommended :—

Alfred Büsse, Barnawatha.

6455. 7 x 7.

Hon. P. L. Van der Byl, Cape Colony.

340. 4 x 4, 5 x 5, or 6 x 6.

Hubert de Castella, St. Huberts, Lillydale.

4336. On the Yarra, 5 x 5; on the Murray, 8 x 8.

Alex. Caughey, Gooramadda.

7296. On wires, 10 x 4; where staked, 8 x 8.

F. G. Docker, Bontherambo.

8614. Has vines at 6 x 6, but prefers 8 x 8.

Richard Dods, Marong.

2689. 9 x 9.

G. B. Federli.

10421. 8 x 8 or 10 x 10.

Hugh Fraser, Brown's Plains.

6820. 7 x 7, but 8 x 8 is preferable.

J. P. H. Gherig, Barnawatha.

6550. Not less than 8 x 8, 10 x 10 is preferable.

Wm. Graham, Rutherglen.

6857. Planted formerly at 8 x 8, but prefers 10 x 10.

Thos Hardy, South Australia.

66. 12 x 20 for currants, 8 x 10 for wine grapes.

L. Levin, Rutherglen.

7182. 8 x 8.

C. H. Morris, Brown's Plains.

6759. Prefers 8 x 8 to 10 x 10.

T. A. Rattray, Tahbilk.

7538. 4 x 4 too close. The proper distance is 10 x 8 or 10 x 10.

Camille Reau, Wahgunyah.

7235. Planted at 5 x 5, but prefers 8 x 8 or 10 x 10.

J. H. Smith, North Barnawatha.

6652. Plants 10 x 5, and roots out every other one later on, so as to make it 10 x 10.

Robert Turner, Rutherglen.

7155. 10 x 10.

G. S. Smith, Wahgunyah.

7494. 8 x 8.

CUTTINGS OR ROOTED VINES.

IN FAVOUR OF CUTTINGS.

Alfred Büsse, Barnawatha.

6459. Prefers cuttings, as once they strike they grow quicker than the rooted vine, which has to form new roots after transplanting.

Hon. P. L. Van der Byl, Cape Colony.

336. Plant cuttings in preference to rooted vines.

R. Caughey, Gooramadda.

7341. In a favorable season prefers cuttings, but rooted vines are less liable to miss.

J. P. H. Gherig, Barnawatha.

6562. Prefers cuttings to rooted vines if circumstances are favorable, as they overtake the rooted vines the second year.

Wm. Graham, Rutherglen.

6869. Prefers cuttings, as in a fair season they are just as good as rooted vines.

D. G. Hamilton, Rutherglen.

7412. Decidedly approves of cuttings in planting a large vineyard.

Camille Reau, Wahgunyah.

7235. Plant 5 x 10 with cuttings; root out every second vine later on, which can be employed to fill up misses.

IN FAVOUR OF ROOTED VINES.

Hubert de Castella, St. Huberts, Lillydale.

4282. Thinks one-year-old rooted vines are the best, as they are more certain to grow. Has seen three-year-old rooted vines produce as good vines as those planted as cuttings.

Thos. Hardy, South Australia.

20. Always plants rooted vines.

G. W. Knight, Bendigo.

9380. Rooted vines are to be preferred to cuttings, as they are far more certain to grow, especially in the northern districts.

C. H. Morris, Brown's Plains.

6765. Thinks cuttings better than rooted vines, but recommends the latter and employs them himself.

Thos. A. Rattray, Tahbilk.

7538. Certainly prefers rooted vines to cuttings, as they save a year.

G. S. Smith, Wahgunyah.

7488. Has employed both systems; the rooted vines are a certainty.

J. H. Smith, Barnawatha.

6659. Prefers rooted vines; not that there is any advantage after the plant has grown, but they are safer to take in the first go off.

APPENDIX B.

LIST OF MEMBERS OF THE CENTRAL VINE-GROWERS' ASSOCIATION, MELBOURNE.

[MAY, 1891.]

Name.	Address.
Adams, Henry	Deep Lead, Wimmera.
Allan, E.	Yates' Seed Farm, Otahuhu, Auckland.
Anderson, E. W. N.	Trymple, Mildura.
Angas, J. H.	Currie-street, Adelaide, S.A.
Angus and Robertson	110 Market-street, Sydney, N.S.W.
Arapiles Shire Council	President.
Barlow, John B.	Retreat Vineyard, Barnawartha.
Barlow, W. A.	*Vigneron*, 109 Pitt-street, Sydney.
Battallani, Jos.	Carmanual Creek, Dunolly.
Battersby, D.	Dargalong.
Bavay, A. de	Victoria Brewery, E. Melbourne.
Bennett, J.	Dookie.
Bernacchi, A. G. D.	Maria Island, Tasmania.
Blayney, Thos.	Nagambie.
Borelli, J. B.	Panton Hill.
Borwick, G. E.	Mount Caraunya Vineyard, Dookie.
Borwick, W. H.	Dookie.
Bowness, E.	217 Heidelberg-road, Clifton Hill.
Boys, Wallace R.	Swan Hill.
Bradbury, S.	London, care of McLean Bros. and Rigg.
Bradshaw, Thos.	Bamawm, Rochester.
Bragato, Romeo	Board of Viticulture.
Brenzing, Ernest	Nagambie.
Bristow, G. B. N.	Vineyard Co., Stawell.
Bruhn, Albert	Emu Vineyard, Emu Creek.
Brunning, William	Somerville, Hastings.
Buchanan, Hon. J.	Berwick.
Buckland, Henry	Moe.
Buckley, Allan R.	Rutherglen.
Burrough, G. C.	Mildura.
Büsse, F., and Sons	Burrabunnia, Barnawartha.
Busst, C. J.	Huntly.
Campbell, John	Rutherglen.
Carolin, J. P.	Sandhurst.
Castella, François de	Board of Viticulture.
Cassuben Bros.	Deep Lead, Wimmera.
Caughey, A.	Mount Prior Vineyard, Gooramadda.
Christians, Wm.	Lake Rowan.
Clarke, Hen.	Lunatic Asylum, Ararat.
Clennett, W. P.	Port Esperance, Tasmania.
Clifford, M. H.	45 Queen-street.
Cook, G. J.	Savings Bank, Melbourne.
Cook, W. F.	The Grange, Narre Warren.
Cook, James	Emu Creek, Sandhurst.
Cook, Saml.	Axe Creek, Axedale.
Cooper, James	Upper Black Dog Creek, Chiltern.

L

Name.	Address.
Cormack, A.	Gannawarra.
Cottnan, H.	Collingwood.
Craike, Thos.	Bowmont, Sandhurst.
Crellin Bros.	Hallam's-road Station.
Cruikshank, Geo.	Witchipool, Donald.
Curtain, John	Dookie.
Daccommun, Emile	Nagambie.
Dall, Jas.	P.O., Sydney.
Darveniza, T.	Excelsior Vineyard, Mooroopna.
Davenport, Sir Samuel	Beaumont, Adelaide.
Davidson, Wm.	Moorondah, Hawthorn.
Delmenico, Giovanni	Terrappee, Boort.
Dick, Dr.	Wodonga.
Docker, F. G.	Bontherambo, Wangaratta.
Doig, J. G.	Bobinawarrah.
Duerkop, Henry	Care of Mr. T. Wilson, Chiltern.
Dugay, Theodore	Rutherglen.
Duncan, Thos.	Tubbo, Narandera, N.S.W.
Dunn, F.	306 Flinders-lane.
Eglie, Fred	Tabilk, Nagambie.
Elms, Wm.	Moyarra, South Gippsland.
Elston, W.	Kangaroo Flat, Sandhurst.
Evans, J.	Buckley-street, Essendon.
Everist, J.	Yarrawonga.
Fitzgerald, R.	3 Catherine-street, Richmond.
Fegely, C. de	472 Little Collins-street west.
Fenton, J. P.	Elcho Estate, Lara.
Formby, R.	Surveyor, Mildura.
Fraser, Hugh	Olive Hills, Brown's Plains.
Frey, H. J.	Tintaldra.
Frowd, Isaac	Tongala, Echuca, Kyabram.
Fyfe, Wm.	Bald Hill, St. Arnaud.
Gardiner, G.	Cashel.
Giovanoni, D.	Spring Creek, Hepburn.
Graham Bros.	Netherby Vineyard, Rutherglen.
Grant, James	Craig Elachie, Elmhurst.
Grant, A. N.	Hillston, N.S.W.
Grant, T. H.	Pakenham.
Grenville, H. K.	Mirboo, Gippsland.
Grosse, Frederick	Emu Creek, Strathfieldsaye, and 6 Collins-street west.
Guppy, Walter	Benalla.
Gues-Willer	Care of Mr. Dugay, Rutherglen.
Haehnell, C. W.	Krambruk, Apollo Bay.
Hague, J. T.	Angastown, S.A.
Haig, Thos.	Beechworth.
Hamilton, D. G.	Rutherglen.
Hardy, Thos.	Bankside, Adelaide.
Harrold Bros.	Adelaide.
Heape, S. F.	Koimburra, Cosgrove.
Henderson, T. S.	Ry. Dept., Wellington, N.Z.
Howell and Green	Bathhurst, N.S.W.
Hutton, M. C. G.	Cooring Yering, Lilydale.
Irvine, Hans W. H.	Great Western
Jeavons, Joseph	Wycheproof, Teddywaddy.
Johns, John	Katandra, vid Rockville P.O.
Johnson, H.	Stony Creek, Rockhampton, Queensland.
Johnson, Thos.	Naringal, Allansford.
Jones, W.	Mooroopna.

Name.	Address.
Kahland, J.	King-street, Sandhurst.
Kelly, T. J. D.	Redan street, St. Kilda.
Kelly, G. P. D.	Viticultural College, Montpellier.
King, Hy.	Taminick.
Lamerock, Jas.	Cosgrove.
Lang, W. H.	Netherby.
Lawrence, A., & Co.	527 Collins-street.
Lenné, Carl	Echuca.
Levin, L.	Rutherglen.
Lockhart, W. P	Park-street west, Brunswick.
Logan, Duncan	Rutherglen.
Long, W. J.	Victoria Hotel, Elmore.
Macey, James	Estcourt, Boorhaman, Wangaratta.
Mackenzie, R. W.	Wynyard, Tasmania.
Mackereth, Edwin H.	Avoca.
Magennis, W. J.	P.O., Yabba.
Maginnis, Jas.	Dookie.
Maher, A.	Arcade, Sandhurst.
Mann, J. G.	South-street, Freemantle, W.A.
Mannes, A.	Axe Creek, Sandhurst.
Martin, R. W.	N. B. and M. Ins. Co., 41 Queen-street.
Matthews, G. V.	Wood-street, Donald.
Manlein, Peter	Primrose Garden, Korongvale.
Mellis, A.	Kyabram.
Minotti, Gustave	Ballarat-road, Guildford.
Mooney, J. & L.	Mooney's Gap, Ararat.
Morris, G. F., & Sons	Fairfield, Rutherglen.
Mueller, Dr. A.	Yackandandah.
Müeller, John	Tabilk.
McBean, Simon	Brown's Plains, Rutherglen.
McIntosh, Jas.	Tabilk.
McFarlane, S.	208 Clarendon-street, S. Melbourne.
McNaughton, John	Burwood.
Neighbour, C. J.	Selborne Chambers.
Newbery, J. Cosmo, C.M.G.	Hotham-street, East St. Kilda.
Nickenson, J. M.	Shepparton.
Nolan, James	Rutherglen.
Norman, Dr. H. H.	Rockville House, 50 N. Terrace, Adelaide.
Nunn, A. L.	Maizena Works, Merimbula, N.S.W.
O'Dea, Michael	Rutherglen.
O'Grady, —	Rutherglen.
Oldham, Hugh	Surveyor, Mildura.
Osborn, A. F.	Cowra, N.S.W.
Osmand, Hon. W. H. S.	Doctor's Creek, Stawell West.
Panton, J. A.	Alexandra-street, East St. Kilda.
Parker, Joseph	Castlemaine West.
Paul, A. W. L.	Briston, Male-street, Middle Brighton.
Pedrini, V.	Yandoit.
Penfold, Dr. O.	Sandhurst.
Petersen, H.	Emu Creek, Sandhurst.
Pooley, Humphrey	Barnawartha.
Power, R. D.	Orbost.
Pownall, W. W.	4 Mill-street, Hanover-square, London.
Poxon, Levi	Lake Marmal, viá Barakee.
Prentice, Jas.	Emu Vineyard, Rutherglen.
Pritchard, J. A.	Gwar-y-Castel, Alma-road, St. Kilda.
Ratcliffe, David	Kyabram, Rodney.
Reade, C.	High-street, Sandhurst.
Reeve, Thomas	Rutherglen.
Rendell, W.	Longfield, Yielima.
Reveree, Alex.	Dark Forest, Waterfall, Illawarra, N.S.W.
Ridout, J. E.	Goorambat East.

Name.	Address.
Ridout, Robert, jun.	Goorambat Vineyard, Benalla.
Rigby, W. C.	74 King William-street, Adelaide.
Ritchie, P. B.	Alphington.
Roberts, John	Fairburn Grange, Cashel.
Ross, G. H. D.	Wethersdane Park, Hallam's-road.
Rough, J. C.	Elive, Gourlay-street, Balaclava.
Ruble, Jacob	View Point Vineyard, Michelston, Tabilk.
Ruedin, A.	Huntly Vineyard, Huntly.
Ryley, F.	Wangaratta.
Schuhkraft, G. F.	Doncaster.
Seal, P.	Mildura.
Shaw, F. K.	Goornong.
Shields, W.	Ethandune, Yielima.
Shillinglaw, John J.	Panton Hill.
Shillinglaw, Esmond B.	Panton Hill.
Shillinglaw, J. Crawford	Panton Hill.
Shillinglaw, F. Flinders	Panton Hill.
Sim, J.	Cosgrove.
Simon, A. C.	Green Bank, Bacchus Marsh.
Smith, Daniel	Eversley.
Smith, G. S., & Sons	All Saints', Wahgunyah.
Smith, Edwin	Rutherglen.
Smith, Elderson	410 Brunswick-street, Fitzroy.
Smith, S., & Son	Yalumba Vineyard, Angaston, S.A.
Snart, Robt.	Gooramadda.
Stevens, John	Mutual Store, Melbourne.
Streckfuss, H.	Goornong.
Stuckey, S. J.	Millicent, S.A.
Stuttard, W.	4 Prince's-park Terrace, Royal-park.
Sutherland, John	Tyrrel-park, Wycheproof.
Swindale, Henry	Runnymede, Elmore.
Tarrant, S.	Rosedale Orchard, Clunes.
Tenner, James	Wodonga.
Tenner, P. A.	Wodonga.
Thompson, H. E.	Cent Arpent, Hay, N.S.W.
Thompson, J. L.	Dookie.
Thompson, G. W.	16 North-street, Richmond.
Tomlinson, H. J.	60 Simpson-street, E. Melbourne.
Traill, J. C.	Enfield-street, St. Kilda.
Treloar, W. G.	Watervale, S.A.
Tribolet, Abraham	Excelsior Vineyard, Corop.
Tully S. S.	Wickliffe-road.
Tyler, E. E.	Tubbo, Narandera, N.S.W.
Van Staveren, J. C.	Nathalia.
Veitch, Christopher	Casterton.
Walker, Francis	St. Ives, Karabeal.
Walker, Thos.	Seaton, Gippsland.
Warnecke, C. H.	Bromley.
Watkin, J. F.	Beaufort-road, Beaufort.
Wattie, Wm.	State School 2565, Leeor.
Webber, J., & Son	Mercer-street, Geelong.
Webster, Graham	Greensborough.
Welham, John	28 Duke-street, Ballarat W.
Wells, H. G	Cheltenham.
Wendell, C. H.	Colbinabbin, Elmore.
Whitehead, J. R.	Barnawartha.
Wickham Bros.	Bullington Vineyard, Wodonga.
Willis, James	South Wangaratta.
Wills, Thos.	Whiteway, Moonambel.
Wilson, Dr. C. M.	Moyarra, South Gippsland.
Wyndham, E.	Bukkulla, Inverell, N.S.W.

APPENDIX C.

LIST OF THE VINE-GROWERS OF VICTORIA.

[May, 1891.]

(Corrections are specially requested, addressed to the Secretary of the Board.)

Name.	Acres.	Address.
Abbott, David	½	Sandringham.
Abbott, J.	4	Indigo, Yackandandah.
Abel, Wm.	¾	Painswick, Goldsborough.
Abell, W.	2	Inkerman, Dunolly.
Ackerman, Walter	½	Lockwood.
Adami, Peter	4	Jamieson-street, Daylesford.
Adams, Henry	¼	Deep Lead, Wimmera.
Adams, John	10	Mooroopna.
Adams, J. S.	6	Alphington.
Adams, P.	7	Wodonga.
Adams, Robt. H.	3	Dromana.
Adams, W. A.	30	Mountain Creek, Moonambel.
Ah Chung	½	Day's Creek, Omeo.
Ah Dan	½	Dimboola.
Ah Fee	½	Dimboola.
Ah Huey, Joney	15	Benalla.
Ah Loy	7	Moliagul.
Ah Shea	4	Moliagul.
Ah Wong	2	Myers' Flat, Eaglehawk.
Alderson, Thos.	7	Bet Bet.
Alexander, J.	5	Toolamba, Tatura.
Allin, Edwin...	½	Bray-street, Long Gully.
Amor, J.	5	McCoy's Bridge, Mooroopna.
Anders, Herman	3	Roseberry, Warracknabeal.
Anderson, John	½	Point Nepean-road.
Anker, W.	¾	Wandin Yallock, Lilydale.
Ansaldo, Emanuel	3	Newtown, Beechworth.
Ansell, Edwin	2	Havelock-road, Beechworth.
Anson, Wm.	¾	Coleraine.
Archer, W. S.	¼	Mooroopna.
Armstrong, Alfred	2½	Marna Vale, Eltham.
Arnold, Jas.	—	Mercer-street, Geelong.
Arnot, E.	½	Bluff-road, South Brighton.
Ashley, William	10	Mandurang.
Audley, H.	10	Rutherglen.
Augustina, A.	1	Bet Bet.
Aumall, Capal	1	Doncaster.
Aumann, August	3½	Doncaster.
Babbage, J. P.	½	Sailor's Gully, Eaglehawk.
Baccala, Antonio	3	Bealiba.
Backons, —	2	Yackandandah.
Bacon, Jas.	12	Great Western.
Bailey, Edgar	13	Rutherglen.

Name.	Acres.	Address.
Baker, Daniel	10	Woosang, Wedderburn.
Baker, George	8	Woosang, Wedderburn.
Banna, Jas.	4	Newtown, Beechworth.
Barassie, Guiseppe	2½	Shicer Gully, Guildford.
Barldaz, Leon	4	Armitage, Christmas Hill.
Barlow, John B.	80	Retreat Vineyard, Barnawartha.
Barnes, Jos.	½	Whim Holes, Napoleon Lead.
Bartels, Henry	3½	Newtown, Beechworth.
Batcheler, Richd.	1	Thomastown.
Battiland, Joseph	7	Dunolly.
Baume, August	13	Rutherglen.
Baumgarten, G.	140	Barnawartha.
Baumgarten, W.	16	Barnawartha.
Bavay, A. de...	—	Beenak.
Bawden, Wm.	2	El Dorado.
Bawm, J. J.	2	Perry River, Stratford.
Baxter, James	3	Barnawartha.
Baxter, John	13	Barnawartha.
Bear, J. P.	—	(See Tahbilk).
Bear, T. H.	40	Castle Hill, Yan Yean.
Beard, David	1¾	Three-mile, Beechworth.
Beck, August	10	Brown's Plains, Rutherglen.
Beck, Fredk.	29	Brown's Plains, Rutherglen.
Becks, Gustave	10	Sunbury.
Bedgood, Charles	½	Perry River, Stratford.
Bedolla, Michael	2	Spring Creek, Hepburn.
Bell, J.	½	Longwood.
Benson, A.	4	Wodonga West.
Bensaschi, Giovanni	2	Talbot-road, Talbot.
Bent, Thomas	½	Union-street, Brighton.
Beper, Alex.	½	Ironbark, Long Gully.
Berger, Godfred	½	Doncaster.
Berryman, William H.	½	Bray-street, Long Gully.
Bersica, S.	15¼	Mooroopna.
Bertran, Francis	4	Newtown, Beechworth.
Best, Henry...	40	Concongella Vineyard, Great Western.
Bieske, Wilhelm	1	Boram Boram, Penshurst.
Biles, Thos.	1½	Maryville, Morwell.
Billieh, Ignatio	1¼	Wedderburn.
Black, Robt.	1	Dunolly.
Blackburn, Thomas	1½	White Hills, Sandhurst.
Blaikie, Alex.	20	North Wangaratta.
Blake, Arthur P.	½	Bambra-road, Caulfield.
Blanckbourne, Wm.	½	Eddington.
Blayney, Thos.	40	Nagambie.
Bloon, Christian	3	Doncaster East.
Bloxham, William	3½	Ivanhoe, Heidelberg.
Blumner, F. F.	5	Bright.
Blumner, Hartman	5	Lockwood.
Bodkin, W.	7	Picola.
Bofil, Martin	8	Waanyarra.
Boland, A.	6	Loddon.
Bolla, Pietro...	½	Hepburn.
Bon, Mrs. A. F.	2	Wappan Station, Doon, Mansfield.
Bond, William	3	Eddington.
Bonning, Wm.	½	Greendale-road, Ballan.
Boreeland, Alex.	6	Laanecoorie, Eddington.
Borelli, J. B.	—	Panton Hill.
Borwick, G. E.	—	Mount Caranya Vineyard, Dookie.
Bossidge, Jasper	1½	Whroo, Rushworth.
Botton, Edward	6	Eddington.
Bourke, John	11	Carlyle, Rutherglen.

Name.	Acres.	Address.
Bowen, Albert	4	Amphitheatre, Elmhurst.
Bowit, William	25	Jackson's Creek, Sunbury.
Bowtell Bros.	4	Sugar Loaf, Great Western.
Boyes, J.	2	Leneva, Wodonga.
Boyes, J. and H. A.	½	Stanhope, Rushworth.
Boyes, T.	7	Middle Creek, Yackandandah.
Braché, C.	—	112 Collins-street west.
Braché, C.	100	Wahgunyah.
Bradshaw, J.	32	Bamawm, Rochester.
Bramston, George	1	Chiltern.
Bray, And.	5	Lilliput, Rutherglen.
Bray, Wm.	¼	Napoleon Lead.
Brennan, C.	10	Emu Creek, Sandhurst.
Brennan, M.	4	Emu Creek, Sandhurst.
Brenzing, Ernest	10	Nagambie.
Brewer, A.	2	Epsom, Sandhurst.
Brewer, A.	5	Huntly.
Briggs, Robt.	21	Narong, Rutherglen.
Bristow, G. B. N.	90	Stawell Vineyard Co.
Broadway, James	1	Lockwood.
Brown, Alfred	½	Lower Tarwin.
Brown, George	2	Gooramadda, Rutherglen.
Brown, George	10	Millewa.
Brown, James John	8	Malakoff-road, Beechworth.
Browne, A. H. L.	—	135 Collins-st. W., agent Chateau Tahbilk.
Broughton, E.	1	Booroopki.
Bruce, Andrew	1	Perry River, Stratford.
Bruhn, Albert	36	Emu Vineyard, Emu Creek.
Bruhn, Otto	¼	Majorca.
Brunning, William	2	Somerville, Hastings.
Bryant, Charles	1½	Muckleford.
Brydie, Alex.	8½	Wahgunyah.
Bubeek, Felix	25	Bald Hill, Sunbury.
Buchanan, Chas.	8	Vine Bank, Beeac.
Buckley, A. R.	71	Rutherglen.
Buckley, John	1	Huntly.
Buckly, John	2	Charlton-road, Wedderburn.
Bull, John E. N.	3½	Castlemaine.
Burgdoff Bros.	4	Barker's Creek, Castlemaine.
Burge, John	6½	Toolamba.
Burger, Johan	6	Yulanga, Boram Boram, Penshurst.
Burne, John	3	Strathfieldsaye.
Burne, J.	15	Axe Creek, Sandhurst.
Burnes, Jos. G.	16	Rutherglen.
Burns, Joseph	20	Carlyle, Rutherglen.
Burns, J. G.	15	Rutherglen.
Burns, Wm.	8	Upper Black Dog Creek, Chiltern.
Burrowes, Wm.	40	Rutherglen.
Burrows, W. and R. J.	45	Rutherglen.
Büsse, F., and Sons	80	Burrabunnia, Barnawartha.
Busst, C. J.	15	Huntly.
Calanchini, G.	½	Hepburn.
Calder, William	5	Natimuk.
Callender, R.	2	Katunga.
Cameron, Alex.	3½	Bailieston, Nagambie.
Cameron, Charles	7	Almond Grove, Bet Bet.
Cameron, Chas.	8	Timor.
Campbell, Alex.	¼	Gordon.
Campbell, J.	75	Rutherglen.
Cannings, W.	¼	Campbellfield.
Carnforth, —	2	Great Western.

Name.	Acres.	Address.
Carnie and Munday	4	Katamatite.
Carroll, S.	8	Wodonga.
Carson Bros.	60	Carlyle, Rutherglen.
Carson, J.	¼	North Mooroopna.
Carson, T. K.	52	Rutherglen.
Cary, Thos.	18	Rutherglen.
Cassubean Bros.	10	Deep Lead, Wimmera.
Castella, Paul De	100	Yering.
Castles, J. J.	6	Narioka.
Cathro, Alex.	1½	Black Spring-road, Beechworth.
Caughey, Alex.	260	Mount Prior Vineyard, Gooramadda.
Cayley, Catherine	¼	Craigie, Majorca.
Cazer, Chas.	½	Talbot.
Celerich, Steven	1¼	St. Arnaud-road, Wedderburn.
Chambers, Geo.	42	Barnawartha.
Chambers, Phil.	20	Rutherglen.
Champion, Adolph	4	Great Western.
Chandler, Geo.	3	Benalla.
Chandler, Geo.	10	Rutherglen.
Chandler, James	45	Rutherglen.
Chandler, William	18	Rutherglen.
Chapman, T. H.	12	Nagambie.
Chapple, Henry	½	Mount Korong-road, Long Gully.
Charlsworth, Joseph	1	Mandurang.
Child, —	—	Doctor's Creek, Stawell.
Christians, Wm.	3½	Lake Rowan.
Clarke and Parry	5	Landsborough.
Clarke, Geo.	1	Somerville.
Clarke, Hen.	3½	Lunatic Asylum, Ararat.
Clements, John	1	Lockwood.
Cleough, —	½	Grassy Flat, Sandhurst.
Clift, W.	1	Huntly.
Clifford, Lewin H.	½	Bacchus Marsh.
Climus, Mrs.	5	Yackandandah.
Cochran, Michl.	1½	Burnside, Tooborac, Heathcote.
Code, B.	3	Axe Creek, Sandhurst.
Coe, William	½	Coleraine.
Cole, Arthur	2	Nicholson-street, Coburg.
Cole, Mrs. Ward	¼	Bay-street, Brighton.
Coleman, S.	12	Shepparton.
Collard, G.	—	Bonegilla.
Collen, John	80	Wahgunyah.
Collie, John	12	Dobie's Bridge, Ararat.
Cone, John	2	Main Lead, Beaufort.
Congdon, William	5½	Wattle Flat, Castlemaine.
Conno, John	9	Gooramadda.
Conroy, Pat.	9	Chiltern West, Rutherglen.
Conroy, Wm.	15	Great Western.
Cook, James	15	Emu Creek, Sandhurst.
Cook, J.	7	Middle Creek, Yackandandah.
Cook, Saml.	2	Axe Creek, Axedale.
Coombes, Wm.	¾	Railway Reserve, Echuca East.
Cooper, Geo.	¼	Bridgewater-on-Loddon.
Cooper, James	8	Upper Black Dog Creek, Chiltern.
Copsey, Alfred	1½	Bet Bet.
Corcoran, Pat.	8	Research Vineyard, Eltham.
Cornelius, J.	17	Rutherglen.
Cornforth, —	3½	Dunbulbalane.
Costello, P. H.	25	Mount Hooghly, Dunolly.
Coupar, Joseph	¼	Mirboo.
Cousens, Benjamin	1	Wedderburn.
Cox, Thos.	½	Lillimur.

Name.	Acres.	Address.
Coyle, Bernard ...	17	... Christmastown, Chiltern.
Craig, W.	2	... Wodonga West.
Craike, Thos. ...	10	... Bowmont, Sandhurst.
Cranny, Fredk. ...	½	... Cockran-street, Elsternwick.
Croft, Robert ...	1	... Waverly-road, Oakleigh.
Crolle, D.	4	... Epsom.
Crooke, James E. ...	½	... Bacchus Marsh.
Crouch, Harry ...	¼	... Yanipy, Kaniva.
Crozier, A.	2	... Kulnine, Yelta.
Crozier, Elliott ...	2	... Yelta.
Cue, Geo.	½	... Casterton.
Cuff, Abraham ...	5	... Taripta, Echuca.
Cummins, J. ...	2	... Bonegilla.
Curnick, F. ...	½	... Mirboo.
Curnow, Jas. ...	2	... Woodstock West, Eddington.
Currie, Capt. ...	½	... Beach, Brighton.
Curry, Mrs. ...	8	... Bet Bet.
Curtain, John ...	700	... Chateau Dookie, Dookie.
Curtis, C. E. ...	½	... Casterton.
Cussen, M. ...	1	... Mooroopna.
Dalberti, Dominich ...	10	... Great Western.
Daley, J. J. ...	½	... Gibson-road, Sandringham.
Daly, H. O'B. ...	80	... Dunolly.
Daly, Jas. ...	½	... Dunolly.
Daly, N. ...	26	... Great Western.
Daravin, J. T. ...	14	... Mandurang.
D'Arcey, Peter ...	½	... Parkin's Reef-road, Maldon.
Darragh, James ...	½	... Ballan.
Darveniza, T. ...	58	... Excelsior Vineyard, Mooroopna.
Davey, H. T. ...	¼	... Kerang.
Davey, T.	2	... Youanmite.
Davidson, John ...	½	... Serpentine.
Davidson, Wm ...	½	... Faraday, Castlemaine.
Deane, John ...	2	... Lockwood.
Dear, Fredk. ...	1	... Dunolly.
Deas, Geo.	19	... Rutherglen.
Deason, John ...	½	... Moliagul.
Deganhardt, G. ...	½	... Murtoa.
Deherert, Reinhold ...	10	... Doncaster East.
Delmenico, Giovanni	17	... Terrappee, Boort.
Deller, Thos.... ...	2	... Constantia, Myers' Flat, Eaglehawk.
Delves, Henry ...	7	... Back Creek, Marong.
Dennis, John ...	½	... Philpot-street, Long Gully.
Denscher, R. ...	4	... Great Western.
Derritt, J.	4	... Indigo, Yackandandah.
Deritt, M., sen. ...	15	... Indigo, Yackandandah.
Deschamp, August ...	4	... Lilydale.
Deschamp, Mrs. C.	18	... Lilydale.
Deschamp, Mrs. L. ...	14	... Lilydale.
Devers, C	15	... Rutherglen.
Dewar, Hugh ...	4	... Great Western.
Dewer, Catherine ...	14	... Rhymney.
De Pury, E. ...	55	... Lilydale.
Dick, Dr.	30	... Wodonga.
Dickson, Robt. ...	40	... Upper Indigo, Barnawartha.
Dickson, Thos. ...	5	... Indigo, Yackandandah.
Dickson and Sons ...	40	... Indigo, Yackandandah.
Dimboola Abor. Mis. S.	½	... Dimboola.
Dixon, John ...	½	... Glen Eira-road, Elsternwick.
Docker, F. G. ...	88	... Bontherambo, Wangaratta.
Dod, R.	2	... Marong.

Name.	Acres.	Address.
Doig, J. G.	20	... Bobinawarrah.
Dominiquez, A. ...	1	... Porepunkah.
Donald, Alex. ...	¼	... Woodford, Dartmoor.
Donaldson, John ...	½	... Chinaman's Creek, Castlemaine.
Donnelly, James ...	5	... Christmas Town-road, Chiltern.
Dookie Agric. Coll. ...	15	... Dookie.
Dorg, Wm.	8	... Elengarden, Myers' Flat, Eaglehawk.
Dorsa, P. D.	½	... Maldon.
D'Orsy, Laurence ...	5	... Doma-Munjie, Chiltern.
Douglas, Thomas ...	23	... Rutherglen.
Drew, William ...	½	... Sparrowhawk, Long Gully.
Drummond, G. M. ...	20	... Carlyle, Rutherglen.
Drummond, Mrs. Margt.	20	... Rutherglen.
Du Boulay, Francis ...	1¼	... Holmes Creek, Beechworth.
Ducommaw, Emil ...	12	... Nagambie.
Duerkop, Henry ...	4	... Chiltern.
Duff, John	1	... Baringhup West.
Dunn, A.	35	... Wahgunyah.
Dunn, John	7	... Gooramadda.
Dunn, Mrs.	9	... Wahgunyah.
Dunn, Saml.	1¼	... Dunlavin, Talbot.
Duscher, Jacob ...	5	... Great Western.
Duscher, Rudolph ...	4	... Great Western.
Duvall, J.	2½	... Wodonga West.
Dyer, John	1	... Kiewa, Yackandandah.
Eaddy, Alfred ...	¼	... Charlton-road, Wedderburn.
Eagle, Wm.	½	... Harcourt.
Eaking, George ...	½	... Duncan-street, Long Gully.
Eaton, Jas.	10	... Rutherglen.
Edmonds, J. H. ...	4	... Clear Lake, Natimuk.
Edwards, J. F. ...	9	... Rutherglen.
Edwards, Mrs. ...	1¼	... Fell Timber Creek, Wodonga.
Edwards, R.	12	... Indigo, Yackandandah.
Eglie, Fred.	12	... Tahbilk, Nagambie.
Eisele, Richd. ...	15	... Kanyapella, *viâ* Echuca.
Eligate, Mrs. ...	5	... Indigo, Yackandandah.
Elliott, E.	6	... Bet Bet.
Ely, Rob.	¼	... Newman, Baringhup.
Emmerson, James ...	5	... Great Western.
Esperson, Gustave ...	2	... Craigie, Majorca.
Estapling Bros. ...	9	... Freestone Creek, Briagolong.
Ettershank, John, and Co.	30	... East Loddon Estate, Serpentine.
Ewins, George ...	8	... Doctor's Creek, Stawell West.
Facey, James ...	½	... Spring Mount Farm, Cranbourne.
Falder, John ...	2	... Murphy's Flat, Tarnagulla.
Falk, F.	1	... Wodonga West.
Fankhauser, Geo. ...	1½	... Belmore-road, Balwyn.
Farkins, August ...	½	... Mount Lonach, Amphitheatre, Lexton.
Farrasi, Joseph ...	1½	... Elevated Plains, Hepburn.
Farrell, Andw. ...	2	... Summer Head, Baringhup
Farrioli, Andrew ...	7	... Snake Hill, Glenlyon.
Faulkiner, John ...	7	... Woosang, Wedderburn.
Felgenhaur, Fredk. ...	8	... Stewart's Bridge, Echuca.
Ferguson, Alex. ...	4	... Mandurang.
Ferguson, Donald ...	3	... Azarby, Yea.
Ferhemann, Auguste	1	... Doncaster East.
Fernando, Joseph ...	1	... Frenchman's, Landsborough.
Field, J. R. A. ...	—	... Kialla West.
Figgins, Jas. ...	4½	... Mollison's Creek, Pyalong, Glenaroua, Pyalong.
Finger, H.	5	... Doncaster East.

Name.		Acres.		Address.
Finger, H., jun.	...	1½	...	Doncaster East.
Fisher, Mrs. Sarah	...	24	...	Gooramadda, Rutherglen.
Fitzgerald, Edward	...	12	...	Castlemaine.
Fitzjohn, Jas.	...	½	...	Broadford.
Fizelle, George	...	1	...	White Hills, Sandhurst.
Fizelle, Theodore	...	2	...	White Hills, Sandhurst.
Fizelle, Thos.	...	¼	...	Botanical Gardens, White Hills, Sandhurst.
Flack, Geo. ...	...	½	...	Ballan.
Fleming, Thos.	...	2	...	Benalla.
Fletcher, Wm.	...	5	...	Warrior Hills, Beeac.
Florentine, Charles	...	2½	...	Mitchelston, Nagambie.
Flowers, David	...	½	...	Talbot.
Foggo, James	...	4	...	Landsborough.
Forster, John	...	½	...	Yallock, Edenhope.
Fortune, M. ...	...	18	...	Rutherglen.
Foux, Peter ...	...	5	...	Dunolly.
Fowles, Wm. F.	...	½	...	Ballan.
Fox, A. ...	...	37	...	Emu Creek, Strathfieldsaye.
Fox, Henry ...	...	¼	...	McCallum's Creek, Majorca.
Francome, E.	...	½	...	Darlimurla, Mirboo.
Franzi, Guiseppe	...	1	...	Newstead-road, Guildford.
Fraser, Hugh	...	20	...	Olive Hills, Brown's Plains.
Frater, Peter	...	6	...	Beechworth.
Frey, H. J. ...	...	¼	...	Tintaldra.
Frowd, Isaac	...	18	..	Tongala, Echuca.
Fuge, R. ...	...	20	...	Rutherglen.
Fulton, Andrew	...	9	...	Mount Fulton, Lilydale.
Fulton and Co.	...	42	...	Wyuna, *viâ* Echuca.
Funcke, Valentine	...	8	...	Rhymney.
Furguson, John	...	2½	...	Hazeldean, Millewa.
Furness, Geo.	...	8	...	Rutherglen.
Gaach, John ...	...	1	...	Moonlight Flat, Castlemaine.
Gaffy, M. ...	...	28½	...	Mooroopna.
Gaggioni, Pietro	...	1	...	Hepburn.
Gale, Danl. ...	...	1	...	Kaniva South.
Gambetta, W.	...	18	...	Deep Lead, Wimmera.
Gambetti, Peter	...	25	...	Elizabeth Creek, Stawell West.
Gammell, Alexander		½	...	Elizabeth-street, Malvern.
Garbeline, Peter	...	7	...	Melbourne-road, Beechworth.
Gardiner, Geo.	...	4½	...	Cashel.
Gardner, James G.	...	20	...	Millewa.
Gasparo, Giovanni	...	1	...	Ringwood, Mornington.
Gee Wah ...	...	½	...	Dimboola.
Gehan, Francis	...	8	...	Mokepilly, Stawell West.
Gehrig, G. P.	...	106	...	Barnawartha.
Gemmell, John	...	6	...	Wooragee, Beechworth.
Gemmil, William	...	9	...	Golden Valley, Bet Bet.
Gemmill, James	...	6	...	Tongala.
Gemmill, J. J.	...	6	...	Mooroopna.
Gentle, Thomas	...	1	...	Tangambalanga, Kiewa.
Gervasoni, Antonio	...	3	...	Yandoit Creek, Yandoit.
Gervasoni, Carlo	...	5	...	Yandoit Creek, Yandoit.
Gervasoni, Lugi	...	5	...	Yandoit Creek, Yandoit.
Gianetti, Baptist	...	5	...	Bealiba.
Gibbs, Alex.	...	¼	...	Campbellfield.
Gieppy, Walter	...	4	...	Goomalibee, Benalla.
Gifford, Wm.	...	½	...	Korong Vale.
Giles, Henry	...	¼	...	White Hills, Sandhurst.
Gillam, James	...	½	...	East Murchison.
Gillet, Paul ...	...	8	...	Great Western.

Name.	Acres.	Address.
Gilliland, Wm.	9	Rutherglen.
Gilmore, G.	½	Woodlands, Napoleon Lead.
Giovanoni, D.	2	Spring Creek, Hepburn.
Glasgow, D.	8	Rutherglen.
Gleddin, Bernard	5	Mandurang.
Gledhill, H.	3	Strathfieldsaye.
Gliddell, Mrs.	2	Strathfieldsaye.
Glisson, S.	4½	Great Western.
Gloss, J.	1	Allen's Flat, Yackandandah
Gloty, J.	¼	Walhalla.
Glover, Mrs.	2	Bullock Creek, Marong.
Goddard, H. S.	5	Taripta, Rodney.
Godley, P. F.	10	Great Western.
Golding, Alfred	5½	Kaniva South.
Goldsworthy, Mrs. Mary	4	Rutherglen.
Gollings, S.	15	Carlyle, Rutherglen.
Goode and Sons	4	Huon's Creek, Wodonga.
Goodyer, E.	5	Indigo, Yackandandah.
Goodyer, Mrs.	30	Indigo, Yackandandah.
Gordon, C.	1½	Wodonga.
Gordon, Miss	¼	Apsley.
Gorse, Thos.	2	Wedderburn.
Gould, Daniel	1½	Doncaster East.
Grace, Mrs. Bridget	5	Gooramadda, Rutherglen.
Graham and Cameron	3	Stawell.
Graham Bros.	190	Netherby Vineyard, Rutherglen.
Graham, George	2½	Wunghnu.
Grant, David	½	Mount Korong-road, Long Gully.
Grant, James	9	Craig Elachie, Elmhurst.
Grant, James	1	Somerville, Hastings.
Grant, Robt.	2	Lowan, Natimuk.
Grant, William	¼	Millbank, Bacchus Marsh.
Gray, Wm.	20	Millewa.
Green, James	1	Mandurang.
Green, John	2	Granite Hill, Talbot.
Green, P.	½	Kitty's Lead, Napoleon Lead.
Greenaway, Joseph	¼	Craigie, Majorca.
Greenham, G.	¼	Dartmoor.
Greenman, J.	4	Huntly.
Gregge, W.	2	Huntly.
Grey, Fredk.	4	Ranter's Gully, Campbell's Creek
Grice, James	1¼	Mornington.
Grieffenhagen, W.	36	Strathfieldsaye.
Griffin, Jeremiah	5	Maidenham, Coghill's Creek.
Griffin, John	6	Strathfieldsaye.
Griffin, Richard	3	Strathfieldsaye.
Griffin, W. and Osmond	3	White Hills, Sandhurst.
Grimmond, John	15	Wahgunyah.
Grosse, Frederick	32	Emu Creek, Strathfieldsaye, and 6 Collins-street.
Groutsch, Mrs. Barbara	2	Runnymede, Elmore.
Gussettie, Fredk.	8	Newbridge.
Hackford, Ed.	16	Lilliput, Rutherglen.
Hadley, Geo.	7	Kiewa, Yackandandah.
Haig, Thos.	18	Beechworth.
Hall, Francis	½	Wattle Flat, Castlemaine.
Ham, J.	¼	Carlsruhe.
Hammil, Pat.	11	Summer Hill, Christmas Town, Chiltern.
Hamilton, D., jun.	30	Clydeside, Rutherglen.
Hamilton, D. G.	78	Rutherglen.
Hamilton. M.	¼	Longwood.

Name.	Acres.	Address.
Hamilton, T.	4	Landon, Yandoit.
Hamling, Thos.	1	Bridgewater-on-Loddon.
Hampton, Josiah	½	Ravenswood, Castlemaine.
Hancock, Chas.	12	Olive Vineyard, Stewart's Bridge, viâ Echuca.
Hanlon, L.	25	Kotupna.
Hannan, Mrs.	46	Rutherglen.
Hannon, John	15	Rutherglen.
Hannon, Mrs.	9	Carlyle, Rutherglen.
Hanton, E.	20	McCoy's Bridge, Mooroopna.
Harbery, Alfred	3	Sheepwash, Strathfieldsaye.
Hardy, Joseph	8	Mooroopna.
Hardy, J.	5	Mooroopna.
Harditch, Geo.	5	Moliagul.
Harris, G. J.	6	Clear Lake, Natimuk.
Harris, Mrs.	8	Axe Creek, Axedale.
Hart, Pat.	16	Marong, Rutherglen.
Harrison, John	40	Brown's Plains, Rutherglen.
Harrison, John	40	Brown's Plains.
Harrison, John	½	Kaniva.
Hartigan Bros.	7	Indigo, Yackandandah.
Hartigan, D.	15	Indigo, Yackandandah.
Hartweek, Carl	3	Hamilton North.
Hasty, Ralph	½	Bungeeltap-road, Ballan.
Headdey, E.	33	St. Ethel's Vineyard, Great Western.
Hedge, Geo.	1½	Everton.
Heedenwag, A.	8	Middle Creek, Wodonga.
Heily, G. D.	1½	Moora, Rushworth.
Helier, John	4	Goulburn Park, Wunghnu.
Helliar, John	½	Stuartmill.
Hempestall, G.	½	Tintaldra.
Henay, Thos.	½	Lillimur North.
Henderson, A.	15	Burnside, Rutherglen.
Henderson, A.	5	Barnawartha.
Henley, James	40	Millewa.
Hennessy, J.	9	Toolleen.
Hennicker, Henric	2	Lower Three-mile, Beechworth.
Henning, John	½	Lockwood, Kangaroo Flat.
Heyfrom, Stephen	20	Upper Black Dog Creek, Chiltern.
Hicks, Joseph	1½	Bromley, Dunolly.
Hicks, —	1½	Burnt Creek, Dunolly.
Hill, James	½	Britannia Reef, Majorca.
Hill, Mrs. Emily	2	Epsom.
Hillier, H. L.	6	Mandurang.
Hindson, John	½	Canterbury-road, Balwyn.
Hiskins, John	3	Rutherglen.
Hintze, G.	15	Rutherglen.
Hives, John	½	Black Lead, Napoleon Lead.
Hobbs, —	6	Yackandandah.
Hodgkinson, J.	6	Strathfieldsaye.
Hodgson, H.	1	Allen's Flat, Yackandandah.
Hole, Mrs.	3	Bet Bet.
Holland, Alfred	2	Strathfieldsaye.
Holibone, Walt.	12	Gooramadda, Rutherglen.
Holloway, G.	15	Barnawartha.
Holmes, John	6	Barrow Vineyard, Strathfieldsaye.
Holmes, Thos.	2	Strathfieldsaye.
Hood, John	2	Huntly.
Horbury, —	2	Strathfieldsaye.
Horseman, Henry	1	Blanket Flat-road, Campbell's Creek.
Horewood, Joel	½	Bridgewater-on-Loddon.
Hoskin, Richd.	3	Royal Farm, Benalla.

Name.		Acres.		Address.
Hossack, Jas.	...	7	...	Rutherglen.
Howard, John	...	22	...	Wahgunyah.
Howell, Mrs. M.	...	12	...	Lilliput, Rutherglen.
Howenstein, And.	...	2	...	Three-mile Creek, Ararat.
Howie, Robt.	...	13	...	Westfield, Moreland-road, Brunswick.
Howlett, Fredk.	...	1½	...	Spring Grove, Merrivale, Morwell.
Houston, Wm. R.	...	7	...	Rutherglen.
Hughes, Mark	...	¼	...	Hamilton North.
Hughes, Wm.	...	68	...	Rutherglen.
Hughes, W. ...	...	60	...	Carlyle, Rutherglen.
Hunt, Frank ...	...	¼	...	Walwa Creek.
Hunter, John	...	¼	...	Wedderburn.
Huntly, John	...	½	...	Thomas-street, Brighton.
Humphreys, Jas.	...	7	...	Gooramadda, Rutherglen.
Hurnell, Mrs.	...	6	...	Great Western.
Hutchins, Geo.	...	¾	...	Coleraine.
Hutton, Harry	...	2	...	Specimen Gully, Campbell's Creek.
Hutton, M. C. G.	...	20	...	Cooring Yering, Lilydale.
Hutton, — ...	...	...	...	Great Western.
Hyland and Wain	...	¼	...	Chiltern.
Ingram, A. ...	...	3	...	Bagshot, Huntly.
Invernezzi, Ambrozio		3	...	Yandoit Creek, Yandoit.
Ireland, De Courcy	...	½	...	Horsham.
Irvine, Hans W. H.	...	83	...	Great Western.
Jacobs, Joseph	...	20	...	Kialla West, Shepparton.
Jack, Rob. ...	...	40	...	Rutherglen.
Jackson, J. ...	...	1	...	Epsom.
Jackson, Mrs.	...	1	...	Runnymede, Elmore.
Jackson, Mrs. Sarah	...	12	...	Rutherglen.
Jacobson, Charles	...	12	...	Rutherglen.
Jamieson, —	...	1	...	Doctor's Creek, Stawell.
Jamieson, R.	...	4	...	Tangambalanga, Kiewa.
Jeavons, Joseph	...	8	...	Wycheproof, Teddywaddy.
Jenkins, —	...	3	...	Epsom.
Jenkin, John	...	½	...	Cambrian Hill, Napoleon Lead.
Jennings, —	...	4	...	Strathfieldsaye.
Jennings, Geo.	...	½	...	Woodside, Casterton.
Jochen, John	...	¾	...	Templestowe, Doncaster.
Johns, John	...	15	...	Katandra, Cashel.
Johns, Thos. M.	...	¼	...	Britannia Reef, Majorca.
Johnson, —	...	½	...	Tubut Station.
Johnston, David	...	5	...	Dookie, Cashel.
Johnston, J. C.	...	16	...	Springvale, Jackson's Creek, Sunbury.
Johnston, J. S.	...	16	...	Sunbury.
Johnston, Robt.	...	2	...	Marmal, Boort.
Johnston, William	...	½	...	Caralulup, Talbot-road, Lexton.
Jolly, William	...	½	...	Bunguluke, Wycheproof.
Jolly, Wm.	...	10	...	Great Western.
Jones, Alfred	...	2	...	Somerville, Hastings.
Jones, H. ...	...	20	...	Rutherglen.
Jones, Henry Geo.	...	2	...	Yarra Yarra Vineyard, Eltham.
Jones, Humphrey	...	4	...	Carlyle.
Jones, James	...	¼	...	Garden Flat, Majorca.
Jones, William	...	20	...	Wedderburn.
Jones, W. ...	...	30	...	Mooroopna.
Kahland, J. ...	...	—	...	King-street, Sandhurst.
Kam, G. ...	...	½	...	Amphitheatre-road, Avoca.
Kane, G. ...	...	½	...	Avoca.
Kapper, Henry	...	2	...	Bonegilla, Bellianga.

Name.	Acres.	Address.
Kavanagh, M.	36	Lake Erie Vineyard, Mooroopna.
Kay, Fong	3	Indigo, Chiltern.
Kegan, Patk.	3	Mokepilly, Stawell West.
Kelly, E.	3	Wodonga.
Kelly, J.	18	Carlyle, Rutherglen.
Kelly, Joseph	26	Rutherglen.
Kelly, M.	8	Wodonga.
Kewly, Thos.	¼	Waterloo.
Keys, —	2	Narioka.
Kilson, Thos.	5	Bealiba.
Kimber, John J.	½	Harcourt, Castlemaine.
King, Daniel	35	Lilliput, Rutherglen.
King, Dan.	65	Rutherglen.
King, E. and Edward	7	Rutherglen.
Kinge, W.	¼	Wodonga West.
Kitchen, A.	1	Donald.
Kitchen, Henry H.	½	Mansfield.
Kitchen, William	½	Waterloo.
Klein, Chas. F.	14	Wyuna, *viâ* Echuca.
Klein, Otto	7	Kanyapella, *viâ* Echuca.
Knight, G. W., sen.	½	Sandhurst.
Knight, Joseph	10	Mooroopna.
Knott, Joseph	¼	Lockwood, Kangaroo Flat.
Koch, F.	4	Christmas Town.
Koenstel, Otto	10	Huntly.
Kreoger, Theodore	¾	Hepburn.
Krutze, Rob.	¼	Hamilton South.
Kurle, Rob.	40	Rosenthal, Sunbury.
Laidlaw, John	14	Carlyle, Rutherglen.
Laidlaw, W.	½	Banayeo, Apsley.
Lamond, R. G.	2	Great Western.
Lampard, —	½	Kadnook, Edenhope.
Lang, Jas.	½	Harcourt.
Lang, John	2	Huntly.
Lang, W.	4	Middle Creek, Wodonga.
Lange, W.	2	Baranduda, Wodonga.
Lapsley, Robt.	3	Lockwood, Kangaroo Flat.
Laub, Louis	1¼	Honeysuckle, Lauriston.
Laurence, John	½	Union-street, Brighton.
Laurence, Joseph	½	Mill-street, Brighton.
Lauson, Robert	4	Kiewa, Yackandandah.
Laver, Alfred	7½	Chinaman's Creek, Castlemaine.
Lawe, Joseph	3	Emu Creek, Strathfieldsaye.
Lawson, John	3	Strathfieldsaye.
Leech, Robert	6	Grange Vineyard, Tooborac, Heathcote.
Leikman, William	½	White Hills, Sandhurst.
Leitch, J.	¼	Wodonga West.
Lennye, Carl	4	Echuca.
Leonard, P.	½	Napoleon Lead.
Lettow, Jas.	—	Dunolly.
Levin, L.	40	Rutherglen.
Leviston, Hy.	½	Enfield, Napoleon Lead.
Lewis, Samuel	4	Mandurang, Strathfieldsaye.
Lloyd, Michael	3	Concongella, Great Western.
Lloyd, Patrick	12½	Concongella, Great Western.
Lloyd, Wm.	5	Alston, Waranga, Rushworth.
Lindlaw, Mrs.	11	Rutherglen.
Lindsey, R.	1½	Sherbourne East, Marong.
Ling, James	1	Dereel, Rokewood.
Little, —	½	Campbellfield.
Lockett, James	7	Waanyarra.

Name.	Acres.	Address.
Longerenong Ag. Col.	—	Dooen.
Longstaff, J.	15	Allen's Flat, Yackandandah.
Looney, Thos.	50	Rutherglen.
Lorimer, John	21	Rhymney.
Lounds, Ambrose	20	Emu Creek, Strathfieldsaye.
Love, J. D.	1½	Tatura.
Loveland, Geo.	1	Eddington.
Lowden, Charles	¼	Mitta Mitta.
Luflow, Wm.	11	Upper Black Dog Creek, Wooragee.
Lynn, —	7	Great Western.
Lyon, Mrs.	¼	Stanmore House, Balmoral.
Macey, James	86	Estcourt, Boorhaman, Wangaratta.
Mackereth, Edwin H.	¾	Avoca.
Magee, —	8	Avoca.
Maguire, J. E.	10	Excelsior Vineyard, Mandurang.
Maguire, Thos.	16	Spring Vale, Rutherglen.
Maher, A.	1	Arcade, Sandhurst.
Maher, J.	6	Bonegilla, Wodonga.
Maher, Laurence	7	Rhymney.
Maling, J. B.	¼	Whitehorse-road, Balwyn.
Malone, Daniel	1	Laanecoorie, Eddington.
Manager, John	12	Great Western.
Maniel, De H.	—	Barnawartha North.
Mann, John	2	Castlemaine.
Manns, G.	10	Leneva, Wodonga.
Mannes, A.	80	Axe Creek, Sandhurst.
Manness, Anthony	20	Strathfieldsaye.
Manson, Jas.	¼	Wattle Flat, Castlemaine.
Margery, G.	55	Barnawartha.
Mariott, Louis	2	Landsborough.
Marriott, John	2	Main-road, Campbell's Creek.
Marshall, Joseph	¼	Muckleford, Castlemaine.
Martin, C.	¼	El Dorado Park, Chiltern.
Martin, F.	50	Rutherglen.
Martin, Geo.	¾	Kaniva.
Martin, James	15	Mooroopna.
Martin, John	5	Kangaroo Creek, Sandhurst.
Martin, John	3	Hawthorne Vineyard, Birregurra.
Martin, J. F.	60	Rutherglen.
Martinoga, Philip	1	Shicer Gully, Guildford.
Maskell, Geo.	¼	Durrant-street, Brighton.
Mason, A. B. and A. C.	12	Shepparton.
Mason, John	½	Mitchell-street, Echuca East.
Massanich, Antonio	2	Ringwood.
Massey, George	8	Wahgunyah.
Mathews, Leonatheous	4	Alma-road, Beechworth.
Matthews, W. H.	3	Epsom.
Matthews, W.	100	Barnawartha North.
Matthewson, John	¼	Dendy-street, Brighton.
Manlein, Peter	6	Primrose Garden, Korongvale.
Maunder, Geo.	15	Barnawartha North.
Maxwell, W. H.	¼	Coleraine.
May, Peter D.	8	Jallukar, Stawell West.
Mayerhoff, Carl	2	Spring Creek, Beechworth.
Mehener, Paul	1	Chinaman's Creek, Castlemaine.
Meiklim, William	8	Mooroopna.
Mellis, A.	4	Kyabram.
Mellon, F.	18	St. Francis' Vineyard, Dunolly.
Melville, Donald	3½	Albion-street, Brunswick.
Merlo, E.	½	South Parkins, Maldon.
Merry, David	4	Wooragee, Beechworth.

Name.	Acres.	Address.
Mertitmeyer, A. E.	4	Chiltern.
Metzger, Jules	2	Doctor's Creek, Stawell.
Metzger, Louis	28	Doctor's Creek, Stawell.
Meyer, Francis	9	Lockwood, Kangaroo Flat.
Meyer, F.	9	Lockwood.
Meyer, H. H.	14	Sheepwash, Mandurang.
Michael, H.	4	Goornong.
Mildura (Chaffey Bros.)	—	Swanston-street, Melbourne.
Milesi, Angelo	1	Smeaton-road, Yandoit.
Millard, Henry	½	Union-street, Brighton.
Millard, John	½	Union-street, Brighton.
Miller, Emma	2½	Honeysuckle, Lauriston.
Miller, James	½	Noorilim East, Arcadia, Murchison.
Miller, Wm. and Geo.	1½	South Brighton.
Millington, F.	½	Enfield, Napoleon Lead.
Mills, Chs.	¼	Hamilton.
Mills, Samuel	8	Mooroopna.
Minogue, Michael	2	South Bundalong, Yarrawonga.
Minotti, Antonio	1½	Hepburn, Mount Franklin.
Minotti, Battista	2	Mill Spring, Franklinford, Yandoit
Minotti, Gustave	3	Ballarat-road, Guildford.
Mirrigan, Pat.	8	Barnawartha North.
Mitchell, Alf.	23	Narong, Rutherglen.
Mitchell, Dav.	40	Gooramadda, Rutherglen.
Mitchell, M. A.	35	Rutherglen.
Mitchell, Mrs. B.	15	Rutherglen.
Mitchell, Wm.	¾	McCallum's Creek, Talbot.
Mole, Geo	2	Terrappee.
Mongan, D.	10	Allen's Flat, Yackandandah.
Monte, —	2	White Hills, Sandhurst.
Montfort, W.	1½	Benalla.
Montgomery, Thos.	13	Rutherglen.
Mooney, J. and L.	90	Mooney's Gap, Ararat.
Moor, T. S.	11	Bellevue, Benalla.
Moore, B.	2	Dunolly.
Moore, John	2½	Dunolly.
Moran, Marcellus	½	White Hills, Sandhurst.
Moran, Martin	2½	Benalla.
Morgan, Mrs.	1	Cherrytree, Kangaroo Flat.
Morganti, Maurizio	8	Eastern Hill, Eganstown.
Moresi, Francesco	21	Terrappee.
Morley, Fredk.	2½	Spring Creek, Beechworth.
Morley, James	24	Rutherglen.
Morris, G. F., & Sons	500	Fairfield, Rutherglen.
Mowatt, Alex. G.	2	Langi-Ghiran, Ararat.
Mueller, Dr. A.	25	Yackandandah.
Mulcare, Joseph	2	Strathfieldsaye.
Mull, Christian	2	El Dorado.
Muller, Mrs. F.	14	Indigo, Yackandandah.
Müller, D. J.	½	Chiltern.
Müller, Jacob H.	½	Wharparilla, via Echuca.
Murphy, B.	2½	Landsborough.
Murphy, Timothy	2	Tongala, Kyabram.
Murray, E. J.	3	Somerville, Frankston.
Murry, C.	1	Somerville.
Murry, Mrs. Ann	10	Gooramadda, Rutherglen.
Murry, William	½	Alma-road, Caulfield.
Mutzig, Charles	6	Deep Lead, Wimmera.
Myer, Christie	2	Spring Creek, Beechworth.
Myers, Albert	5	Mount Fairview, Box Hill.
Myers, H.	16	Mandurang.
Myers, Wm.	6	Epsom.

Name.	Acres.	Address.
Myles, Edward ...	½	... Waanyarra, Tarnagulla.
McBean, Simon ...	30	... Brown's Plains, Rutherglen.
McBride, Alex. ...	12	... Gooramadda.
McCabe, James ...	8	... Lockwood.
McCormack, John ...	½	... Tallarook.
McCrum, R.	1	... Toolamba.
McDonald, John ...	½	... St. Kilda-street, Brighton.
McDonald, William ...	17	... Eclat, Docker's Plains, Wangaratta.
McDugall, Jas. ...	½	... Bambra-road, Caulfield.
McEwin, Peter ...	½	... Dunrobin, Casterton.
McFarlane, C. ...	2	... Fell Timber Creek, Wodonga.
McFarlane, C. ...	2	... Wodonga West.
McFarlane, W. ...	2	... Wodonga West.
McGarrigle, Jas. ...	10	... Gooramadda, Rutherglen.
McGuan, John ...	20	... Concongella, Great Western.
McGill, A.	2	... Toolamba.
McGill, J.	5	... Toolamba.
McGuines, John ...	2	... Mangalore.
McGuire, Thos. ...	10	... Narong, Rutherglen.
McGuire, —	12	... Sheepwash, Mandurang.
McInerny, Mrs. Eliza	8	... Rutherglen.
McInnis, J.	2	... Mangalore.
McIntyre, Hugh ...	10	... Green Hill, Chiltern.
McIntyre, John ...	22	... Wattle Hill, Melbourne-road, Chiltern.
McKay, Wm. ...	¼	... Echuca.
McKenzie, Alex. ...	7	... Booraman, Wangaratta,
McKenzie, James ...	5	... Bet Bet.
McKinley, Chs. ...	20	... Timor West.
McKinnon, Mrs. Anne	¼	... Avoca.
McKirdy, Alex. ...	½	... Somerville, Hastings.
McKnity, Hugh ...	16	... Narong, Rutherglen.
McLennan, J. ...	¼	... Dartmoor.
McLeod, William ...	3	... Little River Vineyard, Little River.
McNaughton, John ...	4	... Burwood.
McNeill, W. H. ...	10	... Barnawartha.
McPhee, John ...	½	... Avoca-road, Lamplough.
McPherson, Donald ...	¼	... Dartmoor.
McPherson, Jas. ...	½	... Nangala, Casterton.
McPherson, Rob. ...	27	... Lilliput, Rutherglen.
McPherson, — ...	3¼	... Tahbilk, Nagambie.
Nation, Philip ...	13	... Gooramadda, Rutherglen.
Neilson, George ...	½	... Horticultural Soct.'s Gardens, Richmond.
Neilson, John ...	25	... Rutherglen.
Nett, Jesse... ...	1½	... Ranter's Gully, Campbell's Creek.
Niblett, Chas. ...	¼	... Lockwood.
Nicholls, Samuel ...	2	... Murphy's Flat, Tarnagulla.
Nicholson, J. C. ..	3	... McCallum's Creek, Talbot.
Nickenson, J. M. ...	11	... Shepparton.
Nicol, John	½	... Mirboo.
Nolan, James ...	14	... Rutherglen.
Norcam, Richard ...	2	... Jallukar, Stawell West.
Norton, Mrs. Margaret	2	... Growtley, Wangaratta.
Nott, Harry	7	... Rutherglen.
Nutske, Henry ...	¼	... Warracknabeal.
Nuttall, Thomas ...	¼	... Craigie, Majorca.
Oates, Wm	2	... El Dorado.
Odgers, R.	½	... Kitty's Lead, Napoleon Lead.
Oliver, Mrs. Marg ...	25	... Carlyle, Rutherglen.
Olney, Jams. ...	2	... Thomastown.
Olsson, Charles ...	3	... Mia Mia, Redesdale.

Name.	Acres.	Address.
Oman, Mrs. Charlotte	¾	.. Doncaster.
Onsley, Chas. ...	½	... Glen Eira-road, Caulfield.
Osborne, W. T. ...	1½	... Cemetery-road, Campbell's Creek.
Osbourne, Henry ...	13	... Emu Creek, Strathfieldsaye.
Osmand, Hon. W. H. S.	¼	... Doctor's Creek, Stawell West.
Ostler and Son, W. H.	⅛	... Mitchelldale, Dayo.
O'Brien, Garrett ...	14	... Rhymney,
O'Connor, John ...	9	... Barnawartha.
O'Dea, Michael ...	22	... Rutherglen.
O'Grady, —	—	... Rutherglen.
O'Neill, —	½	... North-road, Brighton.
O'Shea, John ...	½	... Greendale, Ballan.
O'Sullivan, F. ...	2	... Huntly.
Pagan, George ...	29	... Burnside, Mooroopna.
Pallenger, Henry ...	25	... Wunghnu.
Panton's Freehold M. Co.	5	... Epsom Vineyard, Sandhurst.
Parker, Joseph ...	2	... Castlemaine West.
Parker, Mrs. M. ...	4	... Wodonga West.
Parker, Richard ...	½	... Ballan.
Parnaby, M.	10	... Huon's Creek, Wodonga.
Parry and Clark ...	4	... Cambrian, Landsborough.
Parry, Edward ...	¼	... Garden Flat, Majorca.
Parry, William ...	¼	... Garden Flat, Majorca.
Passalaqua, Prospero	2½	... Shicer Gully, Guildford.
Patterson, J. ...	2	... Leneva, Wodonga.
Payne, Henry ...	1	... Wedderburn.
Payne, H. W. G. ...	½	... Budgeree, Boolara, South Gippsland.
Payne, Mrs. ...	¼	... Kambrook-road, Caulfield.
Payne, Mugleston ...	3	... Kialla West, Mooroopna.
Pearce, Jos. ...	27	... Crumple Horn, Rutherglen.
Peatling, Henry ...	1	... Bagshot, Huntly.
Pedrineini, Pietro ...	1½	... Yandoit.
Pedrini, Vincenzo ...	2½	... Yandoit.
Peerless, H.	3	... Marong.
Pegganette, Peter ...	2	... Dunolly.
Pegler, A. H. ...	2	... Ned's Corner, Yelta.
Pellow, Thos. ...	1	... Baulkamaugh.
Pennington, Harold ...	⅛	... Glen Eira-road, Caulfield.
Peoples, Robt. ...	39	... Wodonga.
Perini, Vincent ...	5	... Spring Creek, Hepburn.
Perry, Mrs. Bridget ...	5	... Carlyle, Rutherglen.
Petchell, Wm. ...	1¾	... Hamilton South.
Petersen, H.	15	... Emu Creek, Sandhurst.
Phelps, Robt. ...	2	... Dunolly North.
Philip, Adam ...	¼	... Bow Flat, Wedderburn.
Phillips, Henry ...	3	... Warracknabeal.
Plum, Albert ...	2	... Docker's Plains, Wangaratta.
Pohl, C.	20	... Emu Creek, Sandhurst.
Pola, Mrs. Ann ...	5	... Rhymney.
Polo, John	23	... Rhymney.
Polo, Peter	31	... Rhymney.
Pollard, G.	½	... Bonegilla, Wodonga.
Pollinelli, Antonio ...	4	... Dunolly.
Pooley, Humphrey ...	24	... Barnawartha.
Porter, Zadok ...	20	... Rutherglen.
Posiner, Philip ...	1	... Dunolly.
Pottenger, H. F. ...	13	... Drumanure, Karpool.
Potter, Robt. ...	14	... Chiltern West, Rutherglen.
Powell, J.	2	... Grassy Flat, Sandhurst.
Power, Thos. ...	¾	... Warracknabeal.
Poxon, Levi	12	... Lake Marmal, *viâ* Barakee.

Name.		Acres.		Address.
Poynton, Wm.	...	6	...	Pyrenees, Amphitheatre, Eversley.
Pratt, James ...	...	85	...	Boorhaman, Wangaratta.
Prentice, Jas.	...	86	...	Gooramadda, Rutherglen.
Prentice, M. J.	...	55	...	Emu Plains, Rutherglen.
Prescott, Thos.	...	½	...	Thomastown.
Price, William	...	2	...	Bealiba.
Pritchard, Alexander...		9	...	Havelock-road, Beechworth.
Pump, John ...	...	8¼	...	Doncaster East.
Purcell, William H.	...	½	...	Bannerman-street, Long Gully.
Pyle, Robert ...	...	5	...	Three-mile, Beechworth.
Quin, Charles	...	8	...	White Hills, Sandhurst.
Quinn, A. ...	...	10	...	Indigo, Chiltern.
Quirk, Thomas	...	4	...	Mooroopna North.
Quirt Bros. ...	...	7	...	Indigo, Yackandandah.
Rainess, H. ...	...	2	...	Castlemaine.
Ralston, Dav.	...	84	...	Rutherglen.
Ralston, Thos.	...	10	...	Rutherglen.
Ramsey, H. T.	...	7	...	St. Andrew, Kangaroo Ground.
Rankin, C. ...	...	½	...	Waterloo.
Ranseyer, F. A.	...	5	...	Telford, Yarrawonga.
Ratcliffe, David	...	12	...	Kyabram, Rodney.
Rathjen, H. ...	...	5	...	Colbinabbin.
Ray, E. ...	...	37	...	Rutherglen.
Reade, C. ...	...	4	...	High-street, Sandhurst.
Reaux, Camille	...	6	...	Wahgunyah.
Reddington, W. R.	...	20	...	Yackandandah.
Redwood, Richard	...	2	...	Barton Farm, Bridgewater-on-Loddon.
Reed, Charles H.	...	3	...	Strathfieldsaye.
Reeve, Thomas	...	35	...	Rutherglen.
Regan, Mrs. A.	...	3	...	Lake Lonsdale, Stawell.
Remsyen, Fredk.	...	7	...	Kangaroo Ground, Eltham.
Renwick, Mrs.	...	½	...	Caulfield.
Rettich, David	...	3	...	Doncaster.
Rey, E. ...	...	13	...	Carlyle, Rutherglen.
Richards, F. ...	...	2	...	Baillieston, Nagambie.
Richards, J. ...	...	3	...	Wodonga.
Richards, — ...	...	½	...	Fawkner.
Richardson, H.	...	5	...	Allen's Flat, Yackandandah.
Richardson, J.	...	7	...	Barnawartha.
Richardson, William ...	...	7	...	Docker's Plains, Wangaratta.
Ridout, J. E. ...	...	2	...	Goorambat East.
Ridout, Robert	...	10	...	Goorambat Vineyard, Benalla.
Righetti, Battista	...	1½	...	Yandoit.
Righetti, Joseph	...	3½	...	Hepburn.
Riley, E. ...	...	1	...	Wangaratta.
Ring, E. ...	...	13	...	Rutherglen.
Roberts, John	...	17	...	Fairburn Grange, Cashel.
Roberts, J. ...	...	2	...	Lockwood.
Roberts, Mrs.	...	2	...	Shelbourne.
Robertson, Geo.	...	½	...	Warrock, Casterton.
Robb, John ...	...	18	...	Carlyle, Rutherglen.
Robbins, Joseph	...	7	...	Barnedown.
Robbins, J. M.	...	4	...	Kangaroo Flat.
Robbins, W. ...	...	3	...	Muskerry.
Robinson, G. W.	...	2	...	Berwick.
Robinson, James	...	10	...	Concongella South.
Robinson, Mrs.	...	80	...	Indigo, Yackandandah,
Robinson, William	...	1½	...	Malakoff-road, Beechworth.
Robinson, Wm.	...	2½	...	Bridgewater-on-Loddon.
Roeder C. ...	...	½	...	Victoria-street, Long Gully.

Name.	Acres.	Address.
Roffins, Martin	1/4	Longwood.
Rogers, Thos.	1½	Ballarat-road, Daylesford.
Rolleri, Guiseppe	6	Spring Creek, Hepburn.
Ronchi, Polo	15	Doctor's Creek, Stawell West.
Roset, John	2	Doncaster.
Rosetti, Barnard	1½	Parkin's Reef-road, Maldon.
Ross, Chas. M.	1	Broadford.
Ross, John G.	1	Serpentine.
Ross, William	4	Big Waterhole, Talbot.
Ross, William	½	Alabama, Coghill's Creek.
Rossia, Thomas	1	Porcupine Ridge, Glenlyon.
Rouse, William	1	Inkerman-road, Beechworth.
Roustan, E.	½	Gordon.
Rowan, Andrew	260	St. Hubert's, Lillydale.
Rowan, John	2½	Bailieston, Nagambie.
Rowan, John	5	Mitchelstown.
Rowe, Edward	¼	Fryerstown.
Rowe, Hannibal O.	1½	Castlemaine.
Rowe, William	10	Chiltern West, Rutherglen.
Rubli, Abraham	1½	Bailieston, Nagambie.
Rubli, Fredk.	20	Bailieston, Nagambie.
Rubie, Jacob	13	View Point Vineyard, Michelston, Tabilk.
Ruske, H.	2	Derrijar, Warracknabeal.
Ruedin, A.	30	Huntly Vineyard, Huntly.
Ruehe, Antony	15	Rutherglen.
Ruhe, Fritz	19	Rutherglen.
Rumbler, A.	½	Napoleon Lead.
Rundel, Mrs. J.	3	Strathfieldsaye.
Rundel, J. T.	2	Emu Creek, Strathfieldsaye.
Rundel, M.	6	Strathfieldsaye.
Rusconie, Charles	2	Tarilta, Vaughan.
Rutland, William	14	Rokewood Junction.
Rutter, J.	2	Fell Timber Creek, Wodonga.
Ryan, John	—	Dookie.
Ryan, M.	2	Bet Bet, Dunolly.
Ryan, Thos.	¼	Nuggetty Gully, Fryerstown.
Ryan, W.	7	Indigo, Yackandandah.
Ryan, —	6	Almond Grove, Bet Bet.
Ryley, F.	—	Wangaratta.
Saines, John	6	Rutherglen.
Saines, Rob.	10	Carlyle, Rutherglen.
Salinger, H.	12	Hochhiem Vineyard, Great Western.
Salvia, Peter	1½	Chewton.
Sanders, Theodore	½	Benevolent Asylum, Ballarat South.
Samblebe, Franz	2¼	Lower Three-mile, Beechworth.
Sargentson, John	10	Big Hill, Stawell West.
Sartori, Lazarus	1½	Yandoit.
Sartori, Peter	5	Yandoit.
Saulter, C. A.	½	Gibson-road, Sandringham.
Scarffe, John	½	Garden Flat, Majorca.
Scarlett, Wm.	½	Mirboo.
Sceilly, Thos.	11	Katunga.
Schache, E.	½	Murtoa.
Schelisky, Henry	1½	Reid's Creek, Beechworth.
Scheuffle, L. F.	4	Epsom, Huntly.
Scheuffle, W.	4	Epsom, Huntly.
Schlemme, Wilhelm	1½	California Gully.
Schlink, A.	12	Huon's Creek, Wodonga.
Schlue, H.	30	Rutherglen.
Schluter, Henry	40	Rutherglen.
Schmede, Chas. F.	2	Muckleford.
Schmitt, Franz	2	Berwick.

Name.	Acres.	Address.
Schnider, Jacob	4	Surrey Hills, Box Hill.
Schramm, M.	2	Doncaster.
Schroder, Ernest	18	Chinaman's Creek, Castlemaine.
Schuhkraft, G. F.	7	Doncaster.
Schutt, Hans	¼	Kangaroo Flat.
Schutt, Henry	1	Kangaroo Flat.
Schwab, Golfred	4	Mitchellston, Nagambie.
Schwarer, Jos.	8	Chiltern West, Rutherglen.
Schweitzer, J.	9	Barnawartha North.
Schwind, J.	2½	Wodonga West.
Scorer, Mrs. M.	½	Woodlands, Napoleon Lead.
Scott, Alex.	2	Somerville, Hastings.
Scott, J.	30	Wahgunyah.
Scott, R. F.	10	Kanyapella, vid Echuca.
Seeber, Christian	1½	Epping.
Segar, Ferdinand	1	Mount Beckworth, Clunes.
Selletti, —	7	Doctor's Creek, Stawell.
Severino, John	2	Caralulup, Talbot, Lexton.
Severino, John	4	Evansford, Talbot.
Sewell, Martin	15	Bet Bet.
Shaw, E.	¼	Korong Vale.
Shaw, F. K.	9	Goornong.
Shaw, Mrs. Sarah	6	Rutherglen.
Shaw, Rinz.	9	Goornong.
Shaw, Samuel	40	Redesdale, North Wangaratta.
Shaw, Saml.	30	Tarrawingee.
Shelly, Wm.	2	Indigo-road, Chiltern.
Shillinglaw, J. J., & Sons	10	Dumbiedykes, Panton Hill.
Shoebridge, Edwd.	3	Havelock-road, Beechworth.
Shoebud, Thos.	6	Holmes Creek, Beechworth.
Shoecraft, Godfrey	4	Doncaster.
Siebel, John	¼	Thomastown.
Silvester, Eugene	½	Coleraine.
Simon, A. C.	½	Green Bank, Bacchus Marsh.
Simon, R.	4	Middle Creek, Yackandandah.
Simons, George	¼	Waterloo.
Simpson, Mrs.	¼	Cabanandra.
Simpson, Thos.	½	Gibson-road, South Brighton.
Sims, —	7	Moliagul.
Sinclair Bros.	½	Rupanyup.
Skene, A. B.	1½	Mildura.
Skinner, John	½	Coleraine.
Skyrme, Geo.	40	St. George Vineyard, Great Western.
Slade, George	40	Fairview, Rhymney.
Small, William	½	North-road, Brighton.
Smart, Rob.	40	Rutherglen.
Smith, A.	½	Napoleon Lead.
Smith, Daniel	15	Eversley.
Smith, G. S. and Sons	250	All Saint's, Wahgunyah.
Smith, H. P.	1	Suffolk Hall Vineyard, Strathfieldsaye.
Smith, James Henry	1½	Hind's Diggings, Redbank.
Smith, John	2	Bridgewater-on-Loddon.
Smith, John Thos.	28	Rose Hill, Howlong-road, Chiltern.
Smith, J. H.	170	Mundadda Vineyard, Barnawartha.
Smith, J.	200	Brown's Plains, Rutherglen.
Smith, Luke	¼	Waterloo.
Smith, Mrs. Christina	¼	Daylesford-road, Ballan.
Smith, Thos.	9	Beechworth.
Snowden, E. G.	6	Monomeath, Canterbury-road, Box Hill.
Somerville, Thomas	7	Strathfieldsaye.
Somerville, William, jun.	4	Strathfieldsaye.
Somerville, William, sen.	8	Strathfieldsaye.
Speakman, —	1	Dunolly.

Name.	Acres.	Address.
Stade, H.	37	Rhymney.
Stafford, Thos.	1	Dunolly.
Stafford, Wm.	2	Deep Lead, Wimmera.
Stanger, T.	8	Fell Timber Creek, Wodonga.
Starr, —	1	Baranduda, Yackandandah.
Stawell Vineyard Co.	110	Watta Wella, Stawell.
Stead, John Jas.	1	Black Dog Creek, Chiltern.
Steen, John	1	Emu Creek, Strathfieldsaye.
Stehn, W.	1½	Lowan, Natimuk.
Stephens, Joseph	½	Three-mile, Beechworth.
Stevenson, Robert	10	Nillumbik, Kangaroo Grd., Queenstown.
Stewart, James	1	Teddywaddy, Wycheproof.
Stewart, J. G.	¼	Craigie, Majorca.
Stiggants, Henry	1	Warrandyte.
Stoaker, Heinrich	32	Carlyle, Rutherglen.
Stone, Edward	2	The Delta, Laanecoorie, Eddington.
Strachen, Thos.	3	Axe Creek, Axedale.
Stranch, F. G.	3	Huntly.
Streckfuss, H.	20	Goornong.
Strickfiss, Edward	18	Eddington, Goornong.
Stuckensmidth, F.	½	White Hills, Sandhurst.
Sullivan, David	23	Rutherglen.
Sullivan, John	20	Carlyle, Rutherglen.
Summers, Albert	10	Newbridge.
Summers, G.	3	Baranduda, Wodonga.
Summers, H.	3	Baranduda, Wodonga.
Summons, P., sen.	5	Baranduda, Yackandandah.
Summons, P. H.	4	Baranduda, Yackandandah.
Sutherland, D.	10	Indigo, Yackandandah.
Sutherland, J.	5	Indigo, Yackandandah.
Sutton, G.	2	Fell Timber Creek, Wodonga.
Sutton, Stephen	1½	Tallarook.
Swan, Andrew	23	St. Leonard, Wangaratta.
Swanton, William	½	Stuartmill.
Sweeney. Terence	12	Rhymney.
Swindale, Henry	½	Runnymede, Elmore.
Synnott, Mrs. E. M.	40	Goonawarra, Sunbury.
Tahbilk (Chateau) Co.	360	Nagambie.
Tait, Samuel	1	Dunolly South.
Tait, William	5	View Bank Farm, Boweya, Lake Rowan.
Tanner, W.	9	Barnawartha.
Telford, Jas.	34	Rutherglen.
Templeman, William	½	Dunolly.
Tennant, George	¼	Kangaroo Flat.
Tenner, A.	5	Wodonga.
Tenner, James	8	Wodonga.
Tenner, P. A.	10	Wodonga.
Tetlow, J.	2	Dunolly.
Thiele, Gottlieb	7	Doncaster.
Thomas, Alfred	½	Thomastown.
Thomas, Francis	3½	Fern Hill, Ascot Vale.
Thomas, T.	5	Allen's Flat, Yackandandah.
Thompson, J. B.	½	Baynton, Kyneton.
Thompson, Mary	7½	Spring Creek, Beechworth.
Thomson, Patrick	½	Daylesford-road, Ballan.
Thomson, W. K.	½	North-road, Brighton.
Thorne, Robert	4	Newbridge.
Thornell, George	1	Somerville, Hastings.
Thornell, Henry	1½	Somerville, Hastings.
Thornell, John	3	Somerville, Hastings.
Thornell, J., jun.	1	Somerville, Frankston.
Thornell, Thomas	1	Somerville, Hastings.

Name.	Acres.	Address.
Toogood, Jane	½	Campbellfield.
Travarsi, Philip	1	Elevated Plains, Hepburn.
Treheir, Nicholas	¼	White Hills, Sandhurst.
Trevise, Benjamin	4	Lockwood South, Kangaroo Flat.
Trewella, John	½	Union-street, Brighton.
Tribolet, Abraham	12	Excelsior Vineyard, Corop.
Trimble, Robt.	25	Rutherglen.
Trinkhaus, Albert	1	Muckleford, Castlemaine.
Trombold, Henry	2	Doncaster.
Trotman, John	10	Federal, Kurraca South, Wedderburn.
Trouette and Blampied	87	St. Peter's Vineyard, Great Western.
Trudewind, A.	4	Nure Creek, Wodonga.
Tuckett, J. R.	15	Rosenberg, Riddell's Creek.
Turner, Robt.	17	Lake View, Rutherglen.
Turnow, William	½	Dane-street, Long Gully.
Turpia, James	1	Lower Tarwin.
Twiddy, Robert	2	Wedderburn.
Tyrell, H.	10	Boggy Creek, Moyhu, Hedi.
Ubergang, Chas.	1	Doncaster East.
Upton, Christop.	20	Lilliput, Rutherglen.
Upton, W.	24	Gladstone, Rutherglen.
Urquhart, James	13	Doctor's Creek, Stawell West.
Vahland, W. C.	80	Charter Vineyard, Runnymede, Elmore.
Valli, Antoni	3½	Goornong South.
Vanina, Charles	1½	Hepburn.
Vanna, James	3	Rock View, Newtown, Beechworth.
Van Staveren, J. C.	—	Nathalia.
Vantravers, Paul	28	Langi-Ghiran, Ararat.
Veitch, Christopher	2	Casterton.
Vickers, Edward	2	Nagambie.
Vince, Daniel	3	Essex Farm, Bridgewater.
Virgoe, Mrs.	½	North-road, Brighton.
Vosti, Antonio	1¾	Ballarat-road, Guildford.
Waldron, Chs.	16	Carlyle, Rutherglen.
Waldron, John	12	Rutherglen.
Walker, Thomas	½	McCallum's Creek, Majorca.
Wallace, John	4¾	Bullock Creek, Marong.
Walsh, Alex.	½	Union-street, Brighton.
Walsh, Thos.	12	Rutherglen.
Ward, J.	—	Bagshot, Huntly.
Warnackie, H.	10	Burnt Creek, Dunolly.
Warne, Fras.	¼	Kangaroo Flat.
Warnecke, C. H.	3	Wunghnu.
Warnicke, C. H.	12	Bromley.
Warren, Henry	10	Rutherglen.
Wass, John	3	Vale Hotel, Moonambel-road, Avoca.
Waterson, James	½	Croft Hill Farm, Baringhup East, Maldon.
Watkin, J. F.	5½	Beaufort-road, Beaufort.
Watson, Hector	½	Dartmoor.
Watson, J. G.	½	Walwa, Tintaldra.
Watson, W.	¾	Napoleon Lead.
Watt, Hugh	8	Cashel.
Watts, Wm.	2	Doncaster.
Webb, George	2	Newtown, Beechworth.
Webb, Wm.	¼	Darling-street, Echuca East.
Webb, W. J.	8	Rochester.
Webster, A.	5	Mooroopna.
Webster, Joseph	10	Moodemere, Rutherglen.
Webster, R., jun.	30	Wahgunyah.
Webster, Rob., sen.	10	Wahgunyah.
Wehsack, Francis	½	Ormond-road, Elwood.

Name.	Acres.	Address.
Weigard, Wm.	2	Lockwood.
Wendell, C. H.	3	Colbinabbin, Elmore.
Wendell, H. E.	1¼	Colbinabbin.
West, John	20	Mooroopna.
Whalley, David	½	Glen Eira-road, Elsternwick.
White, Thos.	2½	Malakoff-road, Beechworth.
Whitehead, J. R.		Barnawartha.
Whitehead, O.	2	Indigo, Yackandandah.
Whitehead, O.	9¼	Upper Indigo, Barnawartha.
Whittingham, Geo.	½	Caulfield.
Wickam Bros.	6	Ballington Vineyard, Wodonga.
Wilcot, John	½	Casley-street, Long Gully.
Wilkins, Jas.	20	Gooramadda, Rutherglen.
Williams, A. J.	3	Dunbulbalane.
Williams Bros.	16	Leneva, Wodonga.
Williams, Daniel	½	Middle Creek, Moonambel.
Williams, D.	18	Middle Creek, Wodonga.
Williams, Enoch	2	Holmes Creek, Beechworth.
Williams, E.	2	Leneva, Wodonga.
Williams, E.	10	Middle Creek, Yackandandah.
Williams, G.	¼	Gordon.
Williams, H.	3	Tarnagulla.
Williams, Jas.	14	Numurkah.
Williams, Joseph H.	3	Stony Creek, Tarnagulla.
Williamson, D. Walter	15	Beau Sejour, Eversley.
Willis, James	2	South Wangaratta.
Wills, John J. B.	4	Bolerch, Moonambel.
Wilson, Dickenson	8	Warrakgeep, Eversley.
Wilson, Hector	6	Vectis Bridge, Natimuk.
Wilson, John	2	Crowlands.
Wilson, M.	4	Upstonville, Mooroopna.
Wilson, M.	4	North Mooroopna.
Wilson, Thomas	10	North Mooroopna.
Wilson, W.	3	Eversley
Wilson, W.	3	Barnawartha.
Wingfield, Wm.	2½	Bridgewater-on-Loddon.
Wingor, William	4	Bullock Creek, Marong.
Winks, H.	3	Winter's Flat, Castlemaine.
Winter, Frederick	3	Doncaster.
Winzar, —	4	Axe Creek, Axedale.
Wise, J.	16	Rutherglen.
Wittig, Ennis	½	Doncaster.
Wood, Thomas	½	Ballarat South.
Work, William	10	Landsborough.
Wornes, William	3	Mooroopna.
Worthy, Mrs.	2	Coleraine.
Wuillemin, Louis	8	Delta Vineyard, Briagolong.
Yackovitey, A.	1	Wandiligong.
Yander, Andrew	5½	Doncaster East.
Yander, Chas.	4	Doncaster East.
York, Edward	3	Three-mile, Beechworth.
Young, Charles	10	Nursery Vineyard, Newbridge.
Young, John	1¼	Rutherglen.
Young, J. F.	32	Mooroopna.
Young, J.	2	Jackass Flat, Eaglehawk.
Young, J.	1½	Parkin's Reef-road, Maldon.
Young, Wm.	2	Baulkamaugh.
Zander, Andrew	8	Doncaster East.
Zander, Charles	5	Doncaster East.
Zerbe, Auguste	3½	Doncaster East.
Zwar, Michael	1½	Broadford.

APPENDIX D.

LIST OF APPLICATIONS FROM VINE-GROWERS IN VICTORIA UNDER THE BONUS REGULATIONS [ACT No. 1043].

[MAY, 1891.]

WITH AREAS PROPOSED TO BE CULTIVATED.

Name.	Parish.	A.	R
Amies, S. J. P.	Horsham	3	0
Aitken, Elizth.	Mildura	4	0
Alexander, Jas.	Toolamba	10	0
Anderson, J. C.	Borung	6	0
Aston, A. W.	Youanmite	80	0
Alexander, Josiah	Terrappee	10	0
Alexander, Jas.	Mildura	4	0
Appleby, A.	Mildura	5	0
Atkinson, H.	Mildura	4	0
Allen, Chas.	Byawatha	4	0
Anderson, Chas.	Kanyapella and Wharparilla	10	0
Bernassochi, J.	Woosang	4	2
Braillard, J.	Tabilk	10	0
Buckley, A. K.	Norong	27	0
Brensing, E.	Tabilk	1	0
Browne, J. H.	Horsham	3	2
Bennett, R. P.	Horsham	4	0
Baker, Geo.	Berrimal	2	0
Burrowes, W.	Carlyle	50	0
Briggs, Mrs. M. J.	Lilliput	5	0
Briggs, R. R.	Norong	18	0
Baldwin, W.	Girgarre East	20	0
Burke, J.	Lilliput	12	0
Burge, J. T.	Toolamba	7	0
Bailey, V.	Glenrowen	18	0
Barlow, J. B.	Barnawartha	18	2
Baumgarten, G. L.	Barnawartha North	40	0
Barnes, G.	Jallukar	10	0
Brache and Co.	Strathfieldsaye	12	0
Blaikie, A.	Carraragarmungee	18	0
Brien, W. R. H.	Wangaratta South	5	0
Bowman, M. J.	Bet Bet	4	0
Batson, G.	Tarranginnie	5	0
Beck, H.	Gooramadda	10	0
Boon, John	Mooroopna	4	0
Bell, R.	Mooroopna	5	0
Brown, D.	Norong	4	0
Bridgefoot, J.	Carraragarmungee	20	0
Brierley, T. W.	Chiltern West	13	0
Brown, G. H.	Oxley	10	0
Bacon, W. H.	Glenalbyn	1	0

Name.	Parish.	A.	R.
Buckland, J. S.	Goornong	7	0
Baum, A.	Boorhaman	4	0
Baumgarten, W. G.	Barnawartha	3	0
Brown, John	Mudgegonga	5	0
Bandy, T.	Corack East	2	0
Baker, Geo.	Bungalally	1	2
Bott, C.	Boomahnoomoonah	11	0
Brehant, Geo.	Concongella	2	0
Burgess, D.	Tallygaroopna	3	0
Bowman, W.	Bet Bet	4	0
Bradley, P.	Carraragarmungee	10	0
Blackburrow, T.	Mildura	10	0
Briggs, R. R.	Waaia	17	0
Byrne and Barry	Mildura	4	0
Ballintine, E.	Dookie	12	0
Baxter, Jno.	Barnawartha North	6	2
Bailey, E.	Carlyle	7	2
Bourke, J.	Carlyle	6	0
Bromley, C. H.	Mildura	8	0
Cox, Elizh. F.	Elmore	4	0
Chalmers, D.	Wychitella	10	0
Chomley, A. W.	Mildura	8	0
Clayton, W.	Barnawartha	12	0
Campbell, Jno.	Lilliput	8	0
Clear, Jno.	Barnawatha North	6	3
Colvin, H.	Boorhaman	6	0
Critchfield, J.	Borung	1	1
Crisp, T. E.	Mooroopna	7	2
Crosthwaite, A.	Mildura	11	2
Costello, J. H.	Bet Bet	20	0
Colvin, J.	Norong	10	0
Coster, C. E. P.	Mildura	8	0
Cau, F. D. B.	Mildura	10	0
Conna, J.	Gooramadda	6	0
Chappell, A.	Pelluebla	2	0
Cameron, W.	Boort	2	0
Clementson, J.	Carlyle	12	0
Cameron, C.	Bet Bet	13	0
Cordner, G.	Miram Piram	2	0
Carson, T.	Huntly	4	2
Clay, W.	Bagshot	5	0
Cocks, J. S.	Woodstock	1	0
Carolin, M.	Waggarandall	6	0
Cooper, J.	Wooragee North	12	0
Culham, M.	Chiltern West	20	0
Chandler, W.	Carlyle	13	2
Charlesworth, J.	Mandurang	6	0
Caelli, B.	Huntly	1	2
Cheesley, R. H.	Barnawartha South	6	0
Chandler, Geo., jun.	Carlyle	16	0
Conroy, B.	Concongella	5	0
Cox, T. J.	Barnawartha North and South	4	2
Cuneen, M.	Runnymede	5	2
Corcoran, J.	Glenlogie	7	0
Crozier, E.	Mildura	4	0
Carver, W. A.	Mildura	3	0
Chaffey, Annie A.	Mildura	10	0
Campbell, T. L.	Mildura	50	0
Chandler, W. J.	Carraragarmungee	25	0
Curtain, John	Dookie	50	0
Clurey, P.	Youanmite	1	0

Name.	Parish.	A.	R.
Dudley, F. J.	Maryborough	1	0
Delves, H.	Marong	8	0
Derry, J. D.	Horsham	13	0
Darveniza, T.	Mooroopna	22	0
Delbridge, T.	Huntly	4	0
Davis, J. A. T.	Yarrawonga	5	1
Day, J.	Pine Lodge	10	0
Dunn, J.	Gooramadda	6	0
Dale, A. A.	Wangaratta North	4	0
Lunne, M.	Youanmite	14	0
Donaldson, J. B.	Woosang	15	0
Daly, H. O'B.	Dunolly	6	0
Downie, R., jun.	Shepparton	4	2
Devitt, P.	Wooragee North	3	0
Davis, J. B.	Shadforth	5	0
Delminico, G.	Terrappee	20	0
Danaher, W.	Barnawartha South	12	0
De Bavay, A.	Woori Yallock	84	0
Dunstan W.	Tarrawingee	2	0
Dalton, T. C.	Horsham	1	0
Dunstan, W.	Bontherambo	5	0
Dormer, J. M.	Norong	10	0
Doig, J. G.	Oxley	8	0
Debney, F. W.	Horsham	1	0
Dagon, P. S.	Wandin Yallock	2	0
Eldridge, G.	Norong	14	0
Eddis, J. E.	Kyabram East	30	0
Ellis Bros.	Lockwood	4	0
Elliott, John	Norong	15	0
Edleston, J. S.	Carapooee	1	0
Eurns, E. J.	Stawell	5	0
Elliott, R.	Bontherambo	8	0
Edmonds, J. H.	Carchap	6	0
Froud, J.	Tongala	15	0
Foster, J.	Mooroopna	8	0
Fraser, A.	Timmering	5	0
Field, J. R. A.	Kialla	6	0
Fisher, T.	Gooramadda	3	2
Fealey, G. A.	Byawatha	25	0
Fraser, Hugh	Gooramadda	40	0
Faulkner, J.	Woosang	10	2
Fairless, W.	Baulkamaugh	4	0
Finnister, J.	Upotipotpon	4	0
Fisher, R.	Chiltern	4	0
Filtoe, R. H.	Mildura	5	0
Foster, J.	Mooroopna	3	0
Falvey, E.	Chiltern West	2	2
Ferguson, G.	Mysia	2	0
Field, J.	Quantong	2	0
Fitzpatrick, M.	Mildura	4	0
Forster, T.	Horsham	4	2
Fortesque, C.	Mildura	6	0
Gordon, D.	Mildura	6	2
Grattan, W.	Gowangardie	45	0
Governa, B.	Moormbool East	40	0
Gordon, G.	Mildura	3	0
Gibbons, R.	Taminick	4	0
Geake, J. E.	Mildura	7	0
Grossman, W.	Wangaratta North	14	0
Gilliland, W.	Goormadda	10	0

Name.	Parish.	A.	R.
Graham, H. P.	Mildura	8	0
Graham, Anne	Carlyle	22	0
Gibbs, J.	Gowangardie South	2	2
Gillham, J. W.	Branjee	2	0
Griffin, A.	Barnawatha	4	0
Gassies, J.	Carlyle	30	0
Gray, W.	Bontherambo	7	0
Garrett, M., jun.	Miepoll	3	0
Griffiths, M.	Tallygaroopna	2	0
Greatorex, T.	Yabba Yabba	10	0
Groom, H.	Berrimal	3	0
Green, J.	Mandurang	6	0
Goulden, M.	Neereman	3	0
Gardiner, G.	Dookie	5	0
Gill, J.	Lilliput	5	0
Graham, Geo.	Drumanure	6	0
Gray, W. M.	Bontherambo	4	0
Gianetti, B.	Bealiba	1	0
Graham, A.	Kialla	10	2
Gorman, J. M.	Yarrawonga	10	0
Garrard, A. F.	Mildura	3	0
Griggs, J. A.	Mildura	7	0
Gamble, E. N.	Watchegatcheca	3	0
Giles, J.	Kewell West	14	0
Hallahan, J.	Lilliput	16	0
Henderson, A.	Lilliput	11	0
Halleen, M.	Norong	18	0
Henshilwood, J.	Mildura	12	0
Hamilton, D. G.	Carlyle	10	0
Hossack, J.	Lilliput	10	0
Humphreys, J.	Carlyle	10	0
Hintze, G.	Carlyle	3	0
Hughes, W.	Carlyle	30	0
Hoare, C.	Mildura	5	0
Howard, K. G.	Mildura	6	2
Harper, J.	Toolamba	5	2
Hicks, W. C.	Bundalong	3	0
Headdey, E.	Concongella	10	0
Harris, T. H.	Kunat Kunat	30	0
Holmes, J. T.	Charlton East	4	0
Hamilton, Mrs. E.	Concongella South	2	0
Howard, J.	Betley	1	2
Howell, Margt.	Lilliput	7	0
Hurnall, C.	Concongella South	11	0
Hicks, J.	Chiltern West	6	2
Hannan, H.	Carlyle	19	0
Heape Bros.	Currawa	5	0
Henrickson, G.	Moliagul	2	0
Hare, W. T.	Murchison North	2	2
Hansen, H.	Lurg	3	0
Hill, W.	Karrabumet	30	0
Hinton, E.	Huntly	12	0
Hardie, C.	Mooroopna	6	0
Hazell Bros.	Oxley	7	0
Hughes, M.	Barnawartha South	6	0
Hanlon, L.	Kotupna	10	0
Hurley, D.	Lexington	1	2
Hayes, T.	Bontherambo	3	2
Hughes, S.	Dooen	1	0
Harriman, T.	Girgarre East	9	2
Hughes, T.	Barnawartha South	4	0

Name.	Parish.	A.	R.
Inchbold, J.	Yarrawonga	34	0
Ireland, De C.	Horsham	8	2
Idiens, A. C.	Mildura	10	0
Irving, F.	Mildura	8	0
Inglis, M.	Mildura	9	0
Jones, W.	Mooroopna	25	0
Jeffroy, A. D.	Echuca North	5	0
Jackson, C. R.	Drouin West	0	2
Jack, R.	Lilliput	40	0
Johns, G. H.	Katandra	10	0
Judd, F. W.	Mildura	8	0
Johns, R., jun.	Carchap	6	2
Jackson, S.	Gooramadda	15	0
Jones, W.	Taminick	8	0
Jacob, J.	Kialla West	20	0
Johns, Jno.	Waggarandall	8	0
Johnston, J. S.		4	2
Jackson, H. H.	Norong	5	0
Johns, R., sen.	Carchap	1	2
Jones, Geo.	Boorhaman	6	0
Jones, F. A.	Bungalally	5	0
Jenner, T. B.	Mildura	2	0
Jeffers, Wm.	Byawatha	3	0
Jackson, A.	Ararat	10	0
Kelly, J.	Carlyle	30	0
König, H. F. V.	Mooroopna	12	0
Kay, E.	Carlyle	14	0
Kidston, W. McF.	Mildura	7	3
King, D.	Lilliput	50	0
Kannenberg, J. H.	Woorak	6	0
Kelly, Jno.	Carlyle	6	0
Kelly, Martin	Wodonga	50	0
Kemp, R.	Yarrowalla	5	0
Keagle, Isabella	Pine Lodge	11	0
Kech, H.	Sandhurst	10	0
Kearney, T. D.	Gooramgooramgong	6	0
Kilburn, J. F.	Mildura	4	0
Keogh, Ed.	Tarrawingee	4	0
Keyte, Ann	Natimuk	5	0
Knight, G. W.	Huntly	5	0
Kelly, Mich.	Carlyle	24	2
Looney, T.	Carlyle	9	0
Lewis, W. E.	Knowsley East	14	0
Lawford, W.	Mokoan	8	0
Long, W. J.	Elmore	9	0
Lyons, Mary	Carlyle	10	0
Lennon, J., sen.	Barrakee	8	0
Lancaster, S.	Kyabram East	6	0
Lane, W.	Shadforth	12	0
Lynch, E.	Yarrawonga	12	0
Lilford, E.	Tongala	17	0
Lilford, J.	Kyabram East	2	0
Lancaster, J.	Taripta	1	0
Lenne, C.	Wharparilla	26	0
Leech, W. H. and T.	Woosang	6	0
Longstaff, J.	Yackandandah	8	0
Lobb, A.	Wahring	4	0
Lamperd, W.	Toolleen	2	0
Laupmann, G. C.	Mildura	4	0
Lawson, P.	Bundalong	10	0
Lynn, J.	Concongella	4	0

Name.	Parish	A.	R.
Moon, R. J.	Bungalally	20	0
Mason, A. C.	Shepparton	50	0
Martin, J.	Mooroopna	15	0
Maddock, J. F.	Mooroopna	2	0
Meehan, W.	Lilliput	16	0
Murray, A. S.	Mildura	30	0
Morris, G. F.	Gooramadda	50	0
Mitchell, Mrs. B.	Lilliput	25	0
Maye, J.	Mildura	6	0
Miller, C.	Karrabumet	50	0
Moylan, M.	Currawa	18	0
Morrison, J. W.	Wangaratta North	1	2
Madder, J.	Mooroopna	8	0
Morrison, Elsie	Wangaratta North	2	2
Magennis, W. J.	Yabba Yabba	8	0
Mayer, K.	Bontherambo	4	2
Millman, S.	Huntly	2	0
Maidling, T. P.	Barambogie	10	0
Maidling, F.	Bontherambo	10	0
Morris, J.	Bontherambo	5	0
Minogue, J.	Estcourt	8	0
Manning, G. H. M.	Horsham	4	0
Mellis, J. J.	Kyabram	5	0
Mandeville, L.	Wedderburn	5	2
Mess, Jas.	Nillumbik	8	0
Manus, G. S.	Wodonga	8	0
Marfleet, J.	Yarrowalla	5	0
Mellis, A.	Kyabram East	2	0
Morin, S.	Wombat	4	0
Manlieu, P.	Borung	2	0
Mannes, A.	Strathfieldsaye	5	0
Mayer, J. C.	Shadforth	5	2
Munro, R.	Undera	10	0
Moss, F.	Maldon	1	0
Miller, C. M.	Mildura	5	0
Morley, M. E.	Carlyle	31	0
Mellords, Jno.	Horsham	1	0
McKay, J.	Chiltern West	10	0
McIntosh, J.	Tabilk	20	0
Macdonald, W.	Lilliput	12	0
McDonald, H.	Dunmunkle	6	0
McLennan, A.	Lilliput	50	0
McQuade, J.	Norong	15	0
McKinty, T.	Boorhaman	20	0
Macguire, T.	Norong	19	0
McPherson, R.	Bontherambo	25	0
McDonald, C.	Wingalook	7	2
McLennan, K.	Mooroopna West	15	0
McFadyen, W. L.	Arapiles	17	0
McEvoy, J.	Lilliput	15	0
McCartie, J.	Lilliput	7	0
McBean, S.	Gooramadda	20	0
MacKay, F. C.	Warragul	1	0
McNeil, J. C.	Undera	6	0
McPherson, J.	Bontherambo	6	0
McRae, M.	Gooramadda	9	0
McMahon, T.	Strathfieldsaye	2	2
McDonald, A. H.	Wangaratta	10	0
McKinnon, C.	Carapooee West	5	0
McGuan, J.	Concongella South	6	0
Mackereth, E. H.	Avoca	14	0
McDonald, J., sen.	Glenloth	3	0

Name.	Parish.	A.	R.
McGuinness, A.	Mount Cole	3	0
McMillan, Mrs. M.	Lexington	7	0
Newsom, J.	Barnawartha South	20	0
Nash, E.	Bungeet	22	0
Neilson, J.	Lilliput and Norong	50	0
Newman, H.	Glenrowen	8	0
Nott, W.	Norong	8	0
Nugent, C.	Echuca	2	0
Nolan, J.	Norong	11	0
Nelson, J. A.	Horsham	2	0
Nickinson, J. N.	Shepparton	1	0
Nason, G. S.	Ararat	3	0
Nicholls, T. A. and H. E.	Waaia	24	0
North, Geo.	Katunga	5	0
Newton, S.	Mildura	7	0
Newcomen, W., jun.	Taminick	11	0
Nonmus, W.	Crowlands	10	0
O'Donoghue, F.	Brimin	20	0
O'Reilly, P.	Marmal	2	0
Owen, J.	Boort	8	2
O'Dwyer, J. J.	Tabilk	6	0
Oliver, J. L.	Norong	12	0
O'Connor, J.	Barnawartha	5	0
Oats, D.	Wooragee North	3	0
O'Grady, J.	Lilliput	44	0
O'Loughlin, J.	Axedale	4	0
Pearce, John	Bontherambo	9	0
Porter, Z.	Boorhaman	10	0
Pogue, S.	Toolamba	7	0
Putland, G.	Duchembegarra	1	0
Pearce, J.	Carlyle	7	0
Pearce, W. R.	Tallygaroopna	10	0
Pressley, C.	Peechelba	5	0
Power, J.	Woosang	5	0
Plum, L. J.	Estcourt	5	0
Patullo, J.	Boomahnoomoonah	20	0
Piper, J.	Buckrabanyule	10	0
Poustie, A.	Kialla	3	0
Pola, P.	Lexington	13	0
Price, W.	Peechelba	20	0
Payne, F. W.	Mildura	2	2
Pointing, T. H.	Mildura	3	0
Pycroft, H. C.	Mildura	10	0
Pleming, T. H. C.	Bontherambo	22	0
Quarrell, J.	Corindhap	1	0
Quinn, W.	Cobram	8	0
Quincy, A. S.	Mildura	8	0
Ratford, J.	Boorhaman	12	0
Ridout, J. E.	Goorambat	3	2
Rowcroft, A. P.	Mildura	14	0
Rüche, F.	Carlyle	12	0
Robinson, G. W.	Heathcote	17	0
Rean, C.	Carlyle	36	0
Raeburn, J.	Wingalook	8	0
Ramseyer, F. A.	Pelluebla	10	0
Rankin, C. H.	Bontherambo	24	0
Reynolds, T.	Youanmite	6	0

Name.	Parish.	A.	R.
Ruedin, A. L.	Huntly	10	0
Roach, C.	Currawa	10	0
Ryan, M.	Bet Bet	12	0
Ribbons, S.	Horsham	1	0
Robinson, J.	Concongella South	8	0
Rough, J. C.	Horsham	2	2
Robinson, A.	Boorhaman	2	0
Roberts, E. J.	Mildura	4	0
Ritchie, J. B.	Mildura	10	0
Rawlings, T. E.	Mildura	10	0
Rundell, M.	Strathfieldsaye	1	0
Skinner and Anderson	Mildura	15	2
Stanilaud, E. W.	Mildura	12	1
Spawn, A. F.	Dooen	3	0
Scott, J. B.	Concongella	2	0
Shillinglaw, John J.	Panton Hill	5	0
Shillinglaw, E. B.	Panton Hill	5	0
Shillinglaw, J. C.	Panton Hill	5	0
Shillinglaw, F. F.	Panton Hill	5	0
Spencer, T. W. B.	Mildura	3	0
Scott, T.	Mundoona	10	0
Stanton, J. L.	Lilliput	21	0
Schluter, H.	Lilliput	11	0
Sewell, W.	Bet Bet	9	0
Smith, G. S.	Carlyle	50	0
Shields, W.	Yielima	10	0
Smith, D.	Bundalong	5	0
Schlue, H., and Sons	Lilliput	34	0
Southon, G.	Katunga	7	2
Stevenson, A.	Lilliput	15	0
Simms, A. J.	Bontherambo	6	0
Stocker, H.	Carlyle	10	0
Smith, P.	Burramine	6	0
Shaw, Sarah	Carlyle	10	0
Scandelera, G.	Teddywaddy	13	0
Sim, J.	Pine Lodge	10	0
Somerville, J.	Strathfieldsaye	4	0
Simpson, P. N.	Euroa	2	0
Strachan, West, and Co.	Mooroopna	42	0
Shea, T.	Ararat	25	0
Stones, M.	Chiltern West	9	0
Swan, A., and Sons	Carraragarmungee	2	0
Shaw, J.	Boohaman	12	0
Schwab, G.	Mitchell	1	2
Stuart, W. C.	Mildura	10	0
Small, J.	Mildura	5	0
Skipper, F. J.	Mildura	3	0
Stevenson, H.	Mooroopna	7	0
Somerville, T.	Strathfieldsaye	1	2
Simpson, D.	Marmal	1	0
Skyrme, Geo.	Concongella	4	0
Sallinger, E. J.	Concongella South	9	0
Tobin, M.	Chiltern West	13	0
Tomlinson, H. G.	Mildura	10	0
Tafft, G.	Lilliput	22	0
Thompson, W.	Strathmerton	20	0
Taylor, A.	Gunbower	3	0
Telford, J. R.	Mooroopna	5	0
Tye, Wm.	Whroo	5	0
Threlfall, R.	Woosang	1	0

Name.	Parish.	A.	B
Taylor, R. S.	Borung	12	0
Tanner, D.	Barnawartha North	15	2
Thompson, J. L.	Dookie	19	0
Thompson, R.	Norong	5	0
Tickner, H.	Ledcourt	9	2
Tickner, F. D.	Ledcourt	8	0
Tanner, J.	Barnawartha	8	0
Tanner, W.	Barnawartha	4	0
Thompson, A. D.	Mildura	10	0
Tolley, G. H.	Mildura	6	2
Taggart, W.	Mildura	4	0
Trouette and Blampied	Concongella	19	0
Upton, C.	Lilliput	40	0
Uhthoff, W. T.	Currawa	2	0
Vaughan, J.	Mildura	6	0
Wilson, J. R.	Mildura	20	0
Whiting, E.	Barp	10	0
Wickham Bros.	Baranduda	5	0
Wilkinson, H. J.	Mildura	10	0
Wilson, W. M.	Mildura	5	0
Wilson, C. D.	Mildura	5	0
Walsh, D.	Norong	5	0
Withers, T.	Lilliput	7	0
Williams, J.	Katunga	14	0
Wilson, A.	Wedderburu	11	0
Wilson, M.	Mooroopna	10	2
Williams, H.	Mildura	20	0
Woollett, G. J.	Norong	25	0
Waite, J. T.	Norong	20	0
Wise, G.	Carraragarmungee	5	0
Wales, C.	Tallarook	7	0
Wall, F.	Burramine	6	0
Worland, C.	Branjee	1	0
Whelan, F.	Gooramadda	9	0
Walther, J. R.	Ni-Ni	2	0
Wicks, A. J.	Horsham	1	0
White, J.	Dunolly	1	0
White, E. S.	Mildura	16	0
Webb, A. W.	Mildura	5	0
Waddington, J.	Mildura	4	0
Wallis, W.	Horsham	2	2
Walker, Y.	Arcadia	15	0
Wenke, M.	Chiltern	8	0
Walsh, J. D.	Chiltern West	7	0
Wallace, C.	Chiltern	12	0
Wormwell, E.	Mildura	4	0
Wuillemin, L.	Briagolong	2	0
Young, T.	Horsham	26	0
Young, Wm.	Boola Boloke	8	0
Young, J.	Tarrawingee	7	2
Young, W. J.	Mildura	5	2

APPENDIX E.

List of Vine-growers' Associations in Victoria, Localities, and Office Bearers, to Date.

Name.	Locality.	President.	Vice-President.	Treasurer.	Secretary.
Central Vine-growers' Association	Melbourne (Board of Viticulture)	..	..	..	J. J. Shillinglaw
Barnawatha Vine and Fruit-growers' Association	Barnawatha	C. H. Morris	J. Baxter, W. Tanner	..	J. R. Whitehead
Bendigo Vine and Fruit-growers' Association	Sandhurst	Wm. Grieffenhagen	Thos. Craike, A. Ruedin	..	J. Kahland
Dookie District Vine and Fruit-growers' Association	Cashel	J. Johns	..	..	C. S. Heape
Dunolly Vine and Fruit-growers' Association	Dunolly	H. O'B. Daly	A. Baccala, P. Pergranetti	P. Faux	R. Clay
Euroa Vine and Fruit-growers' Association	Euroa	E. Chandler	A. Fraser	G. Barrett	J. W. Gillham
Geelong Vine and Fruit-growers' Association	Geelong	C. Craike	J. Deppler, C. Tetaz	H. King	J. H. Dardel, jun.
Goulburn Valley Vine and Fruit-growers' and Special Products Association	Mooroopna	F. J. Young	W. Gibbs, G. Pagan	W. Gibbs	W. Jones
Great Western and District Vine and Special Products Fruit-growers' Association	Great Western	H. W. H. Irvine	J. Lorimer	H. Best	Ed. Headdey
Nagambie and Goulburn River Vine and Fruit-growers' Special Products Association	Nagambie	T. Blayney	E. Vickers, J. McIntosh	..	E. Wild
Nathalia and Lower Moira Viticulture Society	Nathalia	J. C. Van Staveran	..	H. Bryant	R. T. Briggs
Numurkah Vine and Fruit-growers' Association	Numurkah	J. Williams	J. C. Rockliff, S. G. Thompeon	..	W. G McKinney, jun.
Rutherglen and Murray District Vine-growers' Association	Rutherglen	G. S. Smith	R. J. Caughey, R. Burrowes and J. O'Grady	..	H. Audley
Swan Hill Vine and Fruit-growers' Association	Swan Hill	A. F. Ramsay	..	..	C. Perman
Wodonga Wine and Fruit-growers' Association	Wodonga	W. C. McFarlane	A. Schlink, P. Adams	A Schlink	G. S. Manns
Yarra Valley Wine-growers' Association	Lilydale	Paul de Castella	..	M. Hutton	M. C. G. Hutton

Board of Viticulture, 12th May, 1891.

JOHN J. SHILLINGLAW, Secretary.

INDEX.

Adironda, 59
Alicante, 39
Alicante Bouschet, 33
Allens, Hybrid, 63
Altitude, effect on climate, 20
Alvey, 63
American vines as stocks to graft on, 134
,, distinctive characters of leaves, 54
,, foxy taste of fruit, 53
,, resistance opposed to phylloxera, 53
Ampelideæ, 1
Ampelography, 29
Anna, 57
Antiquity of viticulture, 1
Annular incision, 128
Aramon, 30
Aromatic taste of objectionable character diminished by subsoiling, 75
Arragonais (*see* Grenache), 39
Arrangement of vines, 82
Arrouya (*see* Carmenet), 34
Aspect, 20
Aspiran, 31
Aspiran Bouschet, 33
Assimilation, 10
Aucarot, 32
Auvergnat (*see* Pinot Blanc Chardonay), 45
Auvergnat Gris (*see* Pinot Gris), 45
Auvergnat Noir (*see* Pinot Noir), 45
Australian vines, 64
Auxolt (*see* Pinot Gris), 45

Balafant (*see* Tokay), 50
Baloutzat (*see* Malbeck), 40
Balzac (*see* Mataro), 41
Bar, 100
Bark, 5
Baxter's Sherry, 32
Beaunois (*see* Pinot Blanc Chardonay), 45
Bergeron (*see* Roussanne), 47
Beurot (*see* Pinot Gris), 45
Bigney (*see* Merlot), 41
Bignona (*see* Dolcetto), 37
Black Cluster (*see* Pinot Noir), 44
Black German (*see* Canby's August), 60
,, Hamburg, 32
,, July (*see* Devereux), 56
,, Muscadine (*see* Flowers), 63
,, Prince, 32
,, St. Peter, 32
,, Spanish (*see* Jacquez), 56
Blanc Fumé (*see* Sauvignon), 48
Blanche Feuille (*see* Meunier), 45
Blanquette (*see* Clairette), 36
Blauer Klavner (*see* Pinot Noir), 44
,, Trollinger (*see* Black Hamburg), 32
Blocks, extent and disposition of, 86
Blussart (*see* Pulsart), 46
Bois dur (*see* Carignane), 34
Bois Jaune (*see* Grenache), 39
Botanical description of vines, 1
Boudalès (*see* Cinsaut), 36
Bourdalès (*see* Cinsaut), 36

Bouchet Hybrids, 32
Boutelon (*see* Pedro Ximenes), 46
Breton (*see* Carmenet), 34
Buchardt's Prince (*see* Aramon), 30
Bullace (*see* Scuppernong), 63
,, (*see* Vitis Rotundifolia), 62
Bullet (*see* Taylor), 62
Bullet Grape (*see* Vitis Rotundifolia), 62
Burdekin vine (*see* Vitis Opaca), 65
Burger Blanc (*see* Gouais), 38
Burgundy (*see* Pinot), 44
,, of Georgia (*see* Pauline), 57
,, Miller's (*see* Pinot Meunier), 45
,, Smooth-leaved (*see* Pinot Noir), 44
,, White (*see* Pinot Blanc), 45

Cabernet Franc (*see* Carmenet), 34
,, Sauvignon, 33
Calcareous soils, 25
Cambium, importance of ingrafting, 136
Canby's August, 60
Candive (*see* Shiraz), 48
Carbinet (*see* Cabernet Sauvignon), 33
Carignane, 34
Carignan (*see* Carignane), 34
Carmenet, 34
Catalan (*see* Carignane), 34
,, (*see* Mataro), 41
Catawba, 60
"Cepage," 29
"Chaintres" system of pruning, 120
Charnet (*see* Mataro), 41
Chasselas, 35
,, de Falloux, 35
,, de Fontainebleau, 35
,, Golden, 35
,, Musqué, 36
,, Red (*see* Malbeck), 40
,, Rose, 36
,, Violet, 36
Chemical composition of the vine, 24
Chevrier (*see* Semillon), 48
Chicken Grape (*see* Vitis Cordifolia), 58
Chlorophyll, its importance in assimilation, 10
Chlorosis, 23
Choice varieties must be preferred to common, 27
Chrupka (*see* Chasselas), 35
Cigar-box Grape (*see* Jacquez), 56
Cinsaut, 36
Cissus Antarctica (*see* Vitis Baudiniana), 65
,, Opaca (*see* Vitis Opaca), 65
Clairette, 36
Clay soils, 25
Clearing, 77
Climate, 16
Climatic regions of Victoria, 21
Clinton, 61
,, Vialla (*see* Vialla), 64
Cognac grape (*see* Folle), 37
Colombier (*see* Semillon), 48
Commercial considerations, 67
Concord, 60
Conforogo (*see* Sultana), 49
Cordifolia Solonis (*see* Solonis), 62

Corinth Currant, 36
Cot (see Malbeck), 40
Cotticour (see Clairette), 36
"Coulure," 12
Crabutet (see Merlot), 41
Crignane (see Carignane), 34
"Crossettes," 89
Crowns, height of, 105
Cunningham, 55
Cultivation, 130
,, effect on vitality of vine, 2
,, preliminary, must be deep, 74
,, must follow irrigation, 20
Currant, Corinth, 36
,, Zante, 51
Cuttings, 83
,, selection of, 89
,, length of, 90
,, single eye, 91
,, preservation of, 92
,, stratification of, 93
,, means of facilitating emission of roots, 94
Cuttings or rooted vines, 98
,, planting in vineyard, 99
,, inclination of, 99
Cynthiana, 56

Delaware, 64
Devereux, 56
Diana, 60
Dibble, 100
Disbudding, 122
Dolcetto Nero, 37
Doradillo, 37

Edel Clavner (see Pinot Gris), 45
Elbling (see Gouais), 38
Elsinburgh, 56
Elvira, 64
English cleft graft, 137
Enrageat (see Folle), 37
Epinette (see Pinot Blanc Chardonay), 45
Epiran (see Aspiran), 31
Espagnin (see Cinsaut), 36
Espar (see Mataro), 41
Espart (see Mataro), 41
Esparte (see Mataro), 41
Estrangey (see Malbeck), 40
European vines, 30
,, grafting on American stocks, 137
Extent and disposition of blocks, 85

Factors influencing growth and products of vine, 15
Fall of leaves, 14
Fecundation of the ovule, 12
Feigentraube (see Sauvignon), 48
Fendant (see Chasselas), 35
First region, 70
Flouron (see Mataro), 41
Flower, botanical description, 6
,, anormal forms of, 7
Flowering, 12
Flowers, 63
Foex, recommends irrigation of vineyards, 19
,, opinion on value of different grafting stocks, 138
Folle, 37
Forest devil, 77
Forming young vine, 105
Fox Grape (see Vitis Labrusca), 59
"Foxy taste," of American grapes, 43
Franc Pinot (see Pinot Noir), 44

Frankenthal (see Black Hamburg), 32
Frauentraube (see Chasselas), 35
Friability necessary in soil, 22
Fromenteau (see Roussanne), 47
Fromentot (see Pinot Gris), 45
Frontignac (see Muscat de Frontignan), 43
Frontignan (see Muscat de Frontignan), 43
Frost, advantage of late budding varities, 28
,, pruning retarded in consequence, 121
,, grape (see Vitis Cordifolia), 58
Furmint (see Tokay), 50

Gamay, 38
,, Noir, 38
,, Nicholas, 38
,, d'Orleans, 38
,, in Beaujolais, 27
Gentil Aromatique (see Riesling), 46
Goethe, 64
Golden Chasselas (see Chasselas), 35
Gooseberry system, 124
Gordo Blanco (see Muscat Gordo Blanco), 43
Gouais, 38
Goulu Blanc (see Semillon), 48
Gourdoux (see Malbeck), 40
"Goût de terroir," 105
Gouveio (see Verdeilho), 51
Graft, ordinary cleft, 136
,, English cleft, 137
,, splice, 137
Grafting, 134
,, diminishes non setting of fruit, 134
,, time for, 138
Granaxa (see Grenache), 39
Granitic soils, 25
Grédelin (see Maccabeo), 40
Grenache, 39
Gris Cordelier (see Pinot Gris), 45
Gros Cabernet (see Carmenet), 34
,, Gamay (see Gamay), 38
,, Noir (see Tinto), 49
,, Plant Doré (see Morrillon), 43
Grosse Chalosse (see Folle), 37
,, Vinduro (see Carmenet), 34
Gutedel (see Chasselas), 35
Guyot system of pruning, 117
,, opinion on topping, 124

Hailstorms, 69
Hart (see Devereux), 56
Height of vines, 105
Heat, influence of, 17
Hermitage, red (see Shiraz), 48
,, white (see Roussanne), 47
Herbemont, 56
Herbemont's Madeira (see Herbemont), 56
Hoeing, 132
Hybrids, 63
Hybridization of vine, 32
Hyde's Eliza, 60

Iron, its influence on colour of wine, 26
Irrigation of vineyards, 18
,, practised in France and Switzerland, 19
Isabella, 60
Israella, 60
Ives' Seedling, 60
Ives, 60
,, Madeira, 60
Ivanhoe, white (see Shepherd's Riesling), 47

Jaen Blanc (see Doradillo), 37
Jacquez, 56
Jack (see Jacquez), 56

Kittredge (*see* Ives' Seedling), 60
Kechmish (*see* Sultana), 49
Labrusca (*see* Vitis Labrusca), 59
La Souys (*see* Solonis), 61
Lateral shoots, 4
Latitude, influence of, 20
Layering, 94
  ,,   reversed, 96
  ,,   multiple, 96
Laying out of vineyard, 80
Leader, selection of, 116
Leaves, 5
  ,, importance of, in ripening of fruit, 13
  ,, stripping, 128
Length of cuttings, 90
Lenoir (*see* Devereux), 56
  ,, (*see* Jacquez), 56
Levraut (*see* Pinot Gris), 45
Light, importance of, 20
Limestone soils, 25
Lincoln (*see* Devereux), 56
Lindley, 64
Listan (*see* Sweet Water), 49
Little Sweet Mountain (*see* Vitis Berlandieri), 57
Locust, 70
Logan, 61
Long pruning, 115
Long (*see* Cunningham), 55
Long's Arkansas (*see* Solonis), 61

Maccabeo, 40
Maitre Noir (*see* Morrillon), 43
Malaga, 40
Malaga (*see* Semillon), 48
Malbeck, 40
Malbeck bears better grafted on Solonis, 135
Maldoux (*see* Mondeuse), 42
Malvoisie, 41
  ,, (*see* Pinot Gris), 45
Marking out before planting, 85
Marsanne, 47
Martha, 61
Marzemina Bianca (*see* Chasselas), 35
Mataro, 41
  ,, (*see* Carignane), 34
  ,, (*see* Morrastel), 42
Maxatawney, 61
McCandless (*see* Jacquez), 56
McLean (*see* Devereux), 56
Merlot, 41
Mescle (*see* Pulsart), 46
Meunier (*see* Pinot Meunier), 45
Miles, 61
"Millerandage," 13
Miller's Burgundy (*see* Pinot Meunier), 45
Mission Grape, 42
Missouri Bird's Eye (*see* Elsinburgh), 56
Mixed pruning, 118
Moisture, 17
  ,, cultivation retains, 131
Molette (*see* Mondeuse), 42
Mondeuse, 42

Monteith (*see* Canby's August), 60
Morrillon, 43
  ,, Blanc (*see* Pinot Blanc Chardonay), 45
  ,, Noir (*see* Pinot Noir), 44
  ,, Taconné (*see* Pinot Meunier), 45
Morrastel, 42
Mountains, their influence on climate, 21
Mourrastel (*see* Morrastel), 42
Mourvedre (*see* Mataro), 41
Mouteuse (*see* Mondeuse), 42
Mueller, Sir F. von, description of Australian vines, 65

Mulching, 131
Multiple layering, 96
Muscadine, (*see* Vitis Rotundifolia), 62
Muscats, 43
Muscat de Frontignan, 43
  ,, of Alexandria (*see* Muscat Gordo Blanco), 43
Muscat Gordo Blanco, 43
Mustang (*see* Vitis Candicans), 58

Navarre (*see* Cabernet Sauvignon), 33
Nebbiolo (*see* Dolcetto Nero), 37
Neil's Grape (*see* Herbemont), 56
New Zealand Flax for tying vines, 127
Nipping off terminal bud, 127
Noir de Pressac (*see* Malbeck), 40
Noirien (*see* Pinot Noir), 44
Non-setting of fruit, 12
  ,, ,, diminished by annular incision," 128
Non-setting of fruit diminished by disbudding, 123
Non-setting of fruit diminished by grafting, 134
Non-setting of fruit diminished by late pruning, 121
Norton (*see* Cynthiana), 56
Norton's Virginia (*see* Cynthiana), 56
Northern Fox Grape (*see* Vitis Labrusca), 59
Number of vines per acre, 82
  ,, ,, ,, with square system, 83
Number of vines per acre, rectangular system, 84
Number of vines per acre, quincunx, 84

Oeillade, 44
Okorszem Kek (*see* Aramon), 30
Oporto (*see* Tinto), 49
Ouillade (*see* Oeillade), 44

Passolina (*see* Zante Currant), 51
Pauline, 67
Payne's Early (*see* Isabella), 60
Peaty soils, 26
Pedro Jimenez (*see* Pedro Ximenes), 46
Pedro Ximenes, 46
Perkins, 61
Pero Ximen (*see* Pedro Ximenes), 46
Perpignan (*see* Morrastel), 42
Persaigne (*see* Mondeuse), 42
Petiole, structure of, 5
Petit Bouschet, 33
Petit Cabernet (*see* Cabernet Sauvignon), 33
Petit fer (*see* Carmenet), 34
Phormium Tenax for tying vines, 127
Phylloxera resistance of American vines, 52
Physiology of the vine, 9
Picardan (*see* Cinsaut), 36
Picpouille Blanc (*see* Folle), 37
"Pincement," 127
Pinot, 44
  ,, Blanc, 45
  ,, ,, Chardonay, 45
  ,, in Burgundy district, 27
  ,, Gris, 45
  ,, Meunier, 45
  ,, Noir, 44
Piran (*see* Aspiran), 31
Plant d'Arbois (*see* Pulsart), 46
  ,, Doré (*see* Pinot Blanc Chardonay) 45
  ,, d'Arcenant (*see* Gamay), 38
  ,, de Grèce (*see* Folle), 37
  ,, Madame (*see* Folle), 37
  ,, Medoc (*see* Merlot), 41

Plant de Seyssel (*see* Roussanne), 47
Planting, 98
　,,　　cuttings in vineyard, 99
　,,　　　　,,　　nursery, 101
　,,　　rooted vines in vineyard, 103
　,,　　time for, 99
Plateado (*see* Doradillo), 37
Plateadillo (*see* Doradillo), 37
Plough, subsoil, 77
Ploughing, 130
Plutonic soils, 25
Potash, necessity for, 24
Poulsart (*see* Pulsart), 46
Preliminary cultivation, 74
　　,,　　　　　　,,　　depth of in France, 75
Preparation of soil, 74
Prolific buds on vine, 111
Propagation of the vine, 88
Pruning, 110
　,,　　for young vines, 107
　,,　　long or short, 112
　,,　　short spur, 113
　,,　　mixed, 118
　,,　　rod, 115
　,,　　system giving great extension, 119
　,,　　time for, 120
　,,　　instruments for, 121
　,,　　summer, 122
Pulliat's periods of ripening, 30
Pulsart, 46

Queue de Renard (*see* Maccabeo), 40
Quincunx, 83

Rainfall of Europe compared with ours, 69
Rebecca, 61
Rectangular rows, 84
Red Chasselas (*see* Malbeck), 40
　,,　 Hermitage (*see* Schiraz), 48
　,,　 Lenoir (*see* Pauline), 57
　,,　 Muncy (*see* Catawba), 60
　,,　 Wines, demand for, 68
　,,　 River (*see* Cynthiana), 56
Redondal (*see* Grenache), 39
Regions, division of colony into, 21
Respiration, 11
Revalaire (*see* Aramon), 30
Reversed layering, 96
Riesling, 46
　,,　 Shepherd's, 47
Riparia (*see* Vitis Riparia), 61
Ripening of Grapes, 14
Rise of sap, 10
River Grape (*see* Vitis Riparia), 61
Rivesaltes (*see* Grenache), 39
Riveyran (*see* Aspiran), 31
Roads in vineyard, 86
Roanoake (*see* Scuppernong), 63
Rock Grape (*see* Vitis Rupestris), 63
Rod pruning, 115
Rome Noir (*see* Tinto), 49
Roots of vine, 3
Roessling (*see* Riesling), 46
Roussanne, 47
Roussilon (*see* Grenache), 39
Rupestris (*see* Vitis Rupestris), 63
Rushes for tying vines, 126

Salem, 64
Salerne (*see* Cinsaut), 36
Salvagnin Noir (*see* Pinot Noir), 44
Samboton (*see* Isabella), 60
Sand grape (*see* Vitis Riparia), 61
Sandy soils, 25
Sauvignon, Red (*see* Cabernet Sauvignon), 33

Sauvignon, White, 48
Savoyanne (*see* Mondeuse), 42
Scarifiers, 132
Schiraz (*see* Shiraz), 48
Schistose soils, 25
Schwartzer Trollinger (*see* Black Hamburg), 32
Scientific considerations must guide vine-grower in a new country, 16
Scion, 136
　,,　 choice of, 138
Scuppernong, 63
Second region, 72
Seedlings, raising of, 88
　　,,　　variability of, 29
Selection of cuttings, 89
Semillon, 48
Serine (*see* Shiraz), 48
Shepherd's Riesling, 47
Shiraz, 58
Shoots, 4
Short spur pruning, 113
Singleton (*see* Catawba), 60
Sirac (*see* Shiraz), 48
Sirrah (*see* Shiraz), 48
Site, selection of, 66
Smarts (*see* Elsinburgh), 56
Soil, physical and chemical properties of, 22
　,,　 preparation of, 74
Solonis, 62
Spar (*see* Mataro), 41
Spiran (*see* Aspiran), 31
Splice graft, 137
Spofford Seedling (*see* Tokaylon), 61
Square system, 83
Stakes, 126
Stem, 3
　,,　 structure of, 5
　,,　 forming of, 106
Stomata, 6
Stratification of cuttings, 93
Stripping off leaves, 128
Subsoiling, 76
Subsoil plough, 77
Sugar grape (*see* Vitis Rupestris), 63
Sultans, 49
Sultanieh (*see* Sultana), 49
Summer cultivation, 130
Summer grape (*see* Vitis Æstivalis), 55
Summer pruning, 122
Surin Fié (*see* Sauvignon), 48
Surret Mountain (*see* Vitis Berlandieri), 57
Surrounding circumstances, importance of, 16
Sussling (*see* Chasselas), 35
Sweet water, 49
Sweet wines, 67
Syra, (*see* Shiraz), 48

Taylor, 62
Taylor's Bullit (*see* Taylor), 62
Teinturier (*see* Tinto), 49
Tendrils, 8
Terret Bouschet, 33
Third region, 73
Thomas, 63
Thurmond (*see* Devereux), 56
Tinta Francisca (*see* Tinto), 49
Tinto, 49
Tokay, 50
Tokaylon, 61
Topping, 123
　,,　 injurious effects of, 125
Transpiration, 10
Trellised vines, 85
　,,　 overhead, 120
　,,　 relative cost of, 126

Trenching, 76
Tuley (see Devereux), 56
Tying up vines, 126

Ugni Blanc (see Maccabeo), 40
„ Noir (see Aramon), 30
Ulliade (see Oeillade), 44
„ Noir (see Cinsaut)
Uva d'Acqui (see Dolcetto), 37

Valais Blanc (see Chasselas), 35
Variety, its influence on wine, 27
„ must be adapted to other conditions, 28
„ choice of, 66
Veins, 6
Veraison, 14
Verdai (see Aspiran), 31
Verdal „ „ 31
Verdeilho, 51
Verdot, 50
Veronais (see Carmenet), 34
Vialla, 64
Viticulture, antiquity of, 1
„ soils suitable for, 25
Vitis Acetosa, 65
„ Æstivalis, 55
„ Antarctica (see Vitis Baudiniana), 65
„ Arizonica, 65
„ Baudiniana, 65
„ Berlandieri, 58
„ Californica, 58
„ Candicans, 58
„ Cinerea, 58
„ Cordifolia, 58
„ Hypoglauca, 65
„ Labrusca, 59

Vitis Opaca, 65
„ Riparia, 61
„ Rotundifolia, 62
„ Rupestris, 63
„ Vinifera, 30
„ Vulpina (see Vitis Rotundifolia), 65
Vitraille (see Merlot), 41
Vuidure Sauvignonne (see Cabernet Sauvignon), 33

Warren (see Herbemont), 56
Warrenton (see Herbemont), 56
White Burgundy (see Pinot Blanc), 45
„ Hermitage (see Roussanne), 47
„ Ivanhoe (see Shepherd's Riesling), 47
„ Muscadine (see Scuppernong), 63
„ Nice (see Sweetwater), 49
„ Pinot (see Pinot Blanc), 45
„ Syrian (?) (see Doradillo), 37
Wilder, 64
Wild Riparia, 62
Winter cultivation, 130
Winds, 69
Winter grape (see Vitis Cordifolia), 58
Wire, training vine on, 120
Wood upon which fruit grows, 110
Woodward (see Isabella), 60
Worthington (see Clinton), 61
Wyman (see Tokaylon), 61

York's Madeira (see Canby's August), 60
Yellow Muscadine (see Scuppernong), 63

Zante Currant, 51
Zinfandel, 52
Zierfhandler Rother (see Zinfandel), 52

www.ingramcontent.com/pod-product-compliance
Lightning Source LLC
Chambersburg PA
CBHW032225230426
43666CB00033B/1599